The Progressives And The Slums

FOREWORDS BY

Samuel P. Hays & Philip S. Broughton

The Progressives

And The Slums

TENEMENT HOUSE REFORM IN NEW YORK CITY

1890-1917

by

ROY LUBOVE

UNIVERSITY OF PITTSBURGH PRESS

MANUFACTURED IN THE UNITED STATES OF AMERICA BY
BOOK CRAFTSMEN ASSOCIATES, INC., NEW YORK

To the few

Table of Contents

FOREWORDS   IX
    Samuel P. Hays
    Philip S. Broughton

1. The Origins of Tenement Reform, 1830-1865   *1*

2. The Tenement Comes of Age, 1866-1890   *25*

3. Jacob A. Riis: Portrait of a Reformer   *49*

4. The Tenement House Committee of 1894   *81*

5. Lawrence Veiller and the New York
Tenement House Commission of 1900   *117*

6. The Age of Veiller   *151*

7. The Professional Good Neighbor   *185*

8. Progressivism, Planning and Housing   *217*

APPENDICES
    I. Tenement Houses and Population in
       Manhattan, 1864   *257*

VIIICONTENTS

VIII CONTENTS

II. Population, Acreage and Density in Manhattan, 1880, 1894. Number of Tenements in Manhattan, 1893 — 258

III. Tenements, Tenement Population, Ethnic Distribution and Ward Boundaries in Manhattan, 1900 — 260

IV. Tenements and Tenement Population in Brooklyn, Bronx, Queens and Richmond, 1900. Total Tenements and Tenement Population in Greater New York, 1900 — 264

V. Estimated Population of Manhattan Tenements, December 31, 1916 — 265

VI. Tenements in Bronx, Brooklyn, Queens and Richmond, January 1, 1917 — 266

VII. Tenement Court Dimensions Recommended by the Tenement House Commission of 1900 — 267

VIII. Floor Plans of Four Tenements Showing Use of Court Space — 268

IX. Map of Manhattan Island Showing Ward and Tenement House Districts — 272

BIBLIOGRAPHICAL NOTE — 273

INDEX — 275

ILLUSTRATION:

A Child of the Tenements FACING PAGE 1

Forewords

During the past decade and a half the historical analysis of the Progressive Era has undergone considerable change. No longer is the focus on the outward forms of politics, the elections and presidential administrations. Instead, there has been increasing interest in patterns of thought and behavior. Who became reformers and how did they view their world? Most students who have asked such questions, however, have dealt with reformers as a whole, analyzing their common social-psychological reactions. Mr. Lubove's study, on the other hand, uses a different and perhaps more rewarding technique, for by studying the ideas and attitudes of reformers in one particular field of effort, housing, and in one location, New York, he is able to deal with his problem concretely and close to the factual evidence.

In using this approach, Mr. Lubove illuminates the great value of studies in the local history of industrial society, an approach with manifold possibilities. For by observing specific people in specific contexts one can get at the root of social processes which more generalized accounts often obscure or distort. Local history, if purely factual and descriptive, advances knowledge in only a rudimentary fashion; but if local history can illuminate broad processes of social change concretely, then it adds a dimension unobtainable through an emphasis on top-level, nation-wide personalities and events. Mr. Lubove's conclusions are of this nature. Although confined to New York they shed light on both housing and the reform process throughout the Progressive Era, implying generalizations about reform and reform objectives in other urban centers and other contexts.

Housing is typical of a wide variety of historical problems dealing with public policy customarily treated by political scientists rather than historians. Consequently these studies have been concerned more with law, administration or the results of public policy than with historical forces. Their use of history has been limited to "background" material selected not to understand changes over time, but to demonstrate the importance of the current problem under investigation. Historians, long handicapped by dependence on these non-historical studies in their treatment of public issues, should find Mr. Lubove's study useful. He is not primarily concerned with the solution of a social problem at a point in time, but with the understanding of a long-term development in the past. Better housing, in his view, was not the product of righteous cosmic forces, but the contribution of particular people reacting in a particular way to particular circumstances.

Perhaps the most significant aspect of this study lies in its conception of housing reform as a technique of social control. Many developments in modern urban life were ominous to reformers, conducive to social decay rather than growth; and their fears often focused on the slum — the most tangible expression of deterioration. Housing became, therefore, a key to social progress, a device to guide urban growth along desirable lines. Mr. Lubove's work, therefore, does not focus upon the building industry but upon housing in relation to social conditions and ideals of urban reconstruction.

The social control pursued by housing reformers, moreover, was not inspired primarily by a vision of democracy revitalized by such reforms as the direct primary, the direct election of Senators, and the initiative, referendum and recall. It depended, in large measure, upon the increasing influence of professional experts like Lawrence Veiller whose monopoly of detailed and specialized factual knowledge resulted in the assumption that they merited leadership in the crusade of social change and betterment. It is becoming increasingly clear that reform in the Progressive Era was not always the product of mass protest movements as many have described it in the past, but of a relatively small group of people who saw possibilities of "social engineering" through organized and bureaucratic effort, private as well as public. It seems that planned social control was as characteristic of many Progressive reformers as the extension of democracy.

Mr. Lubove's kind of study, with its emphasis on the concrete ingredients of social change, coupled with a broad perspective illuminating large developments in industrial society, is an example of precisely the type of work sorely needed in examining American life in the Industrial Age. We have relied too long on the episodic and the dramatic as well as the nation-wide event, assuming that only in a large and comprehensive study can fundamental processes of history adequately be analyzed. Yet such approaches have often obscured more than they have clarified, and it is increasingly clear that historical understanding depends to a great extent upon the examination of more limited but still significant aspects of society. Historians would do well to follow the combination of intensive analysis and imaginative synthesis which Mr. Lubove's study represents.

SAMUEL P. HAYS

University of Pittsburgh

Social history is valid in its own right as insight into the past, but it can be much more. Mr. Lubove deals with an aspect of city development that prefaces decisions American cities are making today. The only function of this foreword is to suggest how his book can best be read as prologue.

It was said of Rousseau that although he often found the wrong answers, he nearly always asked the right questions, and therein was his greatness. The American city has reversed this process. Our city governments and civic leaders have all too often engaged in dedicated efforts to find the right answers to the wrong questions. Nowhere has this curious aberration had more devastating results than in land use planning and in the housing of people.

The fault does not lie with the politicians, for within the limits of their leadership they must reflect their constituents. Neither does the fault lie with those earnest citizens who serve municipal governments in many advisory capacities, for they reflect the society that made them and have too little political influence on the decisive mass of voters. The traditions of our society are not geared (except rhetorically at banquets) to asking, "What kind of a city do we want? What is our purpose? How can we design law, policy, and a city plan to create the intended quality of life?"

These questions are never asked because the deeply ingrained inarticulate major premise of our society is that a city is merely an area divided into parcels of land which are bought and sold for economic advantage. Americans do not buy homes to live in and cherish but buy them as houses to sell later at a profit; and they feel that they have somehow been betrayed if this doesn't happen. To ask fundamental questions would violate the principle that all other civic values are subordinate to the self-determination of the market place.

Only slowly have we begun to recognize that today's monumentally expensive urban redevelopment arises because we asked the wrong questions yesterday and got the right answers to the wrong questions. The evidence is all about us. The public investment required to enlarge the automobile capacity of the downtown area of a typical large city has been estimated at $23,000 per automobile. Yet faced with traffic congestion, city fathers do not ask, "How can this influx be reduced to numbers appropriate to practical street patterns?" They ask, "How can we finance bigger and better limited access highways and create more central city parking places?" It is as though one sought to lower the level of Chesapeake Bay by dredging its bottom.

Or turn to the question of land use. There is an American

myth that public land is unproductive and that privately held land brings taxes and is therefore, *ipso facto*, productive. A new bowling alley or drive-in-theater is regarded as a sign of prosperity; a new school, a library, or a swimming pool is a tax burden. If this statement seems extreme, watch what happens if your town council should boldly propose to designate marginal land for park purposes: the outcry will suggest that the constitutional rights of realtors, builders, and owners are being ruthlessly invaded. The *reductio ad absurdum* of this reasoning occurred in Pittsburgh recently when promoters wanted to build a giant stadium over the Monongahela River because if put there, it would take no land out of taxation. This reasoning might well be extended and the entire river turned into a covered sewer.

Unlike those of Chesapeake Bay, the tides that flow in and out of the city are not beyond human control provided the right questions are asked. Cities which have created open space at their central core and parks in their suburbs find that the total assessment of their real estate rises. As for riverfronts: do the glorious embankments of Paris and London cost those cities money, or do they pay economic as well as civic dividends? Even economic questions must therefore relate to the total economy of the city.

A re-examination of the questions we ask ourselves about our cities and our housing is overdue because the wrong answers have not merely cost city, state and federal money, but have helped change the character of our Republic. The tax cost of traffic control, the cost of health protection, social welfare, policing, education and juvenile delinquency are related to the kind of cities we have. Wastes which reflect answers to the wrong questions have bankrupted our cities. "Federal encroachment" on local affairs is not a conspiracy or even a philosophy of government: it reflects the fact that we have developed cities which are not financially viable on their own. The umbilical cord of the Federal government is the only alternative they can take.

The Progressives and the Slums should, therefore, be read as a record of the public policy questions citizens of civic intelligence and good will in other times have asked about housing. In two splendid introductory chapters Mr. Lubove tells of the origin of tenement reform from 1830 to 1890. He, thus, begins in a period when the market place was supreme: the construction, condition, and facilities of housing, and the rent and tenure of the occupant were nobody's business but that of the landlord. He shows step by step the reasoning of men as they began to ask public policy questions. Honorable, moral, usually men of churchly conscience, they did not ask, "What kind of a city do we want and how can we make it so?" They asked about guilt. Some saw the slums as the result of sloth, sin, and bad character. Slum families got exactly what they deserved for competitive *laissez faire* (like big-time college football today) was not only character building but character revealing. Any justification for public intervention arose only because the slums bred disease which might strike the more deserving portions of the community, or lower land values, or threaten public order. Others took a more charitable view of their fellow men and argued environmental determinism: the slums were not the result but the contributing cause of sloth, sin, and bad character. The landlord was the villain. Basic questions about community purpose were largely lost in the debate over blame.

The classic example of asking the wrong question and getting the right answer is, of course, the case of the notorious "dumbbell tenement" which Mr. Lubove describes in Chapter 2. It won a prize in a housing competition conducted by a high-minded reform group, and laws were designed to encourage it. The prize competition sought "a tenement on a 25 x 100 foot lot which best combined the maximum facilities and convenience for the tenant and maximum profitability for the investor." Thus, there were two questions to be answered: first, a question on behalf of the tenant family; second, a question on behalf of the landlord. The distinguished judging committee declared that the "requirements of physical and moral health could *not* be satisfied by a tenement on a 25 x 100 foot lot." But they awarded the prize anyhow. This reflects the dominant social ethos. One could not, after all, refuse to answer the really fundamental question for the landlord, just because the social, civic, and moral question would inevitably get the wrong answer.

It was hard for America to ask the right questions about its cities and even harder to do anything about them. American legislatures reflected the rural bias that cities are depraved and all their problems are to be deplored. Reform legislation was voted, not out of social vision, but as an attack on the sinful city political machine. Even the city reformer sought little beyond a limit on the malevolence of the market place. The heavier public architecture of Athens and Rome might be copied but not their creative civic concepts. The abatement of Sodom and Gomorrah set the tone. And beyond the biblical perfidy of the city was a new scapegoat to prejudice the debate: the immigrant, the alien intruder.

Lawrence Veiller was among the first to bring into focus certain economic dimensions of the problem. When he dubbed New York "The City of Living Death" and showed how thirty-nine tenements could record forty cases of tuberculosis and 660 applications for charitable aid, he could establish that this was expensive, neither compatible with the conservative "stake in society" nor with the tenants' "responsibilities of citizenship." A very few might speculate (intellectually, not financially) about the long-range questions of land use, the prospects of planning, or even urban decentralization. But these were not real questions voters and city governments were willing to face in guiding policy.

Mr. Lubove has enabled us to see the Progressive Movement in its historical context as a transition, not arrival but growth. In his perceptive Retrospect and Prospect he sees it as the climax of an earlier reform era, but still "captive to the classic." To what extent did the Progressives realize that city planning and housing must be intimately connected and that long-range housing programs must consider the relationship between housing and other elements of urban life? Even more than Jacob Riis before him, Veiller's emphasis was upon restrictive control legislation and did not constitute a public philosophy of the city. Cities were not ready for that; indeed, we have not yet achieved it.

Anyone who has ever heard even a minor tax or zoning issue discussed will recognize in every chapter that we have passed this way before: self-interested resistances to change, fragmented issues and deep reluctance to ask the fundamental questions about land planning law and public policy which would give municipal decisions an ultimate significance.

PHILIP S. BROUGHTON

Pittsburgh, Pennsylvania

Acknowledgments

This book has benefited immeasurably from the kindness and cooperation of many people. I am indebted to the staffs of the Cornell University Library, the manuscript divisions of the New York Public Library and Library of Congress, and the Columbia University Oral History Project. The Community Service Society of New York placed important archival material at my disposal. Parts of Chapter I and Chapter V appeared, respectively, in the *New-York Historical Society Quarterly* and in the *Mississippi Valley Historical Review*, and this material is reprinted with permission of the editors.

Several persons contributed to my understanding of contemporary housing and social work problems, a necessary accompaniment to any meaningful evaluation of the past. In this connection I wish to thank Barbara Reach, Staff Associate, Committee on Housing and Urban Redevelopment, Community Service Society of New York; Louis Mucciolo, Assistant Manager, Vladeck Houses; George E. Edinson, Housing Assistant, Vladeck Houses; Helen M. Harris, Executive Director, United Neighborhood Houses; Gladys McPeek, Director, Hartley House; Agnes Preston, Assistant to the Director, Union Settlement; Jose Villegas, Director, LaGuardia Community Project; H. Daniel Carpenter, Director, Hudson Neighborhood Guild;

Margaret B. Shipherd, Assistant Director, Morningside Heights, Inc.

Dr. Irving Rappaport, Director of Laboratories and Attending Pathologist, Beekman Hospital in New York, read and criticized the discussion of public health and medical progress in Chapter IV.

Miss Frances Perkins related to the author her memories of Lawrence Veiller and the spirit of Progressive social reform.

Professor David B. Davis of Cornell University read the manuscript several times, with great profit to the author. Also at Cornell, Kermit C. Parsons, Thomas W. Mackesey, Douglas F. Dowd and Andrew Hacker contributed a number of useful suggestions. The perceptive comments of Professor Robert H. Bremner, Ohio State University, improved the manuscript at many points.

Despite great pain from vertigo, gout, and other afflictions, Mr. Veiller entertained the author at his home on several occasions before his death in the summer of 1959. He patiently answered dozens of questions relating to his career, personal life, and housing. Realistic and tough-minded to the end, Mr. Veiller predicted he would not survive the summer, but he accepted the fact gracefully; it did not in the least affect the wit and earthy skepticism of one of America's outstanding municipal reformers.

Although Mr. Veiller and the others I have mentioned must accept credit for their assistance, they are absolved from any responsibility for errors of fact or interpretation. These belong to the author alone. I end these acknowledgments with a word of appreciation to my wife Carole, a woman of exemplary patience.

A CHILD OF THE TENEMENTS

PHOTOGRAPH BY JACOB RIIS

Courtesy of the Museum of the City of New York

The Origins of Tenement Reform, 1830-1865

Crazy old buildings — crowded rear tenements in filthy yards — dark, damp basements — leaky garrets, ships, outhouses and stables converted into dwellings, though scarcely fit to shelter brutes — are the habitations of thousands of our fellow-beings in this wealthy Christian city.

ASSOCIATION FOR IMPROVING THE
CONDITION OF THE POOR, 1853

[1]

It is difficult to conceive of New York as a small, semirural city of 60,000 population. Yet in 1800 the narrow, cavernous streets of today's downtown Manhattan were lined with the unpretentious homes and shops of merchants and artisans, the prosperous and ambitious middle class of the period. The open country could be reached after a short stroll along Broadway or the Bowery Road. Brooklyn and Queens to the east, the Bronx to the north, were vast green tracts of forest and meadow. Land upon which to build homes and raise families was not yet one of the most precious commodities in New York. Its inexhaustibility could be taken for granted, like the waters of the rivers which clamped Manhattan on either side. The merchants, lawyers, sailmakers, silversmiths, and pewterers elected to the City Council faced the usual, but not yet insuperable, problems characteristic of an urban community: police and fire protection, street and dock maintenance, health and housing regulation.[1]

1. New York at the end of the eighteenth century is described in Sidney I. Pomerantz, *New York, An American City, 1783-1803: A Study of Urban Life* (New York, 1938).

1

The city's population and wealth increased steadily during the next three decades. In the 1820's the opening of the Erie Canal and the aggressive campaign of the city's merchants to wrest for New York the lion's share of the import trade, insured the future commercial and financial suzerainty of the metropolis. The immigrant flood into the United States after 1830, which deposited a substantial residue in New York before filtering west, provided the unskilled labor force necessary to the economic and physical expansion of the city.

Most of the newcomers were Irish and German. Often destitute upon arrival, they had urgent need for work and shelter. Work was most likely to be found in the lower wards of the city, where the shipping, mercantile, and wholesale trades were concentrated. Since hours were long and tenure often uncertain, immigrants naturally lived in those districts closest to their sources of employment. For the first time, housing the city's population became a serious problem.[2]

Increasingly after 1825 native New Yorkers vacated their one-family dwellings in the lower wards and moved to more favored northern portions of Manhattan Island. Sometimes their homes were demolished to make room for commercial structures. Otherwise they were sold or leased. The new owners and lessees, alert to the economic potentialities represented by thousands of immigrants in no position to haggle over the quality and location of their housing, partitioned the homes of the displaced Gothamites. Thus houses originally designed to accommodate one family soon bulged with three or four. In order to squeeze maximum profits out of their investment, housing speculators erected dwellings upon the spacious yards and gardens which had adorned the landscape.

Although a state assembly investigating committee in 1857 characterized the "primary reconstructions or adaptations" of one-family homes as "the lowest of tenant houses," the tenements built especially to house the poor were hardly superior.

2. An excellent account of the immigrant in New York before the Civil War is Robert Ernst, *Immigrant Life in New York City, 1825-1863* (New York, 1949).

By the 1850's one might notice squat three- and four-story boxes of wood or brick in the downtown area, filled with workingmen and their families. These flimsily constructed railroad flats contained as many as twelve or sixteen families. No ray of sunlight penetrated the tiny interior bedrooms, not much larger than closets. Those who could not afford the luxury of an apartment in a reconverted one-family home or in a tenement frequently landed in dark, damp cellars or renovated stables and warehouses.

The urban housing problem which arose in New York during the Jacksonian era had its roots in the same ethos which determined western land development. The counterpart of the speculator in western lands was the urban jerry-builder, eager to exploit his opportunities and move on. The city's land, the housing of its people, represented his rich lode of speculative profits. Just as the western land speculator resented any government interference, such as John Quincy Adams's program of regulated land disposal, the urban real estate speculator resented community control over his domain. He, not the community, would determine the level of structural and sanitary standards. The community acquiesced. In an age of liberal capitalism, the right of one kind of entrepreneur to pursue his economic destiny was the same as any other. The Jacksonian entrepreneurial ethos and land use control by the community were mutually exclusive. Jacksonian liberalism precluded any planned and orderly development of the human and material resources of the urban community.

Although New York City at the end of the Jacksonian era bore little resemblance to the semirural, relatively homogeneous society of 1800, many of the attitudes of the earlier period persisted. There was little understanding of the distinctive nature of a complex urban civilization and the demands which it makes upon government to preserve the general welfare. The large city required governmental services and controls which the small town could ignore, or leave to the individual, volunteer and amateur. Consequently, New York staggered into the industrial age with housing regulations appropriate to the colonial era. It left its health service in the hands of amateurs and politicians. The pressure of population upon the land, combined with the influx of thousands of immigrant poor, created health and housing problems which neither the entrepreneurial ethos of Jacksonian America nor the small town ethos of self-help could solve.

[2]

New York's housing troubles in the nineteenth century officially date from 1834. The City Inspector, chief health officer of the city, stated in his annual report for the year that "some cause should be assigned for the increase of deaths beyond the increase of population, and none appears so prominent as that of intemperance and the crowded and filthy state in which a great portion of our population live. . . ."[3] His words were echoed many times over in the next two decades by the New York Association for Improving the Condition of the Poor (AICP). The Association, established in 1843, launched a private crusade against the slums and the disease, vice, and crime which seemed to characterize their inhabitants. Led and financed by wealthy merchants and businessmen, the Association became the principal source of organized opposition to New York's rapidly deteriorating housing conditions in the years before the Civil War.

The founders of the AICP were troubled by the multiplicity of private charities in the city, each working within a limited geographical area or else dedicated to some specific project such as the relief of indigent Episcopalian widows. No agency coordinated the work of these charities to prevent duplications and fraud. Preoccupied with relief, they neglected the fundamental issue of the causes and cures for poverty. In contrast the AICP was designed to serve as a city-wide agency whose general objective was "the elevation of the moral and physical condition of the indigent." The "relief of their necessities" was secondary.[4]

3. Quoted in Lawrence Veiller, "Tenement House Reform in New York City, 1834-1900," in Robert W. de Forest and Lawrence Veiller, eds., *The Tenement House Problem* (New York, 1903), I, 71.
4. For an analysis of the origins and early work of the AICP see my "The New York Association for Improving the Condition of the Poor: The Formative Years," *New York Historical Society Quarterly*, XLIII (1959), 307-27.

The Association, reflecting the view of many middle-class Americans, was convinced that a chief source of poverty was defective character. The indolence, improvidence, and above all the intemperance of the poor resulted in a squandering of their earnings, in a lack of concern for the future, in an inability to take advantage of America's limitless economic opportunities. Since they had to acquire the virtues of industriousness, frugality, and sobriety, character reformation was infinitely more important than relief, which often only rewarded laziness. Thus the Association suggested to its "visitors" responsible for examining applicants for aid that they endeavor to arouse the self-respect and inner moral resources of the poor.[5] They could perform no greater service.

Very often a distinction was made by the AICP between the "worthy" and the "unworthy" poor or between "poverty" and "pauperism." The worthy poor included those willing but unable to work because of sickness or other circumstantial misfortune, and also those who could not make ends meet no matter how much they sweated. The unworthy poor were comprised of those who preferred to live off begging and charitable largess instead of working. Despite this theoretical distinction, the AICP frequently regarded all poverty with a certain measure of contempt. The worthy poor discovered that no matter how hard they struggled, they were condemned as moral failures.

The Association stressed a moral interpretation of poverty but at the same time tended to attribute many woes of the impoverished to their housing. Indeed it leaned toward an environmentalist interpretation of poverty when it examined the slums and their social consequences. If one read simply the opinions of the AICP upon the subject of housing, he might reasonably conclude that it blamed the environment predominantly for the imperfections of the poor: "What they are . . . they are made to a greater or less extent, by circumstances over which they have but little control; and vain will be the effort to elevate their character, without first improving their physical condition." [6]

5. AICP, *First Annual Report*, 1845, Visitor's Manual, 26.
6. AICP, *First Report of a Committee on the Sanitary Condition of the Laboring Classes in the City of New York, With Remedial Suggestions* (1853), 24. Hereafter cited as AICP, *Committee on Sanitary Condition*.

The AICP, however, was never conscious of any contradiction in its position. When examining the slums in particular, it simply advanced an environmentalist interpretation of the causes of poverty and the vice which seemed to be associated with it. When it considered the subject of poverty in general — its causes, consequences, and remedies — it stressed a moral causation, blaming the intemperance, indolence, improvidence, and ignorance of the poor for their predicament. But the Association was consistent in one respect. No matter what caused poverty in the first place, the moral reformation of the poor was necessary for their salvation. This was the real challenge. Only such a reformation would enable the poor to transcend their environment. If they were incapable of resisting the temptations which abounded in slum districts, they could never hope to elevate their status. Thus the Association's interest in housing reform originated less from its conviction that inferior housing caused poverty and vice than from its conviction that persons raised and acclimated to the squalid moral and social atmosphere of slums would remain impervious to the Christian middle-class doctrine which the Association strove to inculcate.

The AICP reviled the slums for their pernicious influence upon health and morals. They were overcrowded. They lacked air, light, and ventilation. The fetid atmosphere which enveloped the slum dweller produced disease and intemperance. The personal habits of slum residents combined with inadequate water, sewerage, and sanitary facilities resulted in an odoriferous accumulation of filth which offended the senses and caused untold suffering. "Physical evils produce moral evils," thundered the AICP. "Degrade men to the condition of brutes, and they will have brutal propensities and passions." It is not difficult to understand why the Protestant middle-class gentlemen of the AICP were repulsed by the slums. In them were concentrated and intensified all those concomitants of poverty which respectable Gothamites found reprehensible: filth, crime, sexual promiscuity, drunkenness, ribaldry, disease and, of course, improvidence and indolence. Could law-abiding children be raised by tippling mothers and vicious fathers? "The connection of juvenile depravity . . . with the wretched conditions of [slum] life" was obvious.[7]

No single feature of slum culture received such condemnation as the overcrowding. Here was a capital offense against middle-class standards of moral deportment. "The absence of all necessary accommodations in many dwellings, and the crowded state of the rooms, which defies all attempts at decency and modesty," the AICP complained, "breaks down the barriers of self-respect, and prepares the way for direct profligacy." [8] In crowded tenements entire families often slept and dressed in the same rooms. They shared their quarters with strangers, lodgers who were taken in to supplement the family income. Such iniquities, together with the steady growth of poverty and pauperism in the 1840's and 1850's, ominously threatened the safety of the whole community. Unless conditions improved, the Association warned, it was certain that the poor would "overrun the city as thieves and beggars — endanger public peace and the security of property and life — tax the community for their support, and entail upon it an inheritance of vice and pauperism." [9]

In an era which placed few restrictions in the way of the entrepreneur, the Association's fulminations against the slums rebounded against a wall of indifference. Although the AICP was prepared to restrict entrepreneurial freedom in housing in order to improve that environment, it seemed unjust and discriminatory to others to single out the real estate speculator, and not the manufacturer or merchant, as guilty of some heinous crime against humanity. Why should a man's housing be any more an issue of community concern than the way he dressed? The law of supply and demand determined the quality and quantity of housing. If the ignorant Irish and German peasants crowding into Manhattan's slums did not relish what was available, they could do themselves and the city a favor by migrating to the country.[10]

7. *Ibid.*, 21, 26.
8. *Ibid.*, 20.
9. AICP, *Thirteenth Annual Report*, 1856, 24.
10. The AICP itself advised immigrants: "Escape then from the city — for escape is your only resource against the terrible ills of beggery; and the farther you go, the better." AICP, *The Mistake* (Pamphlet, 1850), 4.

As events would prove, unregulated enterprise did not suffice. The municipality for several decades only deluded itself in thinking that it could remain aloof indefinitely from its responsibility to ensure adequate housing for the working-class population. The fact was that housing in a populous, heterogeneous community like New York could not be left entirely to the beneficent laws of supply and demand. It was, in a sense, a kind of public utility, as essential to the health, comfort, and safety of the citizens as were the transportation, sewerage, and water systems or the police and fire departments, and not, as the AICP perceived, simply an ordinary market commodity. The quantity and quality of the housing supply after 1830 became as much a public as a private matter because it affected the physical well-being of vast numbers of people, because congestion in the lower wards of Manhattan made it nearly impossible for the worker to afford an apartment which offered a minimum of light, air, privacy, and other necessities, and because enforced overcrowding intensified the dangers to human life from every fire, every case of contagious disease, every neglected privy.

Although the leaders of the AICP were more conscious than most New Yorkers of the need for improved housing, and thus justified the right of the municipal authorities "to enact and enforce all such sanitary regulations, as the peculiar position and condition of this great metropolis requires," the Association also assumed that an enlightened capitalism combining philanthropy and profits could inaugurate a new era in housing.[11] In this connection, the AICP promulgated the ideal of the model tenement. This it described as a tenement built by the individual capitalist or company which voluntarily limited profits in favor of higher structural and sanitary standards than those found in the ordinary speculative tenement. Model tenements, sound investments rather than speculative adventures, might reap diminished profits but investors would be rewarded by the pleasure of having served the poor.

In order to prove that model tenements could pay their way and were not simply charities, the Association sponsored one.

11. AICP, *Eleventh Annual Report*, 1854, 43.

The AICP organized a subsidiary company in 1854 which erected a model tenement in the vicinity of Elizabeth and Mott Streets. It contained eighty-seven suites of apartments, two stores, and a large hall. Rents ranged from $5.50 to $8.50 per month, which was expected to return 6 per cent on the original investment of $90,000.[12] This tenement, occupied by Negroes rather than white American or immigrant workers, did not in fact prove either a financial or social success. It degenerated into one of the worst slum pockets in the city, and was sold in 1867. In the 1880's, ironically, a committee of the AICP condemned the "big flat" it had sired as unfit for human habitation.[13] The AICP, however, never lost faith during its formative years that much of the initiative for the abolition of the slum would spring from capitalists motivated by humanitarianism and enlightened self-interest.

The model tenement idea represented less a solution to the housing problem than an evasion. There was no reason to expect that capitalists, as a group, would prove more self-sacrificing in housing than any other avenue of investment. Maximum profits in tenement construction involved the most intensive use of the land. This meant packing as much humanity as possible in a building containing the smallest room space possible, built as many stories high as possible, and as cheaply as possible. Most builders subordinated the pleasure of serving humanity to the maximization of profit.

In 1853, nineteen years after the City Inspector first complained of the housing accommodations of the poor, the AICP summarized the situation in these words: "The dwellings of the industrious classes in this City are not generally adapted to the wants of human organization, nor compatable [sic] with the health, or the social or moral improvement of the occupants."[14] At no time had the State of New York intervened with its police powers to halt the tenement blight in its seaport metrop-

12. AICP, *Thirteenth Annual Report*, 1856, 45ff.
13. The decline of the "big flat" is described in Robert H. Bremner, "The Big Flat: History of a New York Tenement House," *American Historical Review*, LXIV (1958), 54-62; AICP, *Forty-third Annual Report*, 1886, 44-53.
14. AICP, *Committee on Sanitary Condition*, 14.

olis. In 1856, however, the state shed its indifference when the assembly appointed a select committee whose mission was to "examine into the Condition of Tenant Houses in New-York and Brooklyn."

After several months of investigation, the committee submitted its report to the legislature. In angry words the shocked investigators condemned the capitalist "avarice" and the public "lethargy," which they blamed for the housing evil. The slums, the committee charged, were the "offspring of municipal neglect." "Had the evils which now appall us, been prevented or checked in their earlier manifestation, by wise and simple laws," the committee argued, "the city of New-York would now exhibit more gratifying bills of health, more general social comfort and prosperity, and less, far less expenditure for the support of pauperism and crime."

The assembly committee prophesied that continued municipal neglect of the alien tenement population would result in total moral decay: "Of a surety, we must, as a people, *act* upon this foreign element, or it will act upon us. Like the vast Atlantic, we must decompose and cleanse the impurities which rush into our midst, or . . . we shall receive their poison into our whole national system. American *social virtue* has deteriorated . . . through the operation of influences connected with the influx of foreigners, without corresponding precautions to counteract them."[15] The slum, quite obviously, did not represent simply an economic or sanitary problem. Its critics feared that the moral integrity and the unity of the community were endangered by the alien tenement population, ignorant of American ways, dirty and diseased, whose thieving, whoring, and drinking threatened to disrupt social stability and order. The tenement slum, even at this early date, was viewed as a problem in social control. Reformers assumed that improved housing conditions would assist in transmitting to the immigrant and working-class

15. "Report of the Select Committee Appointed to Examine into the Condition of Tenant Houses in New-York and Brooklyn," *New York Assembly Documents*, No. 205, Mar. 9, 1857, 10-11, 49.

population of the city middle-class culture, manners, and mores.[16]

The dire warnings of the AICP and the assembly committee of 1857 spurred neither the state legislature nor New York City into action. The committee's recommendation for the establishment of a "Board of Home Commissioners" to regulate sanitary and structural standards was ignored. The pleas to enlightened capitalists to erect decent dwellings at rents which the poor now wasted on "holes and dens" met a faint response. The people of New York were not yet prepared to admit that the housing of the poor was a matter of legitimate community responsibility.

[3]

On July 26, 1849, George Templeton Strong noted in his diary that cholera had been the "all-pervading subject" for a fortnight; people were dying at the rate of 100 a day.[17] In the 1830's and again in the 1840's, New York was host to serious cholera epidemics. The cholera raged most fiercely in the crowded tenement districts, where such scourges as typhoid and typhus fever, pulmonary and diarrheal diseases were also common. The city's inordinately high sickness and mortality rate alarmed physicians. Their concern was augmented by their contempt for New York's inefficient health department. In the 1860's a small but determined group of physicians strove to modernize the municipal health service and force the city to acknowledge its responsibility for the supervision of tenement conditions. For the first time the sanitary and housing reformer was not isolated. The middle class, driven by fear, united in support of improved sanitary control.

It was not simply the danger of epidemic stalking out from the downtown ghettos that panicked the middle class. True, the "stinks of Centre Street [lifted] up their voices," [18] but important

16. John H. Griscom, *The Sanitary Condition of the Laboring Population of New York* (New York, 1845), 23.
17. Allan Nevins and Milton Halsey Thomas, eds., *The Diary of George Templeton Strong* (New York, 1952), I, 358.
18. *Ibid.*, II, 177-78.

also after 1863 was the memory of the terrible July days when the poor streamed out from their gloomy haunts to burn, murder, and pillage. The draft riots, a turbulent protest of the immigrant poor against what they believed was discriminatory conscription, helped prove to New Yorkers that they could not permanently ignore the social and moral condition of the immigrant.

It was in the year after the riots, 1864, that the Council of Hygiene of the Citizens' Association inaugurated its campaign to improve housing and sanitary standards.[19] The Citizens' Association had been organized in 1863 to combat corruption and inefficiency in municipal government. Led by some of the most prominent men of New York, including William B. Astor, James M. Brown, Peter Cooper, Hamilton Fish, August Belmont, and John Jacob Astor, Jr., the Association soon broadened its focus to include sanitary reform. This resulted in the establishment of a subordinate body, the Council of Hygiene.

The Council's immediate objective was to abolish the office of City Inspector, the chief health official of the city. The only continuous supervision over New York's sanitary condition was concentrated in the authority of the Inspector to collect vital statistics, clean the streets, and appoint wardens to investigate and eliminate local nuisances. As evidence before a state investigating committee in 1865 revealed, the City Inspector's department was mostly a preserve for deserving politicians ignorant of even the rather primitive sanitary and medical science of the time.

The health warden for Manhattan's ninth ward in 1865 was Albert J. Terhune, a carpenter by occupation. When asked by the committee to list the books he had read on the subject of

19. In its introduction to the *Report* of the Council of Hygiene, the Council of the Citizens' Association took note of the draft riots: "The mobs that held fearful sway in our city during the memorable outbreak of violence in the month of July, 1863, were gathered in the overcrowded and neglected quarters of the city." Council of Hygiene and Public Health of the Citizens' Association of New York, *Report Upon the Sanitary Condition of the City* (New York, 1865), xv. Hereafter cited as Council of Hygiene, *Report.* A lively account of the draft riots can be found in Herbert Asbury, *The Gangs of New York: An Informal History of the Underworld* (Garden City, N. Y., 1927), 118-73.

"sanitary measures," Terhune revealed that "common sense is the work I read on that subject." Terhune could not explain the difference between typhus and typhoid fever. He did not know if cholera infantum prevailed in his district because he did not know what it was.[20]

John Donnelly had been a grocer before his appointment to the post of health warden for the sixth ward. When asked to defend the fitness of his assistant warden, Donnelly replied that the gentleman in question could "write a legible hand, and read writing plain." The testimony of James Lawrence, warden for the fifth ward, left little doubt that a man's political qualifications were more relevant for service in the Inspector's department than his medical abilities:

> Q. Who was appointed your successor?
> A. A man named Michael McManus.
> Q. Do you know how you came to be put out after serving for twelve years?
> A. I don't know, any further than it is usual to give the spoils to the victors, and my successor was appointed by the new alderman in the district. . . .
> Q. According to the usage of the department, the patronage is given to the alderman of the district?
> A. Yes, Sir; I was removed for that cause, so far as I understand it.[21]

The Council of Hygiene in 1864 had petitioned the state legislature to create a new health department for New York City. The petition failed, in part, because the City Inspector opposed any such innovation. According to Dr. Smith, a distinguished surgeon, "the City Inspector . . . was a grossly ignorant politician, but as he had upwards of one million dollars at his disposal, he had a prevailing influence in the Legislature when any bill affected his interests." The New York *Times* sug-

20. "Proceedings of a Select Committee of the Senate of the State of New York, Appointed to Investigate Various Departments of the Government of the City of New York," *New York Senate Documents*, No. 38, Feb. 9, 1865, 454, 455, 457. Hereafter cited as New York Senate Committee to Investigate New York Departments, 1865.
21. *Ibid.*, 464, 475, 478.

gested that the expenses of rural candidates to the legislature were "entirely paid by the parties who support the present unsanitary condition of the city." [22] John Donnelly, warden for the sixth ward, admitted in his testimony before the investigating committee that the City Inspector assessed officeholders to insure his department's survival:

> Q. Has there been any amount of money collected from the health wardens this year, or have they been made to contribute to a fund?
> A. I don't know what fund you refer to.
> Q. Have you given a month's pay?
> A. Yes, sir. . . .
> Q. Do you know what was the purpose of raising that fund?
> A. For the purpose of defraying the expenses incurred by the wanton raid that has been made on the department.[23]

The standards of efficiency and honesty in the City Inspector's office were probably no lower than in most municipal departments. The Tweed regime was not distinguished by a careful discrimination between public and private interests. Yet New York's health and housing problems cannot be ascribed to corrupt and ignorant politicians or "greedy" speculators and landlords. A rapidly expanding, heterogeneous, urban-industrial society posed problems of control—physical and social—which overwhelmed its citizens. They had to learn, through experience, which of the multitudinous specialized activities of an urban community could be left entirely in private hands, which required government monopoly, which needed government regulation, and finally, how to organize the system of government services and controls most efficiently. Equally important, municipal health regulation was dependent upon progress in medical science and engineering technology, a fact with significant implications for housing policy. One must remember that the

22. Stephen Smith, *The City That Was* (New York, 1911), 42; New York *Times*, Nov. 4, 1865, 6.

23. New York Senate Committee to Investigate New York Departments, 1865, 462.

bacteriological origins of disease were not understood until the 1870's and that housing regulation depended, in part, upon the ability of engineers to insure a supply of pure, fresh water and adequate sewerage facilities. Similarly, if housing reformers frequently complained of disease-breeding stables interspersed among residences, they could do little until the city found alternatives to the horse as the primary mode of urban transportation.

The tenement landlord or builder can hardly be blamed for ignoring these broader issues. Someone had to provide accommodation for the poor, and he assumed the responsibility for determining the quality and quantity of the city's housing by default. He had no zoning or minimum standards legislation to guide him, no municipal controls correlating the housing supply with the water and sewerage system, no clear-cut community policy defining private and public obligations in housing. The housing reformer's task was to ensure that the profit motive alone did not determine the city's housing development. It is not surprising that physicians assumed leadership in the struggle. Dr. John Griscom, for example, had been active in the AICP's campaign since the 1840's, and physicians provided the testimony which induced a select committee of the New York State Senate to recommend the establishment of a separate health department in 1859. Physicians such as Stephen Smith and Elisha Harris sparked the efforts of the Council of Hygiene a few years later. Medical men were not only more conscious than most laymen of the relationship between health and environment, but viewed public health as a specialized responsibility of government. They not only objected, therefore, to the corruption of the City Inspector's department, but resented the fact that his duties included sanitation, regulation of public markets, and inspection of weights and measures, as well as health. Closely linked with their efforts to limit entrepreneurial freedom in housing were the attempts of physician-reformers to establish public health as a specialized function in the complex urban community, a specialization they regarded as a prerequisite to efficient and scientific administration. "The duties of a health department in such a city as New York," argued the select senate committee in 1859, "if properly constituted and arranged, could possess a magnitude and importance sufficient to occupy the time and talents of the best educated men to be found in the ranks of the medical profession. None other than such should be entrusted with so delicate and responsible a service; none other can perform it with proper efficiency, and when selected they should be relieved of every extraneous duty." [24]

In 1859 the select committee failed to loosen the City Inspector's grip upon New York's public health services and substitute a separate department controlled by experts. After the Council of Hygiene's petition was likewise rejected in 1864, it decided to undertake an intensive investigation of New York's housing and sanitary condition. Perhaps the weight of scientific fact and truth could undermine the City Inspector's influence in the state legislature. The investigation, which commenced in July 1864, was directed by Dr. Stephen Smith; the thoroughness of the Council's work owed much to his intelligence and unflagging zeal. One of America's great sanitarians and public health reformers, Smith was born in Skaneateles, New York, in 1823. He acquired his medical education at Geneva Medical College in up-state New York, Buffalo Medical College and the College of Physicians and Surgeons in New York City. Smith was a long-time member of the Bellevue surgical staff and the author of two standard surgical texts. His work in connection with the establishment of the New York Metropolitan Board of Health and his service as its commissioner, 1867-75, were the first of many distinguished contributions in public health that ended with his death in 1922, at the awe-inspiring age of ninety-nine.

Like Smith, Dr. Elisha Harris, secretary to the Council of Hygiene, was an able physician with a pronounced social conscience. He, too, was determined that the triumphs of medical science should benefit the people of New York in the form of an efficient organization of the community's health services. Probably best remembered for his work with the United States Sanitary Commission during the Civil War, Harris was ap-

24. "Report of the Select Committee Appointed to Investigate the Health Department of the City of New York," *New York Senate Documents*, No. 49, Feb. 3, 1859, 10.

pointed to high posts in the Metropolitan Board of Health. Harris succeeded Smith as president of the American Public Health Association and rounded out his career as a commissioner of the New York State Board of Charities and as state superintendent of Vital Statistics.

Under Smith's direction, the Council of Hygiene divided New York City into twenty-nine districts. Each was placed in charge of an experienced physician. These men were instructed to make a house-by-house inspection of their assigned areas, to examine the topography, drainage, condition of the buildings, character of the population and, above all, the incidence of disease and mortality. The Council requested details concerning the medical history of every sick individual, including a record of those who had been exposed to him. Although the inspection was concentrated into the period July-December 1864, the dedicated little band of sanitary reformers extended their painstaking examinations into disease and mortality well beyond that date. The Council was determined to prove that much of New York's sickness and death was preventable. In their eyes, it was inexcusable that the city's death rate "invariably keeps above the highest average of other American cities" and "continues to be higher than that of the largest cities of Great Britain and France."

One of the presumably fecund sources of preventable disease stressed by the Council were the many "special nuisances" scattered about residential neighborhoods. These included cattle pens and stables, filthy public markets, the cattle and swine that shared the public thoroughfares with pedestrians, and "the accumulation of dumping-grounds and manure yards in the vicinity of populous streets." Among the tenements of Hell's Kitchen, in the area bounded by Eighth and Tenth Avenues, 37th to 40th Streets, the Council located three slaughterhouses, a varnish factory, a distillery, and a hides-and-fats plant. Breweries, packing plants, and swill milk factories were common in residential neighborhoods. The Council complained, on the basis of such evidence, that the atmosphere of the entire city was being polluted by a combination of "putrefying masses of animal and vegetable matter, together with dead animals . . . and poisonous exhalations from manufactories of various kinds."[25]

The condition of the streets was next in line for the Council's denunciations. They abounded with filth and garbage. The physician-inspector for the twenty-third sanitary district, situated between Sixth Avenue and the East River, 33rd to 40th Streets, observed that not a single thoroughfare was properly cleaned. Random piles of dirt were scattered in all directions by the wind. Grocers, oystermen, and other merchants tossed their refuse into the streets "with impunity." Overflowing garbage cans remained undisturbed for weeks at a time. Most inspectors also criticized the sewerage systems in their districts. Sewer gases leaked from defective pipes into streets and homes. Culverts were frequently glutted with mountains of miscellaneous filth.

Rounding out its indictment, the Council of Hygiene turned to the tenements of New York. These it defined as dwellings containing three or more families who rented their apartments by the month or for shorter periods of time. The Council counted 15,511 such tenements at the end of 1864. They housed approximately 500,000 people, a large majority of New York's total population of 800,000. Over 15,000 people still resided in cellars and basements. The following capsule description of the tenements is testimony to the ultimate fruits of the rapid but unplanned and unregulated urban growth of Jacksonian America:

> Not only does filth, overcrowding, lack of privacy and domesticity, lack of ventilation and lighting, and absence of supervision and of sanitary regulation, still characterize the greater number of them; but they are built to a greater height in stories, there are more rear tenant-houses erected back-to-back with other buildings, correspondingly situated on parallel streets; the courts and alleys are more greedily encroached upon and narrowed into unventilated,

25. Council of Hygiene, *Report*, xlv. The Council observed that these nuisances encroached upon the most select neighborhoods as well as the living quarters of the poor. *Ibid.*, xciii.

unlighted, damp, and well-like holes between the many-storied front and rear tenements; and more fever-breeding wynds and *culs-de-sac* are created as the demand for the humble homes of the laboring poor increases.[26]

An examination of one of the sanitary districts illustrates the deterioration which occurred as the result of the city's failure to establish minimum housing and sanitary standards. The fourth district, the domain of Dr. Ezra R. Pulling, corresponded to Manhattan's fourth ward. Fronting on the East River, bounded also by Peck Slip, Park Row, and Catherine Street, this river-front ward had been a choice residential district in the eighteenth and early nineteenth centuries. George Washington had lived in its fashionable Cherry Hill neighborhood after his inauguration as President. Over the years, however, Irish and German immigrants drove out the native Gothamites, and the neighborhood became a disrespectable, pugnacious ward, lined with shabby tenements and dives. Water Street, according to Herbert Asbury, became the "scene of more violent crime than any other street on the continent."[27] The ward became the hangout of such notorious river gangs as the Hookers, Swamp Angels, Slaughter Housers, and Patsy Conroys. Cherry Street blossomed with boarding houses whose proprietors were not averse to robbing and murdering their maritime and hobo guests.

An impressive total of 446 liquor stores and dives, located in residences, brothels and sailors' dance houses, catered to the thirsty. Junk shops and stables abounded. Local grocery and butcher shops hawked a quality of goods typical of the worst tenement districts: "Unwholesome meat, particularly *slunk* veal, is constantly vended and consumed. Piles of pickled herrings are exposed to the air till the mass approaches a condition of putridity; and this slimy food, with wilted and decayed vegetables, sausages not above suspicion, and horrible pies, composed of stale and unripe fruits, whose digestion no human stomach can accomplish, all find ready purchasers." The in-

26. *Ibid.*, lxxv-lxxvi.
27. Asbury, *The Gangs of New York*, 49.

gredients for a suspicious fourth ward sausage included "frag-
ments of bread and other farinacious food, decaying potatoes,
cabbages, etc., interspersed with lifeless cats, rats, and puppies,
thus introduced to a *post mortem* fellowship."[28]

The ward contained 714 tenements in 1864, mostly of brick.
No less than 474 had originally been constructed to house
single families or to serve some commercial purpose. The rent
for two or three tiny rooms averaged $9.00 per month. On
Cherry Street loomed the notorious Gotham Court, a reputedly
prolific breeder of crime and disease. This was a tenement five
stories high, 234 feet deep and 34 feet wide. Ironically, a benevolent Quaker had erected the building in 1851 as a kind of
model tenement. By 1865, however, it had become a haunt of
outlaws and an incubator of smallpox, tuberculosis, dysentery,
and other scourges. Pulling believed that Gotham Court represented "about an average specimen of tenant-houses in the
lower part of the city in respect to salubrity." Although some
were roomier, better ventilated and cleaner, there were many
"in far worse condition," with even a higher incidence of
disease and mortality.[29]

[4]

The Council of Hygiene's vitriolic denunciation of the sanitary condition of New York was balanced by a perceptive
insight into the social origins of the housing problem. In modern
terms, the tenement was the product of a complex process of
acculturation to an urban, increasingly industrialized society.
The acculturation process involved the uprooted immigrant,
on the one hand, and the American — his need to adapt older
rural attitudes, institutions, and patterns of thought to an urban
civilization — on the other. The Council of Hygiene recognized
that, for better or worse, the fortunes of the immigrant and
native communities were inseparably linked. The best interests

28. Ezra R. Pulling, "Report of the Fourth Sanitary District" in Council of
Hygiene, *Report*, 59, 60.

29. *Ibid.*, 49, 54, 55. The apartments in Gotham Court contained two rooms.
The larger of these was only 14'8" long, 9'6" wide and 8'4" high. The smaller
had the same dimensions except for a foot less in width.

of the entire community, not simply the immigrant's, demanded municipal supervision of his housing and sanitary condition.[30] Given the congestion and the demand for cheap living quarters, the absence of control over building development, and the irresponsibility of tenement landlords, the tenement neighborhood inevitably degenerated into a dirty, oppressive slum. Even if a particular immigrant possessed high personal standards of domestic cleanliness and order, he was handicapped by circumstances beyond his control. What could he do to overcome the inadequate sanitary facilities, the enforced overcrowding, the prevading dinginess, the ignorance or carelessness of his neighbors, the unwillingness of the landlord to make necessary repairs and improvements, the paucity of light, air and ventilation? Similarly, who would teach the ignorant peasant, accustomed to the make-shift sanitary arrangements of his European village, his responsibilities to himself and his neighbors in an urban society? Left to himself, as the Council of Hygiene perceived, the immigrant often followed the path of least resistance. His habits reflected the low sanitary, moral, and cultural tone of the tenement neighborhood.

The farsighted physician-reformers of the Council of Hygiene realized not only that the immigrant could not be allowed to shift for himself in matters of health and housing, but that an urban society required new institutions and new habits of thought to cope effectively with its problems. "Unless the resources of Sanitary Science and the beneficient operations of widely-administered sanitary regulations are interposed," the Council warned, "the evils attendant upon overcrowding and the aggregation of vast numbers will be continually augmented as the population increases." The self-sufficient individualism of the frontier or farm, the Jacksonian devotion to entrepreneurial freedom, the application of small town standards of efficiency to municipal services, were outmoded. The welfare of the large city like New York depended upon some sacrifice of individual economic freedom. It demanded a disciplined social conscience and the use of government powers and re-

30. Council of Hygiene, *Report,* xlvii.

sources to assist (or control) those unable or unwilling to adapt to an urban way of life. Thus the Council of Hygiene insisted that the people of New York apply "forethought, inquiry, science, art and good governmental regulations" to their social problems. It proposed that the true measure of municipal progress, the "index of social advancement," be "a careful regard for human life and welfare."[31]

In justifying the sanitary reforms which it advocated, the Council of Hygiene followed the trail first marked out by the AICP. Like the Association, the Council viewed the slums as detrimental to morals as well as health, pointing out that "the sanitary wants and the social evils of this city have become fearfully centralized in the densely-crowded tenant-house districts."[32] The Council also reaffirmed the rather simple environmental faith of the AICP by assuming that if one removed oppressive physical evils, then social evils would disappear as well. And like the AICP, the Council of Hygiene was prepared to accept restrictions upon entrepreneurial freedom in order to advance the welfare of both the immigrant and native-American community.

The Council of Hygiene's greatest contribution to the struggle for sanitary and housing improvement was its stress upon careful and methodical investigation of existing conditions as a prelude to reform and the establishment of adequate machinery to administer sanitary regulations. Without the first, no satisfactory legislation could be enacted; without the second, it could not be enforced. Thus the Council of Hygiene served as a model for the "scientific" housing reform of the Progressive era.[33]

After it had issued its *Report* early in 1865, the Council of Hygiene renewed its efforts to win Albany's support for a new health department. Armed with facts and figures, Dr. Smith labored to convince the legislature that the proposed

31. *Ibid.*, xxxix, xxxviii, cxliii.

32. *Ibid.*, lxviii.

33. Lawrence Veiller, the country's most distinguished housing expert for the two decades after 1900, referred to the work of the Council of Hygiene as a "tremendous influence" upon his own, Interview, July 13, 1959.

Board of Health was imperative for the health and safety of the city. Once again the influence of the City Inspector and his cohorts proved decisive.

This time, however, the Inspector's triumph was short-lived. In the summer of 1865 cholera appeared in Europe. New Yorkers feared that its terrible sickle would soon sweep across the Atlantic and add more bodies to the toll already collected by the Civil War. In November, Strong noted in his diary: "What we need is practical sanitary reformation of back streets, tenement houses, and pestiferous bone-boiling establishments. Thereby, and by nothing else, can the inevitable epidemic be mitigated. The city government will not do this, or any other good work, honestly and thoroughly, for it is rotten to the core. The 'Citizens' Association' will do what it can." An editorial in *Harper's Weekly* reflected the community's alarm when it prophesied that the "imminence of the cholera" assured the passage of a health bill in 1866. Otherwise, "the city of New York will be literally left to its own destruction."[34] At the first session of the legislature the panicky fears of New Yorkers were translated into law. A Metropolitan Board of Health was created for the New York area. Terror had succeeded where reason, enlightened self-interest and the pleas of humanitarians had failed. The new Board would not single-handedly solve New York's health and housing problems. It represented, however, an end to the era of *laissez-faire* and unqualified incompetence in these critical provinces of the city's life.[35]

34. Strong, *Diary*, IV, 44; *Harper's Weekly*, Jan. 20, 1866, 35. On the impending cholera and sanitary reform see also *The Nation*, I (1865), 250; New York *Times*, Oct. 20, 1865, 4, and Nov. 4, 1865, 6.
35. George Rosen, *A History of Public Health* (New York, 1958), 247.

2. The Tenement Comes of Age, 1866-1890

*They generally go hand in hand, poverty
and uncleanliness, because these poor people
have not the facilities to keep themselves
clean; I do not wish to cast any odium on
the poor, but unfortunately the poor have
not got the facilities to keep themselves
clean; they have no baths, or servants, or
many other things that money can secure.*

JOHN C. COLLINS,
Health Department Inspector, 1884

[1]

The jurisdiction of the newly-established Metropolitan Board
of Health extended over New York, Kings, Westchester, and
Richmond counties and a few towns in the present Borough
of Queens. The Board consisted of nine commissioners — four
appointed by the governor, three of whom had to be physicians; the health officer of the Port of New York; and four
police commissioners. A sanitary superintendent, appointed by
the Board, supervised the work of fifteen sanitary inspectors.[1]

The Board's authority to regulate tenement conditions was
embodied in the Tenement House Law of 1867. This law was
enacted upon the recommendation of a state legislative committee which had investigated the New York and Brooklyn
tenements shortly after the establishment of the Metropolitan
Board of Health. The committee discovered that the 15,511
tenements reported by the Council of Hygiene had increased
to over 18,000. More than half were in "bad sanitary condition." The squalor of basement and cellar habitations defied
imagination. In the lower streets of the city they were "subject

1. In 1870 the Board was reorganized to include only the City of New York
(Manhattan and the Bronx).

to regular periodical flooding by tide water, to the depth of from six inches to a foot; frequently so much as to keep the children of the occupants in bed until ebb-tide."[2] The committee's findings generally confirmed the low estimate placed upon New York's sanitary condition by the Council of Hygiene.

The housing act of 1867 defined a tenement as follows:

> A tenement house within the meaning of this act shall be taken to mean and include every house, building, or portion thereof which is rented, leased, let or hired out to be occupied, or is occupied as the home or residence of more than three families living independently of another, and doing their cooking upon the premises, or by more than two families on a floor, so living and cooking, but have a common right in the halls, stairways, water closets or privies, or some of them.[3]

The "more than three families" provision was a serious error. Some of the city's worst tenements were occupied by only three families.[4] Twenty years passed before this fault was corrected. Otherwise, the legal definition of a tenement remained the same into the twentieth century.

On the whole, the standards established by the Tenement House Law of 1867 were low. Many of its provisions were vague, leaving too much discretionary authority with the Board of Health. In relation to fire protection, for example, the law required all tenements to have a fire escape *or some other means of egress* approved by the inspector of public buildings in Manhattan and in Brooklyn by the assistant sanitary superintendent. An inconveniently located wooden ladder thus satisfied the legal requirements, if approved by these officials. To ventilate dark interior bedrooms, the law compelled only the construction of a window connecting with a room which did communicate with the outer air. The law set no limit to the

2. "Report of the Committee on Public Health, Medical Colleges and Societies, Relative to the Conditions of Tenement Houses in the Cities of New York and Brooklyn," *New York State Assembly Documents*, No. 156, Mar. 8, 1867, 3, 4, 6.

3. *New York State Laws*, Ninetieth Session, 1867, Chap. 908, Sec. 17.

4. This was the conclusion reached by the New York State Tenement House Commission of 1884. "Report of the Tenement House Commission," *New York State Senate Documents*, No. 36, Feb. 17, 1885, 9. Hereafter cited as Tenement House Commission of 1884, *Report*.

percentage of the lot which a tenement might cover. Although ten feet had to separate the rear of any building from another, a tenement might extend to the lot line if no other building existed. The Board of Health was authorized to modify even this modest ten foot requirement.

The reports of the inspectors for the Council of Hygiene were glutted with uncomplimentary references to the poor sanitary and drainage systems in tenement districts. Privies, often unconnected to sewers and located in rear yards, overflowed. In some places, the contents seeped through rotten foundations into cellars.[5] The sanitary requirements set by the act of 1867 represented little progress. Cesspools were forbidden — except where unavoidable. Water closets and privies had to connect with sewers — where such existed. A landlord was obligated to provide only one water closet or privy for every twenty inhabitants, and it could be located in the yard. The manner and material of water closet construction was left again to the discretion of the Board of Health. Finally the tenement landlord satisfied the law if he furnished a water tap somewhere in the house or yard.

The Tenement House Law of 1867 at least had symbolic value. It represented the acceptance in principle of the community's right to limit the freedom of the tenement landlord and builder. However, the low standards of the law and its successors through 1901 involved a very shaky compromise between entrepreneurial rights and the rights of the community to protect its citizens. Housing legislation before 1901 was also characterized by inadequate provision for enforcement. An understaffed Board of Health, often subject to political pressures from landlords or builders influential with Tammany, found it difficult to ensure compliance with the law.[6] Burdened with many other duties, the Board of Health had not the time or resources to inspect periodically thousands of tenements or to prod indefinitely uncooperative landlords. It was difficult to force elusive "estates, receivers, agents and non-residents" to

5. Council of Hygiene, *Report*, 151.
6. New York *Times*, Mar. 25, 1879, 40, May 25, 1879, 6.

obey the legislation, and the "poverty of small owners, struggling to retain property heavily mortgaged" intensified the problems of enforcement.[7] Legal compulsion was at best a slow and often futile procedure. Two major problems inherited by Progressive housing reformers were an ineffective tenement code and the creaky machinery of enforcement.

[2]

Housing reformers of the post-Civil War decades experimented further with the model tenement program which had its small beginnings in the AICP's "Workmen's Home" and in the program of sanitary legislation urged by the Council of Hygiene. A key development of the period was the emergence of Alfred T. White of Brooklyn as the chief spokesman for the model tenement ideal. The example of White's three groups of model tenements, built between 1877 and 1890, greatly influenced a generation of reformers seeking a solution to the problem of the ever-expanding tenement slums.

The discrepancy in standards between the model tenements erected by White and other "investment philanthropists" and the ordinary commercial tenement built under the housing laws, was very apparent; but the few built housed only a small fraction of New York's tenement population and the vast majority had to depend for their protection upon legislative restrictions over builders and landlords. Conceivably, had the housing reformer not overestimated the potentialities of the model tenement, he might have pressed harder for legislation which would make all tenements model, at least in relation to such basic necessities as light, air, ventilation, fire protection, and sanitary facilities. One consequence of the minimal legislative controls over building development was the birth and proliferation after 1879 of the notorious dumb-bell tenement. The dumb-bell, indeed, did not even originate in the minds of

7. See the testimony before the Tenement House Commission of 1884 of Roger S. Tracy, a sanitary inspector for the Board of Health, and William P. Prentice, attorney and counsel to the Board. Tenement House Commission of 1884, *Report*, 170, 132, 135.

building speculators, but was the contribution of reformers willing to accept the terms imposed by the commercial builder.

The history of the dumb-bell begins in 1877 when Henry C. Meyer established a trade journal, the *Plumber and Sanitary Engineer*. Shortly after the Civil War, Meyer had founded a company which manufactured water, gas, and steam installation supplies. Anxious to boost sales, he hoped that his journal would convince architects, plumbers, and engineers of the safety of his type of equipment. Meyer chose Charles F. Wingate, a civil engineer, as his editor. A relative of the secretary of the AICP, Wingate had assisted in the preparation of the Association's annual reports and in the process had become an authority on the housing problem. Wingate interested Meyer in housing reform, and the latter decided that a competition for an improved tenement sponsored by his journal would increase circulation. Accordingly, the *Plumber and Sanitary Engineer* in December 1878, announced a prize competition for a tenement on a 25 x 100 foot lot. The design which best combined maximum safety and convenience for the tenant, and maximum profitability for the investor, would win.[8]

In the next few months approximately two hundred plans were submitted by architects. Exhibited at the Leavitt Art Gallery on Clinton Place, they aroused considerable public interest.[9] The plans were judged by a committee of five: R. G. Hatfield, a consulting architect;[10] Charles F. Chandler, president of the Board of Health; Robert Hoe, a printing press manufacturer; and two clergymen, Dr. Potter of Grace Church and Dr. John Hall, Meyer's own clergyman. The gentlemen of this committee, despite their explicit denial that the "requirements of physical and moral health"[11] could be satisfied by a

8. For Meyer's account of the founding of his journal see Henry C. Meyer, *The Story of the Sanitary Engineer, Later the Engineering Record. Supplementary to Civil War Experiences* (New York, 1928). On the contest itself consult the *Plumber and Sanitary Engineer*, II (1878), 1, 32.

9. New York *Times*, Feb. 10, 1879, 8; *American Architect and Building News*, V (1879), 57; *Plumber and Sanitary Engineer* II (1879), 90.

10. Hatfield died before the awards were made. He was replaced by James Renwick.

11. *Plumber and Sanitary Engineer*, II (1879), 90.

tenement on a 25 x 100 foot lot, awarded first prize to the dumb-bell design of James E. Ware.

The widespread adoption of the dumb-bell by builders was assured by a provision of the Tenement House Law of 1879. Partly as a result of the interest in tenement reform stimulated by the *Plumber and Sanitary Engineer* competition, a group of clergymen and laymen held a conference early in February 1879. This conference, which included Dr. Stephen Smith, Alfred T. White, and Charles Loring Brace of the Children's Aid Society, resolved that the clergy of the city would preach on the tenement problem on Sunday, February 23. After the ministers had spoken, two public meetings were held in the evening and various speakers explained the pressing urgency of tenement reform. The following week Mayor Cooper presided over an important public meeting at Cooper Union, which resulted in the formation of a Committee of Nine to plot a reform strategy. Upon the recommendation of this committee, an Improved Dwellings Association was formed to provide housing for "persons unable to pay more than eight to ten dollars per month." The "New York Sanitary Reform Society," a voluntary private association designed to work for the improvement of tenement conditions, also originated in the Committee's recommendations. Finally, the Committee of Nine prepared and introduced into the state legislature a bill amending the Tenement House Law of 1867. After considerable delay "owing to the vigorous opposition of many landlords through the agency of their representatives at Albany,"[12] the legislation passed. It required, significantly, that every tenement bedroom

12. For the sequence of events beginning with the conference at the home of D. Willis James to the formation of the Committee of Nine and the enactment of the Tenement House Law of 1879, consult the following: Committee of Nine, *Final Report*, May 31, 1879; James Gallatin, *Tenement House Reform in the City of New York* (Boston, 1881); Henry E. Pellew, "New York Tenement Houses," *The Sanitarian*, VII (1879), 107-11; *Plumber and Sanitary Engineer*, II (1879), 89. The members of the Committee of Nine were H. E. Pellew, W. Bayard Cutting, R. T. Auchmuty, D. Willis James, C. P. Daly, C. Vanderbilt, W. W. Astor, James Gallatin, and F. D. Tappen. Most of these served on the Board of Directors of the New York Sanitary Reform Society and were connected in some capacity with the Improved Dwellings Association. The quotation is from Gallatin, 6.

have a window opening directly to the street or yard unless sufficient light and ventilation could be provided "in a manner and upon a plan approved by the board of health." This provision of the law requiring a window in all tenement bedrooms, combined with the discretionary authority granted to the Board of Health, paved the way for the dumb-bell tenement.

Ware's prize tenement, with various modifications, was the characteristic type of multiple dwelling erected for the working class in New York between 1879 and 1901. The dumb-bell was essentially a front and rear tenement connected by a hall. Situated on a pinched 25 x 100 foot lot, the dumb-bell was usually five or six stories high and contained fourteen rooms to a floor, seven on either side running in a straight line. One family occupied the first four of these seven rooms, a second family the remaining three rooms to the rear. The dumb-bell thus harbored four families to a floor. The hallways and stairwell were dimly lit by windows fronting upon the air shaft. Water closets, two to a floor or one to every two families, were located opposite the stairs.

Of the fourteen rooms on each floor, ten depended for light upon the narrow air shaft. This was an indentation at the side of the building about twenty-eight inches wide and enclosed on all sides. It proved to be not only inadequate for the purpose of providing light and air, but a positive hindrance to the health and comfort of tenants. The shaft was a fire hazard, acting as a duct to convey flames from one story to the next. It became a receptacle for garbage and filth of all kinds. It was noisy with the quarrels and shouts of twenty or more families. Its stale air reeked with the cooking odors from twenty or more kitchens.

Meyer and his associates had attempted the impossible; the architect could not reconcile the tenant's welfare and the investor's profit. Two dozen families could not be housed comfortably in a six-story building compressed into a lot 25 x 100 feet in dimension. The building occupied 75 per cent to 90 per cent of the lot. The front parlor, the most spacious room, measured only 10½ x 11 feet. Bedrooms were about 7 x 8½ feet in size. Amenities such as landscaping or children's play areas were out of the question.

Meyer explained his acquiescence in the 25 x 100 foot lot on the grounds that "the problem in New York then was the single lot, and that any architect could make a design for a large block; but that it was an attempt to emphasize and solve the New York problem that the competition was instituted."[13] Far more useful, however, would have been an attempt by Meyer or the Committee of Nine to condemn the single lot as unfit for tenement construction. The 25 x 100 foot lot mostly benefited land owners, speculators, realtors, builders, and landlords who found it a convenient parcel to buy, build upon, and sell. This narrow subdivision may have made sense in 1800, when most dwellings were built for single-family occupancy. By 1879 it had outlived its usefulness.

The prize awards of the *Plumber and Sanitary Engineer* were criticized by contemporaries who realized that the dumb-bell was a negative contribution to the solution of the housing problem. The New York *Times* observed that if the prize plans were the best possible, then the housing problem was virtually insolvable. Perhaps, the *Times* sardonically reflected, "the gentlemen who offered the prizes really desired to demonstrate this to the public before proposing any other scheme." Dr. A. N. Bell, editor of the *Sanitarian*, complained that "the prizes were won by the most ingenious designs for dungeons." If the dumb-bell is the best, then "how much is the best worth?" wondered the *American Architect and Building News*.[14]

[3]

The housing legislation between 1879 and 1890 contained some useful provisions, but did nothing to alter the dumb-bell pattern. The 1879 law limited, for the first time, the amount of lot space a tenement could occupy. The 65 per cent limitation, however, was nullified by the discretionary authority

13. Meyer, *Story of the Sanitary Engineer*, 13.
14. New York *Times*, Mar. 16, 1879, 6; *The Sanitarian*, VII (1879), 226; *American Architect and Building News*, V (1879), 81, 97.

granted the Board of Health. A provision requiring a window of at least twelve square feet in any room used for sleeping was also diluted by discretionary power given the Board of Health, which could approve a substitute. Finally, the law provided for thirty sanitary police, under the Board's supervision, to enforce the housing code.

The widespread interest in housing conditions stimulated by the *Plumber and Sanitary Engineer* competition subsided until 1884, when a series of lectures by Felix Adler, founder of the Ethical Culture Society, again aroused and coalesced the energies of reformers. Growing out of Adler's denunciation of the tenement blight in 1884 was the first of a series of official state tenement house commissions. The investigations and report of the Tenement House Commission of 1884, which included Adler and Charles F. Wingate among its membership, resulted in further amendments to the tenement code in 1887, mostly of a superficial character. The number of sanitary police was increased from thirty to forty-five. The law established a standing (and quite ineffectual) tenement house commission composed of New York's mayor and several department heads. Tenement landlords now had to provide one water closet for every fifteen instead of every twenty inhabitants, as well as running water on every floor. For administrative purposes, the law required owners of tenements to file their names and addresses annually with the Board of Health. Moreover, the Board was required to make semiannual inspections of every tenement. Neither of these latter provisions was successfully enforced.[15]

We have suggested, although it would be difficult to prove, that reformers might have labored for higher standards of restrictive legislation had they not been so dazzled by the potentialities of the model tenement. The intense interest in model tenements throughout the period was always disproportionate to the actual accomplishments of "investment philan-

15. The Tenement House Commission of 1884 included, besides Adler and Wingate, Joseph W. Drexel, chairman; S. O. Vanderpoel; Oswald Ottendorfer; Moreau Morris; Anthony Reichardt; Joseph J. O'Donohue; Abbot Hodgman; William P. Esterbrook.

thropy." The model tenement, in theory, had many advantages over restrictive legislation. It circumvented the troublesome task of enacting and enforcing housing codes, a process which often involved the compromise of standards and principles. Second, even if restrictive legislation prevented the worst tenements from being built, it did not guarantee a sufficient supply of good ones at moderate rentals. The model tenement, a strictly private venture accompanied by voluntary limitations upon profit, promised a safe, sane solution to the housing problem in a capitalist society.

One of the first notable model tenement projects after the Civil War emerged not in New York but in Boston, where Dr. H. P. Bowditch helped organize the Boston Cooperative Building Company in 1871. Limiting dividends to 7 per cent, the Company opened its first buildings in 1872 and ultimately constructed five tenement estates. The tenements were small, with one family to a floor, and each apartment contained running water. This latter convenience, however, was canceled out by cellar toilets. A few years after the Company began operations, Robert Treat Paine decided to offer workers the benefits of model homes rather than tenements. He financed the construction of four- to six-room single-family homes, with bath, and arranged for long-term mortgage payments. Paine organized a limited-dividend Workingmen's Building Association in 1880 to expand his operations.

Despite the work of Paine and the Boston Cooperative Building Company, the undisputed evangelist of model-tenement gospel in the postwar period was Alfred T. White of Brooklyn. Born in 1846, White was educated at Rennselaer Polytechnical Institute. After the Civil War he joined his father as a partner in the importing firm of W. A. and A. M. White. A wealthy man in search of a philanthropy, White discovered in housing reform an outlet for his benevolent impulse: "It is time to recognize that if the intelligent and wealthy portion of the community do not provide homes for the working classes, the want will be continually supplied by the less intelligent class and after the old fashion." In White's estimation, the need for improved low-income housing had become imperative, for "the badly constructed, unventilated, dark and foul tenement houses of New York . . . are the nurseries of the epidemics which spread with certain destructiveness into the fairest homes; they are the hiding-places of the local banditti; they are the cradles of the insane who fill the asylums and of the paupers who throng the almshouses; in fact, they produce these noxious and unhappy elements of society as surely as the harvest follows the sowing. . . ."[16]

In 1872 White began preparing plans for a model tenement when he learned of Sir Sydney Waterlow's philanthropic work in London. Waterlow in 1863 had erected a tenement whose distinctive features were an exterior stairwell and two-room-deep apartments. White patterned his own buildings after the Langbourn Estate of Waterlow's Improved Industrial Dwellings Company, including the outside stairwell which dispensed with the "foulness of interior dark unventilated halls and stairways," and served as a sturdy, accessible fire escape.[17] Located in Brooklyn and completed in 1877, White's initial tribute to "philanthropy and 5 per cent" was an immediate, influential success. He demonstrated, presumably, that a capitalist could provide "well-ventilated, convenient, and agreeable" housing for workers.[18] According to White, his "Home Buildings" on Hicks and Baltic Streets near the Brooklyn waterfront swiftly captured the attention of the Children's Aid Society, the AICP, and the State Charities Aid Association. Among the visitors, "keen in their interest," were Theodore Roosevelt, Sr., and Louisa Lee Schuyler, both of the State Charities Aid Association, D. Willis James, at whose home the first conference leading to the formation of the Committee of Nine had been

16. Alfred T. White, *Improved Dwellings for the Laboring Classes: The Need, and the Way to Meet It on Strict Commercial Principles*, in New York and other Cities (New York, 1879), 41, 2.

17. Alfred T. White, *Thirty-Five Years' Experience as an Owner* (New York, 1912), 3.

18. New York *Times*, Nov. 5, 1877, 4; *American Architect and Building News*, IV (1878), 208; Tenement House Commission of 1884, *Report*, 75; Charles L. Brace, "Model Tenement Houses," *Plumber and Sanitary Engineer*, I (1878), 48.

held, and Josephine Shaw Lowell, founder of the New York
Charity Organization Society, who referred to the new tenements as a "realization of an Arabian Night's Dream."[19]

The "Home Buildings" accommodated forty families; and
each apartment, only two rooms deep to ensure sufficient light
and ventilation, included a sink and water closet. White completed a second adjoining unit the same year and then purchased a 200 x 250 foot tract on the next block. The "Tower
Buildings" arose on this site (Hicks, Warren, and Baltic
Streets) in 1878-79. Finally, White compressed thirty-four
cottages into a narrow alley or passageway running from
Warren to Baltic Street. These were attached six- to nine-room
houses, arranged in two parallel rows. Altogether White was
landlord to 267 families. He prohibited boarders or lodgers, set
high standards of maintenance and upkeep for his tenants, and
demanded prompt weekly payments of rent in advance.

Following White's lead, others promoted model tenement
companies in the next decade. The Improved Dwellings Association, organized in 1879 as a consequence of the Committee
of Nine's recommendations, opened its Manhattan tenements
for occupancy in 1882. The Tenement House Building Company, organized in 1885, was ready for business two years later.
Its property was located on squalid Cherry Street in the fourth
ward. Pratt Institute inaugurated another philanthropic venture
in 1887, when it opened its Astral Apartments in Greenpoint,
Brooklyn, and White rounded out the decade's good works
with his "Riverside Buildings" in 1890.

White's objectives were representative of most other model
tenement enthusiasts of the period. He insisted, above all, that
such tenements must be profitable. Otherwise, they would not
inspire imitators. And if model tenements failed financially,
opponents of restrictive legislation would use this as an argument "*against* efforts to secure legislative action seeking to
impose healthful restrictions on existing or future buildings."[20]
Furthermore, the reformer must never view housing as a charity

19. White, *Thirty-Five Years' Experience as an Owner*, 4, 5.
20. Alfred T. White, "Better Homes for Workingmen," National Conference of Charities and Correction, *Proceedings*, 1885, 368.

in which the poor got something for nothing, thus weakening their character and self-reliance. It was a business venture; the purpose of the model tenement was to prove that good housing paid.

White advised prospective investors to build in districts already invaded by speculators. "You can afford to pay as much for land as they can; and high cost is no detriment, *provided* the value is made by the pressure of people seeking residence there."[21] White's insistence upon profitability and his advice to philanthropists to emulate the example of the speculative builder indicate his essentially conservative outlook. Neither White nor his contemporary housing reformers were radicals, toying with imaginative reconstructions of the social and economic order. Their aim was more modest — to provide safe, comfortable, and even pleasant housing for low-income groups within the framework of the capitalist-profit system. Apart from the genuine structural merits of the model tenement, it is not surprising that the businessmen, clergymen, and social workers who participated in the housing movement were so united in its endorsement. The model tenement represented no challenge whatever to economic orthodoxy. It was a painless and ostensibly effective solution to the housing problem.

White recommended that model tenement investors determine the prevailing rents in the neighborhood selected for construction. The buildings should then be planned to return the same average rentals and simultaneously assure tenants "as many conveniences as this average rental will allow."[22] White's last unit, the "Riverside Buildings," are a good example of his objectives in practice and they indicate, generally, the kind of accommodations which the model tenement companies hoped to provide. The Riverside Buildings were six stories high. They contained 3 one-room, 91 two-room, 161 three-room and 23 four-room apartments. Rents ranged from $1.40 a week for a single room with scullery on the ground floor to $3.60 a week for a four-room apartment. These rents, which the unskilled worker could

21. *Ibid.*, 370-71.
22. *Ibid.*, 371.

afford to pay, were unusually low even by the standards of the model tenement. White, of course, built in Brooklyn, where land prices were much cheaper than in Manhattan. The Riverside Buildings provided a separate water closet for each family and such outdoor amenities as children's sandboxes, grass-lined courts and summer band concerts. Most important of all, White broke from the confines of the 25 x 100 foot lot and grouped his buildings around a large central court. They covered only half the land and since no apartment was more than two rooms deep, every room was assured plentiful light and ventilation.[23]

Model tenement zealots like White were certain that the policy of investment philanthropy would inspire widespread emulation. After all, the model tenement idea courted two of the strongest instincts in human nature — self-interest and altruism. By helping the poor at a profit, one served both humanity and one's pocket. Unfortunately, capitalists in the 1880's were no more prepared to minister to humanity in this fashion than had been their counterparts in the 1850's, when the AICP had sponsored its model tenement. Why should wealthy businessmen with loose capital accept dividends of only 4 or 5 per cent in an age of great material expansion when more profitable investments beckoned elsewhere?

Housing, as a rule, did not attract the large aggregations of capital necessary to build model tenements in contrast to the cheaper dumb-bells with their smaller lot dimensions and lower structural standards. Concentrated ownership of tenement land or property, such as that of the Astor family or Trinity Church, was not typical. Low-income housing appealed mostly to the capitalist (builder or landlord) of relatively small means.[24] It required a comparatively modest equity, which was all he could afford. Yet the tenement landlord might anticipate average profits of 6 or 7 per cent on his investment. Tenement property

23. For a description of the Riverside Buildings see E. R. L. Gould, *The Housing of the Working People*, Eighth Special Report of the Commissioner of Labor (Washington, D. C., 1895), 177-81.

24. Gustavus Myers, *History of the Great American Fortunes* (Modern Library: New York, 1936), 160-62. Henry C. Meyer, testifying before a Royal Housing Commission in England, claimed that New York's 21,000 tenements were divided among 18,000 owners. Meyer, *Story of the Sanitary Engineer*, 33.

in the 1880's sometimes paid much more — even 15 or 18 per cent.[25] In effect, those who could afford the large capital investment required to build model tenements were not particularly interested; they had better uses for their capital which did not involve the annoyance of dealing with ignorant or careless tenants. On the other hand the small entrepreneurs, sometimes immigrants themselves, who owned the lion's share of New York tenements, were not prepared to sacrifice their profits for the sake of humanity. The altruism and self-restraint upon which model-tenement enthusiasts depended were remote from the realities of the market place. Until reformers could incorporate the standards of the model tenement in restrictive legislation, housing conditions would not 'improve for the majority of workers.

[4]

Why was it that an affluent and comfortably situated gentleman like Alfred T. White devoted so much time, energy, and money to improving the housing of the poor? Why, in the words of the AICP, was there "no social question, except that of labor itself, of deeper interest to the community at large?"[26] We cannot wholly appreciate the attitudes and goals of housing reformers until we grasp the full social implications of the tenement problem. The tenement slum was the product of mighty social and economic upheavals in American society. For most reformers it was also a 'cause.

The quality of a city's housing is inextricably linked to broader social and economic trends. It is related, for example, to the generally accepted standard of living, the pace of urban and industrial expansion, the level of technology, the accepted role of government in the urban economy, and social and moral ideals. The decade or two after the Civil War has been described as the age of the robber barons, the gilded age, the age of enterprise, the great barbecue. Its dominant features — industrialization, urbanization, immigration, westward expansion — were not

25. Tenement House Commission of 1884, *Report*, 83, 105, 106.
26. AICP, *Forty-fifth Annual Report*, 1888, 21.

new phenomena in American life, but their magnitude was un-precedented. In 1860 there were only nine cities with over 100,000 population. By 1880 there were twenty. The nine cities in 1860 contained a little over 2,500,000 inhabitants. The corresponding figure for the twenty cities in 1880 was 6,000,000. In 1854, some 400,000 immigrants from Europe landed in the United States, the record number before the Civil War. After 1880, yearly immigration rarely fell below 400,000. In 1859, approximately 1,300,000 wage earners toiled in 140,000 industrial establishments. By 1889, over 4,000,000 labored in 355,000 factories. The value of manufactured products in the same thirty-year period rose from less than two billion dollars to more than nine billion.[27]

However one might characterize the two decades after the Civil War, one thing is certain. The machine and the city had shattered the Jeffersonian-Jacksonian vision of the yeoman, agrarian republic. The economic vitality of the new era centered in the factory, not the farm. The city, rather than the small town, became the undisputed symbol of America's productive energies, cultural and intellectual attainments, economic and social opportunities. New men of wealth in the great cities superseded the older planter and merchant aristocracy and, as Veblen explained, created new canons of consumption. The stone and marble palaces of the rich lined Fifth Avenue in New York. The lavish excesses of the wealthy excited the imagination of *hoi polloi*. It became the custom on New Year's day, for example, to leave window curtains partly undrawn on Fifth Avenue, permitting strollers to view "the richly furnished, brightly lighted drawing rooms, with their elegantly dressed occupants."[28] The excitement and diversity of city life, its economic possibilities most vividly manifested by the *nouveau riche*, attracted those persons dissatisfied with the stale routine of the farm or village.

27. The statistics were drawn from U. S. Department of Commerce: Bureau of the Census, *Historical Statistics of the United States, 1789-1945* (Washington, D. C., 1949).

28. James D. McCabe, *New York by Sunlight and Gaslight, A Work Descriptive of the Great American Metropolis* (New York, 1882), 174.

But the color of the city, the avenues it opened to material success and cultural stimulation, were balanced by less glamorous features. The city reflected as well the acute social tensions and maladjustments of an expanding and fluid industrial society.

The Jeffersonian-Jacksonian ideal had been that of a roughly equalitarian society. A nation composed of small property owners, mostly farmers and artisans, would insure political democracy, widely diffused intelligence, virtue, and patriotism. Although extreme Jacksonians had certain qualms about the unsettling effects on the economy of business enterprise, most Americans could easily reconcile enterprise with stability and virtue. Men would be rewarded for their toil in proportion to their thrift, initiative, ability, and sobriety. Work and business were thus tests of character, and the entrepreneur the instrument of the community's moral and economic progress. Even the most doctrinaire Jacksonian agreed that the threat to social stability came not from business enterprise as such, but from monopoly and special privilege.

What happened to the certainties of the equalitarian society in an industrial-urban age? They lingered on in men's minds, but they obviously had less applicability in the urban metropolis, with its striking contrasts between wealth and poverty. The artisan became a wage earner in a factory. No longer the master of his economic destiny, he found that his standard of living and his range of opportunities were increasingly controlled by remote and impersonal forces — the absentee capitalist, the laws of the market place, technological innovations. A permanent laboring class had formed that owned neither its homes nor the tools of its trade. But the equalitarian dream was based upon a nation of men who owned their homes, worked for themselves, and lived close to the soil. Could the new proletariat be relied upon to exercise sound political judgment when it had no material interest in honest government? No wonder corruption and bossism pervaded urban politics. Could such a class appreciate the rights of property and not look with envy upon the acquisitions of the more prosperous and successful? No wonder the middle class reacted furiously to such assertions of working-class discontent as the railroad strikes of 1877 and the Haymarket explosion of 1886. Were these a portent of the future—a nation of cities filled with a rootless, ignorant proletariat ogling the wealth of their betters and prepared to expropriate it by violent means? "The city's beautiful homes, splendid with costly furniture; the prancing horses and sparkling carriages; the silks and seal-skins and the bright and dainty dresses of rich children," seemed to the worker "to have been filched from his own poor fireside and from his shabby little ones." What did one have in common with a man who believed that "you and your class have wronged him?"[29]

At the same time that the city exposed the breakdown of America's ideal of the classless society, it revealed a corresponding division by race and nationality. Large cities like New York, Chicago, and Boston developed foreign quarters whose life and culture seemed to diverge at every point from that of native, middle-class Americans. Here was another serious menace to America's social homogeneity and the stability of her institutions.

Could these foreigners, most of them belonging to the wage-earning proletariat and many of them Catholics, be depended upon to preserve the "pure high faith of our fathers," the faith that had "promoted at once free-thinking and right-thinking, power and purity, personal liberty and personal responsibility?" How many of these same foreigners — whose ranks after 1880 increasingly included the hot-tempered, unpredictable Italian and the querulous, clannish Jew plucked from the Pale and ghettos of eastern Europe — would "join the ranks of the misguided and incorrigible men who openly or secretly long for the coming of anarchy and chaos?" The presence of the foreigner not only intensified the "great and growing gulf . . . between the working class and those above them," but created an even worse class problem than existed in Europe. In America dis-

---

29. Samuel L. Loomis, *Modern Cities and Their Religious Problems* (New York, 1887), 61. Josiah Strong complained that "socialism not only centers in the city, but is almost confined to it; and the materials of its growth are multiplied with the growth of the city." Josiah Strong, *Our Country: Its Possible Future and Its Present Crisis* (New York, 1885), 132; New York *Tribune*, Jan. 16, 1885, 4.

parities in wealth were intensified by "still greater differences in race, language, and religion."[30]

Within the urban community, the most vivid expression of the class and ethnic tensions troubling American society was the slum. Here the working-class and immigrant population concentrated. Measured by American standards of physical health, moral deportment, language, customs, traditions, and religion, the tenement population almost seemed to belong to a different species of humanity. The housing reformer believed that if he could improve the housing of the poor, this would reduce the class and ethnic conflict splitting the urban community into enemy camps. Better housing was needed not only to protect the health of the entire community, but to Americanize the immigrant working-class population, to impose upon it the middle-class code of manners and morals.

[5]

Charles F. Wingate, former editor of the *Plumber and Sanitary Engineer*, included among the moral disadvantages of tenement life "the growth of intemperance and immorality," "the disruption of families, the turning of children into the street, the creation and fostering of crime." If such charges were true, then New York had indeed allowed a civic Frankenstein to gestate within its womb. By 1890, the city's 81,000 dwellings included 35,000 tenements. These tenements, however, contained an overwhelming percentage of the city's total population of approximately 1,500,000. Those tenements alone which housed twenty-one persons or more contained a total population in excess of 1,000,000.[31]

In the American hierarchy of values, stable and harmonious family life loomed high. Whatever else failed, the moral influence of the family unit over the individual would maintain the

30. Loomis, *Modern Cities and Their Religious Problems*, 81, 66; New York *Times*, May 2, 1887, 4.

31. Charles F. Wingate, "The Moral Side of the Tenement-House Problem," *The Catholic World*, XLI (1885), 160; "Dwellings and Families in 1890," Extra Census Bulletin, No. 19, *U. S. Census*, 1890, 17, 27.

integrity of the community. But New York was a city of the homeless. Many of its people grew up "without the education, discipline, and moral influence of a separate family life and the interest in the community which the owning of a bit of land gives." These were the "natural tool of demogogues." A generation of tenement life had already "destroyed in a great measure the safeguards which a genuine home erects around a people." This left "vice and ignorance as the foundation stones of the municipality."[32]

As in the past, the feature of tenement life which critics singled out most frequently was the enforced overcrowding. The tenement heaped people and families together; by force of example, the impure infected the virtuous. As Wingate explained: "Every tenement-house is a community in itself, and the malign example of vice cannot fail to exert its full influence. The drunkard, the wife or child beater, the immoral woman, and the depraved child infect scores of their neighbors by their vicious acts. How is it possible to preserve purity amid such homes, or to bring up children to be moral and decent?"[33]

There in the tenements "young girls are found sleeping on the floor in rooms where are crowded men, women, youths and children. Delicacy is never known; purity is lost before its meaning is understood. . . ."[34] Boys growing up in the company of thieves and vagabonds formed into gangs of "toughs" who roamed the city in search of thrills. These, the children of immigrants, were described by Charles Loring Brace as "the

32. New York *Times*, Mar. 2, 1879, 6; Edward Crapsey, *The Nether Side of New York; or, The Vice, Crime, and Poverty of the Great Metropolis* (New York, 1872), 116. Also New York *Tribune*, Apr. 20, 1884, 6; New York *Times*, Mar. 1, 1879, 8.

33. Wingate, "The Moral Side of the Tenement-House Problem," 160-61.

34. New York *Times*, Dec. 3, 1876, 6. Charles Loring Brace, founder of the Children's Aid Society, expressed a similar point of view: "If a female child be born and brought up in a room of one of these tenement-houses, she loses very early the modesty which is the great shield of purity. Personal delicacy becomes almost unknown to her. Living, sleeping, and doing her work in the same apartment with men and boys of various ages, it is well-nigh impossible for her to retain any feminine reserve, and she passes almost unconsciously the line of purity at a very early age." Charles Loring Brace, *The Dangerous Classes of New York, and Twenty Years' Work Among Them* (New York, 1880), 55.

dangerous classes of New York." Ignorant and insensitive, they were "far more brutal than the peasantry from whom they descend."[35] When the parent could no longer control his child, the tenement indeed had sapped the roots of the family.

The tenement environment responsible for crime, hoodlumism, and sexual impurity also fostered alcoholism. Poor food, filthy surroundings, and "the constant inhalation of vitiated air" poisoned the organism and predisposed "these unfortunates to a continual desire for stimulation."[36] The environment was more responsible for intemperance than any inherent addiction of the tenement poor to liquor. If "Mr. Millions" had to suffer through life in a cramped tenement apartment, one sympathetic observer noted, he would very likely be inclined to send for his bottle of rum and "solace himself with the great East Side comforter."[37]

How could the immigrant and his children develop into desirable citizens, how could they be assimilated into the American community if the tenement warped their personalities? It even warped their bodies. The poor fell prey to "the slow process of decay . . . called 'tenement-house rot'." Infantile life was "nipped in the bud." Deformed youth gave way at the age of thirty to "loathsome" decrepitude. The typical immigrant was "a European peasant, whose horizon has been narrow, whose moral and religious training has been meager or false, and whose ideas of life are low." How could he possibly be rescued if, segregated in his tenement ghetto, he remained impervious to the elevating influence of American moral and cultural doctrine? Perhaps it was necessary to restrict immigration, the source of so much turmoil. The foreigners who came here to "herd together like sheep in East Side tenement-houses" were more an incubus than a boon to the nation.[38]

35. *Ibid.*, 27. Josiah Strong complained that "the hoodlums and roughs of our cities are, most of them, American-born of foreign parentage." Strong, *Our Country: Its Possible Future and Its Present Crisis*, 41-42. See also Edward Self, "Evils Incident to Immigration," *North American Review*, CXXXVIII (1884), 85.

36. "The Sanitary and Moral Condition of New York City," *The Catholic World*, VII (1868), 556.

37. New York *Times*, Jan. 7, 1883, 9.

38. Wingate, "The Moral Side of the Tenement-House Problem," 162; Strong, *Our Country: Its Possible Future and Its Present Crisis*, 40; New York *Times*, May 15, 1880, 4.

Although the American middle-class community and the immigrant worker were conscious of each other's existence, there was little personal association between them. The city became a world marked by physical proximity and social distance.[39] The American reacted with hostile contempt to the foreigner's unwillingness or inability to shed his old world customs, language, and companions. He blamed the foreigner for having caused the tenement blight. He resented the fact that "all forms of misgovernment and political corruption in the City feed on this un-Americanized mass, which has now grown so great that the native element is merely tolerated."[40] The foreigner, for his part, could either ignore or rankle under the whiplash of such criticism. Whatever his reaction, he could not suddenly shed his foreignness and merge silently into the American community. The city was divided into two worlds.

If the homogeneity of urban society had disintegrated under the strains caused by industrialism and immigration, the tenement system in the eyes of reformers thwarted any possibilities of reintegration. Since "the bad almost inevitably drag down the good; and the good have not the chance to lift up the bad,"[41] it was impossible for the foreigner to adopt the standards of personal cleanliness and behavior essential to his Americanization.

The tenement reformer had great faith in the reformatory powers of an improved housing environment. It was true, as some complained, that many "perfectly honest and virtuous" persons conscientiously abstained from soap and water, twisted out balusters for kindling wood, and unhesitatingly emptied garbage from the nearest window.[42] Reformers replied to such

39. For a sociological analysis of the physical proximity and social distance which characterize urban life, consult two essays in Ernest W. Burgess, ed., *The Urban Community* (Chicago, 1926). The first is E. S. Bogardus, "Social Distance in the City"; the second is Nicholas J. Spykman, "A Social Philosophy of the City." Useful also is Louis Wirth, "Urbanism as a Way of Life," *American Journal of Sociology*, XLIV (1938), 1-24.

40. New York *Times*, May 15, 1880, 4.

41. J. O. S. Huntington, "Tenement-House Morality," *Forum*, III (1887), 516.

42. *American Architect and Building News*, XV (1884), 205. For similar sentiments see the remarks of Henry Bergh quoted in the New York *Times*, Mar. 7, 1879, 3, and the remarks of several speakers at a meeting at Cooper Union Institute on Mar. 11, also quoted in the *Times*, Mar. 12, 1879, 2.

pessimism that the poor could not always help themselves, that they "never knew cleanliness or comfort or anything but squalor." It was their normal condition. On the other hand, such squalor not only served to "prevent the adoption of better habits," but threatened to "produce a race adapted to the surroundings." Thus John Cotton Smith, rector of Ascension Church, admitted that is was useless to carry on mission work among the poor until their physical conditions had been improved. They would only remain impervious to elevating moral influences. In words reminiscent of the AICP, the New York *Times* argued that it was futile to expect "decency, purity of life, and obedience to moral and political law" to arise out of wretched physical squalor.[43]

Conceivably, housing reformers placed excessive faith in the potency of a changed physical environment. The latter cannot necessarily transcend the limitations imposed by historical and cultural conditioning. The slum, after all, was a way of life, not simply houses. Habits and attitudes of the tenement population were affected by such fundamental influences as ethnic background, level of education, employment opportunities, and personal ambitions. The immigrant's adaptation to American life was influenced also by what he expected from this country. The immigrant who viewed his residence here as only temporary did not always care how he lived, so long as he found work, and this transient immigrant would remain especially resistant to efforts to transform his life.[44] Because the quality and tone of tenement life were moulded by factors other than overcrowding, poor sanitary facilities, a paucity of light or ventilation, and similar inconveniences, housing reform had limited applicability as an instrument of social control. As Thomas and Znaniecki have explained in their analysis of the Polish peasant, changes of material environment will not necessarily affect

43. New York *Tribune*, Feb. 6, 1884, 4; New York *Times*, July 1, 1878, 2, Feb. 24, 1879, 4.

44. David Brody has pointed out that the "one essential" for immigrant steelworkers was "not wages, working conditions, or living standards, but employment itself," *Steelworkers in America: The Nonunion Era* (Cambridge, Mass., 1960), 105.

"mentality and character of individuals and groups." A change of material conditions might "help or hinder . . . the development of corresponding lines of behavior, but only if the tendency is already there, for the way in which they will be used depends on the people who use them."[45]

Tenement reformers, however, did not usually ponder such subtleties. They exposed the moral and physical condition of the tenement population and arraigned the tenement itself as the nursery of the squalor and degradation spreading incessantly before their eyes. They transmitted their faith in the beneficent powers of better housing conditions to most reformers of the Progressive generation.

45. William I. Thomas and Florian Znaniecki, *The Polish Peasant in Europe and America* (Dover Publications: New York, 1958), I, 13.

3. Jacob A. Riis: Portrait of a Reformer

I already knew Jake Riis, because his book "How the Other Half Lives" had been to me both an enlightenment and an inspiration for which I felt I could never be too grateful.

THEODORE ROOSEVELT,
Autobiography

[1]

Jacob A. Riis, a dozen years after publication of *How the Other Half Lives*, was described as the man "who has done more than any one else to alleviate the condition of the poor of New York by revealing their misery to a sympathetic world." Lincoln Steffens, surveying the former Danish carpenter's achievements up to 1903, observed that "if any rich man could mark a city with as many good works as Jacob A. Riis has thrust upon New York, his name would be called good and himself great." In 1922, eight years after Riis's death, the crusading Episcopal minister, W. S. Rainsford, remembered him as one of the two men most beloved by the poor in his time.[1]

No housing reformer before Riis so successfully captured the public's imagination and affection. One cannot explain Riis's eminence through the novelty of his message — he certainly did not discover the tenement problem. Furthermore, Riis erected no scaffolding of theory to which disciples could turn for inspiration and guidance; he was unsystematic, almost impressionistic, in his thought. Riis never held public office, with

1. Joseph B. Gilder, "The Making of Jacob A. Riis," *The Critic*, XL (1902), 64; Lincoln Steffens, "Jacob A. Riis, Reporter, Reformer, American Citizen," *McClure's Magazine*, XXI (1903), 419; William S. Rainsford, *The Story of a Varied Life: An Autobiography* (New York, 1922), 369. The other was Father McGlynn, described by Rainsford as "a saint, a crusader born ahead of his time."

its accompanying power and prestige. In part, the architect of Riis's fame was history. It is significant that *How the Other Half Lives* was published in 1890, the first year of a decade of turbulence such as the nation had not experienced since the Civil War.

The social and economic problems which had troubled the postwar generation exploded in the 1890's with accumulated fury. Agricultural prices sank to new lows. Southern and western farmers organized a political party which promulgated such radical doctrines as the free coinage of silver and government ownership of utilities. The Homestead strike of 1892 foreshadowed the labor strife of the lean years of depression beginning in 1893. The Pullman strike in 1894 and Coxey's industrial army, only one strike and one army among many others in that convulsive year, suggested that power, violence, and disciplined organization were fast becoming the arbiters of our industrial life. The Pullman strike, for the time being at least, suggested also that workers would no longer accept the paternal benevolence represented by George M. Pullman as a substitute for their right to organize. The widespread unemployment and pervasive poverty of the depression years seemed to prove, once and for all, that America would not be spared "the discipline of poverty and inherited misery."

It was not only in agriculture and labor-capital relations that the 1890's witnessed a challenge to the old order. The alleged conquest of the West signalized by Frederick Jackson Turner's 1893 essay on the significance of the frontier troubled those who believed that American character and institutions had been shaped by the process of westward settlement. Significantly, the ardent immigration restrictionist, Francis A. Walker, based his argument in part upon "the important fact of the complete exhaustion of the free public land in the United States."[2]

Perhaps more important in the eyes of Riis's contemporaries than the passing of the frontier was the conquest of the town and farm by the big city. Although the growing influence of the city disturbed Americans before 1890, as we have seen, in-

2. Francis A. Walker, "Restriction of Immigration," *Atlantic Monthly*, LXXVII (1896), 826.

terest in the role of the urban colossus reached a new pitch of intensity after that date. It was not only the city's inexorable expansion in population and wealth that attracted attention, but the fact that many Americans regarded the city as a kind of parasite, draining the hinterlands of their vitality. Youth poured into the city seeking jobs, cultural and social stimulation. The old, the weary, the complacent remained in the country. Unless something were done, America faced the appalling prospect of breeding a "rural American peasantry, illiterate and immoral, possessing the rights of citizenship, but utterly incapable of performing or comprehending its duties."[3] The American was forgetting that his roots lay in the soil: "Not only has he left the pasture and wood, but in the towns his shelter lifts higher and higher, nearer the stars, but surely not nearer heaven."[4]

This "silent tragedy" being enacted in the 1890's — the depopulation and decline of the countryside — represented for many a profound social and economic catastrophe. People forsook the pure air, cheap homes, and equalitarianism of the countryside, heedlessly pouring into cities which deprived them of these advantages. The defenders of country life argued that the city would, in the end, pay dearly unless the balance was restored, for "the degeneration of the rural population means the later degeneration of the urban population also." The city could not survive without the infusion of sturdy, energetic rural stock.[5]

Connected with practically every major social and economic issue of the 1890's was the immigrant. Americans, never so fearful and pessimistic about the future welfare of the Republic since the Civil War, scrutinized the relationship between the immigrant and national life with the deepest misgivings. If the

3. Josiah Strong, *The New Era or The Coming Kingdom* (New York, 1893), 174. See also Henry J. Fletcher, "The Doom of the Small Town," *Forum*, XIX (1895), 223; and A. C. True, "The Solidarity of Town and Farm," *Arena*, XVII (1896-97), 544.

4. Anna R. Weeks, "The Divorce of Man from Nature," *Arena*, IX (1893-94), 230.

5. Henry J. Fletcher, "The Drift of Population to Cities: Remedies," *Forum*, XIX (1895), 738; quotation from Strong, *The New Era*, 177; True, "The Solidarity of Town and Farm," 544. Also Alfred H. Peters, "The Depreciation of Farming Land," *Quarterly Journal of Economics*, IV (1889-90), 32, 33.

immigrant was not entirely responsible for such developments as urban congestion and crime, industrial warfare and machine politics, he certainly contributed his share.

Two features stand out conspicuously in the immigration controversy of the decade. The first was the pervasive nativism affecting South and West as well as East; the second was the growing sentiment in favor of halting unrestricted immigration. The anti-Italian riots in New Orleans, the anti-Chinese agitation on the West coast, the fear of eastern workers that great immigrant hordes threatened their jobs and standard of living, the rapid growth of the anti-Catholic American Protective Association, the anti-semitism of western and southern agrarians which focused upon the "conspiracy" of Jewish bankers and financiers to exploit the productive classes, the racism circulating in the writings and salons of eastern patrician intellectuals like Henry Cabot Lodge and the Adams brothers, all point to the conclusion that Americans of disparate classes and sections viewed the immigrant as a grave threat.

It seemed as if the immigrant had become a national scapegoat upon whom frustrated Americans could focus their wrath. Hostility to the immigrant provided at least one policy upon which normally antagonistic groups could unite; thus nativism cut across the class and sectional strife of the 1890's. The employer, fearful of imported European anarchy and radicalism, could join with the worker troubled about the threat to his economic security, in common hostility to the immigrant. Conservative patrician intellectuals who parted company with southern and western agrarians on economic issues, shared with them a mutual dislike of Jews and other corrupters of American racial purity. In effect, the broad scope and fiery intensity of the nativism of the 1890's cannot be explained by reference only to the conflict between American and foreigner on concrete economic or political issues. In an era of intense sectional and class disharmony, nativism was a psychological palliative — a means of affirming national unity in the face of obvious disunity. The immigrant became the victim of an internally directed nationalism, just as the Spaniard became the victim of an externally directed nationalism and jingoism in 1898.[6]

The decade, understandably, gave rise to a vigorous conviction in favor of closing the gates so indifferently guarded since the nation's founding. With the frontier at an end and our cities already overcrowded, many feared that we were losing our capacity to absorb and assimilate the immigrant. It was "obvious that the time must come when by the advance of population we shall lose the very advantages that now make this country attractive to European emigrants." Opponents of free immigration argued that the recruiting activities of steamship agencies and the extension of rail facilities to interior portions of Europe made immigration too easy. As a result, it was "now among the least thrifty and prosperous members of any European community that the emigration agent finds his best recruiting-ground."[7]

Given the temper of the time, restriction would probably have been an important issue in the 1890's no matter what the source of the immigration. As it happened, the trickle from southern and eastern Europe in the 1870's increased over the next decade and leaped to the crest of the wave in the 1890's. Italians, Jews, Poles, Russians, and Slavs superseded the arrivals from the British Isles, Scandinavia, and Germany for the first time. The "new immigration" — 650,000 Italians over the decade compared to 500,000 Germans; 500,000 Russians compared to 250,000 Britons; 600,000 from Austria-Hungary in contrast to 300,000 from Norway and Sweden — was received

6. An excellent account of nativism in the 1890's is contained in Chapter Four of John Higham, *Strangers in the Land: Patterns of American Nativism, 1860-1925* (New Brunswick, N. J., 1955), 68-105. Also informative is Richard Hofstadter, *The Age of Reform: From Bryan to F.D.R.* (New York, 1955), 70-93.

7. New York *Times*, Jan. 30, 1893, 4; Walker, "Restriction of Immigration," 827. On the restriction controversy consult, besides Higham, the following: National Conference of Charities and Correction, *Proceedings*, 1890-1900; New York *Times*, Sept. 5, 1892, 4; Peri Ander, "Our Foreign Immigration. Its Social Aspects," *Arena*, II (1902), 269-77; Prescott F. Hall, "Immigration and the Educational Test," *North American Review*, CLXV (1897), 393-402; Edward G. Hartmann, *The Movement to Americanize the Immigrant* (New York, 1948).

by many Americans with fear, contempt, and hostility. Opponents of the new immigration doubted that this flock of uneducated peasantry could be assimilated within the foreseeable future, if at all. The new immigrants were described as "beaten men from beaten races; representing the worst failures in the struggle for existence." They had no inherent aptitude for self-government in contrast to those "descended from the tribes that met under the oak-trees of old Germany to make laws and choose chieftains." Their habits were "of the most revolting kind." Contact with them was "foul and loathsome."[8] Even the moderate and dignified New York *Times* complained of this invasion of "the physical, moral, and mental wrecks" of Europe.[12]

The new immigrants poured into our northern industrial cities and towns at a time when Americans already feared that urban pauperism, vice, crime, and political corruption menaced the welfare of the nation. They augmented the unskilled labor force at a time when labor-capital relations were undergoing severe strains. At best the new immigrants — a motley crew of peasants, illiterates, and incompetents in the eyes of extremists — intensified the class and ethnic divisions which were corrupting the ideal of the classless and homogeneous society. At worst it reinforced the numbers of those who actively menaced the law and order of the urban community. New York, for example, sheltered the "hatchet-faced, pimply, sallow-cheeked, rat-eyed young men of the Russian-Jew colony," who drank the "pestiferous milk of Nihilism and dynamite throwing."[9] It bulged also with Italians who imported with them the sinister Mafia and code of personal vengeance. The Italian too often considered himself above the laws and courts of justice.[10] Americans "pretty well agreed," the New York *Times* concluded, that the

8. Walker, "Restriction of Immigration," 828; New York *Times*, Feb. 17, 1890, 4.

9. New York *Times*, Aug. 23, 1893, 1.

10. "Most of the illiterate immigrants from the southern provinces of Italy, having had no feeling save contempt and hatred for the courts of their native land, do not import with them any disposition to respect the processes of civil tribunals in this country. Taught to seek redress with stiletto or blunderbuss at home, they cannot easily be educated to outgrow that inclination. . . ." New

Russian and Italian immigration was "of a kind which we are better without."[11]

The new immigrants demonstrated an unusually "great resistance to being assimilated and Americanized." This was their greatest fault. Their clannishness negated whatever virtues they may have possessed as individuals or whatever economic utility they may have had. The new immigrants crowded into cities, clustering in ghettos where "the mother tongue is carefully preserved, the English language is ignored, the institutions of the home country are revered, and American habits are despised."[12] In an intensely nationalistic decade, the shadow of the new immigrant seemed to cover the land with the darkness of un-Americanism.

[2]

The success of Jacob Riis as a housing reformer is incomprehensible apart from the historical context just described. Americans in the 1890's were anxious to learn about those things which he described in his books and lectures. Puzzled and fearful, they needed social critics like Riis to interpret the significance of the big city and immigration, poverty and tenement life; to explain how America could safely make the transition from an agrarian-rural society to an urban-industrial one.

Born in Ribe, Denmark, in 1849, Riis spent his youth in a pre-industrial society. His boyhood town was situated on a wide plain, separated from the nearby river by a marsh. On summer evenings, Riis recalled, he and his companions drifted down the river in a boat "listening to the small talk of the mother duck with her young, and to the chattering of uncounted thousands of starlings in the reeds." True, a cotton

York *Times*, May 16, 1893, 9. Also Robert E. Park and Herbert A. Miller, *Old World Traits Transplanted* (New York, 1921), 238-58; Jacob A. Riis, *How the Other Half Lives: Studies Among the Tenements of New York* (Sagamore Press: New York, 1957), 40-41.

11. New York *Times*, Mar. 6, 1892, 4. Working in favor of the immigrant during these troubled years were such influences as the long tradition of free immigration and the continuing need for cheap labor. It was not until World War I that restrictionists finally triumphed.

12. New York *Times*, Mar. 6, 1892, 4; John T. Buchanan, "How to Assimilate the Foreign Element in Our Population," *Forum*, XXXII (1901-02), 689.

mill had invaded Ribe, but it was "grotesque in its medieval setting, and discredited by public opinion as a kind of flying in the face of tradition and Providence at once. . . ."[13]

Riis grew up in an environment in which primary group ties centering in the family and neighborhood circle of friends and peers exerted a powerful influence over personal behavior. Through the network of primary group relationships the community transmitted its conventions, customs, and traditions, and in this way exercised a social control comparable to that of statutory law in a more stratified, complex society. How different from New York was Ribe where "neighbor knew neighbor and shared his griefs and his joys." There "no one was rich, as wealth is counted nowadays; but then no one was allowed to want for the daily bread." Although the daily salutations, "Good day and God help," were only figures of speech, they were typical of the "good feeling that was over and above all the sign of the Old Town and its people."

Before Riis set down his recollections of his Danish boyhood, many decades had intervened. No doubt his memory was influenced by the nostalgia which afflicts the old when they remember their youth, and by Riis's inveterate romanticism and sentimentality; it was easy for him to believe of faraway Ribe than of Hester Street in New York that "the sun shone always in summer," and that "the autumn days were ever mellow." The important thing, however, was that for Riis the social ideal always remained the warm, friendly life which Ribe personified in his mind.[14]

At the age of sixteen Riis went to Copenhagen to learn carpentry. After four years he returned to Ribe in possession of a certificate from the carpenter's guild. Unfortunately, both the gods of love and trade frowned upon the ambitious young artisan. His childhood sweetheart, Elisabeth, rejected his protestations of love, and work was difficult to find. These setbacks inspired Riis's decision to leave for America in 1870.

For seven years the young Danish immigrant shuffled from

13. Jacob A. Riis, *The Old Town* (New York, 1909), 6, 7-8.
14. *Ibid.*, 24, 25, 229.

job to job. He tried, among others, carpentry, coal mining, and advertising. Having acquired a taste for journalism by helping his father edit the local Ribe paper, Riis gained additional experience working for Brooklyn and Long Island newspapers. An opening on the New York *Tribune* staff in 1877 marked the turning point in his fortunes, for despite the low pay and long hours, it was a triumph to be hired by a metropolitan daily. After only a few months, Riis became the *Tribune's* police reporter. He held the position until 1888, when he joined the *Evening Sun* in the same capacity.

Two years later he published *How the Other Half Lives: Studies Among the Tenements of New York*. In this vivid and impressionistic series of sketches, Riis described the residential environment and ethnic traits of New York immigrant colonies, the weary struggle for subsistence in the tenement sweatshop, the dangers confronting the tenement child and working girl, the lure of the saloon and street gang, the degradation of the stage-beer dive, cheap lodginghouse, and opium den, and the human garbage dumped unceremoniously into the workhouse, almshouse, charity hospital, penitentiary, and Potter's Field. Seven lean years flittering from one unsatisfactory job to another, more than a decade as a police reporter exploring the life of the outcasts, criminals, and the poor of New York — these were the experiences which Riis distilled into his book. He, too, had gone hungry many days and had slept many nights in the doorways and alleys of the East Side. When Riis described the case of the "hardworking family of man and wife, young people from the old country, who took poison together in a Crosby Street tenement because they were 'tired,' " he could understand the roots of such a tragedy more than most people. He had contemplated suicide once when he was unemployed and despondent.[15] Riis understood also that a man's poverty did not justify an affront to his dignity. Scorched in his memory was the treatment he had received at the Church Street police lodginghouse, the dormitory of last resort, filled

15. Riis, *How the Other Half Lives*, 9; Jacob A. Riis, *The Making of an American* (New York, 1901), 70.

with tramps and beggars who could not afford a cot even in one of New York's frowsy downtown rooming houses. He was ejected by a German police sergeant who had heard him express sympathy for the French in the Franco-Prussian war. This was after Riis had complained to the sergeant that his gold watch had been stolen, only to be called a thief for possessing such a valuable.

In part, *How the Other Half Lives* was a plea for understanding and sympathy drawn from Riis's own experiences. He implored his contemporaries to join in an assault against the degrading influence of poverty and the tenement environment upon the individual. Riis appealed to the conscience of the middle class, asking it to raise "a bridge founded upon justice and built of human hearts."[16] He argued that the indifference and greed of the respectable elements of the community were as responsible for the social catastrophe he described as any ignorance or vice which might be ascribed to the poor themselves. One can always detect in Riis's work a plea for brotherhood and Christian love.

In addition to sympathy for the sufferings of the poor and the indignant demand for elementary justice, there is another dimension to *How the Other Half Lives*, just as there was to Riis's subsequent interpretations of poverty. One reviewer complained that his first book revealed certain "serious limitations": "a lack of broad and penetrative vision, a singularly warped sense of justice at times, and a roughness amounting almost to brutality." This criticism is exaggerated, but it contains an important kernel of truth. Riis sometimes displayed a singular lack of patience with certain groups. For example, he had nothing but contempt for the beggar, tramp, pauper, or whoever, in his estimation, preferred to live off charity rather than earn an honest living. Such outcasts, he said, were the responsibility of the police and workhouse, not the sociologist or social worker.[17]

Riis's career sheds considerable light upon his attitude toward

16. Riis, *How the Other Half Lives*, 226.
17. *The Critic*, XVII (1890), 332; Riis, *The Making of an American*, 75.

the tramp and pauper. His own life personified the promise of America. His was an American success story in the classical vein. A poor man, handicapped because he was an immigrant, Riis in time achieved local and national fame. Like Horatio Alger, he lifted himself out of the mire by force of brains, ambition, and will power. He took advantage of America's limitless freedom and opportunities to reward himself and reward America by becoming a useful and respected citizen. Did he not thus prove his loyalty to his adopted country by justifying the opportunities she lavished upon the individual? By the same token, were not tramps and paupers little better than traitors and parasites? Their laziness and social irresponsibility seemed to mock the ideals and institutions which afforded Riis and other ambitious individuals a chance to advance in life.

For all his social consciousness, Riis was squarely in the American entrepreneurial tradition. His basic economic and social creed was individualism, but tempered by justice, moral responsibility and Christian love — the kind of restraints upon individual assertiveness presumably found in the primary-group. The nation did not need socialism, communism, or any other form of collectivism to cure its social ills so much as the creation of an environment which insured the individual a chance to realize his potentialities; an environment that did not, like the tenement, stifle his moral sensibilities and choke off his ambitions. Riis believed fervently in all the contemporary entrepreneurial, individualistic cliches: "Nothing is more certain, humanly speaking, than this, that what a man wills himself to be, that he will be"; "Luck is lassoed by the masterful man, by the man who knows and who can"; "All the little defeats are just to test . . . grit. It is a question of grit, that is all."[18] Here was the spirit which was to find its most elaborate expression in Wilson's New Freedom.

Individualism and love of nature were two basic components of Riis's moral *Weltanschauung*. They were closely related. "For hating the slum what credit belongs to me?" Riis asked.

18. Jacob A. Riis, *Theodore Roosevelt the Citizen* (New York, 1904), 15, 63-64, 125.

"When it comes to that, perhaps it was the open, the woods, the freedom of my Danish fields I loved, the contrast that was hateful." Despite a lifetime spent in New York, Riis never reconciled himself to the complexity and impersonality of city life. The city, generally, and the tenement slum in particular, he equated with physical and spiritual decay. The city hindered the individual from growing into a moral and sensitive human being. Too often, it elicited the worst instead of the best in his nature. The child, especially, suffered damnation in the urban wilderness. Any "plan of rescue for the boy in which the appeal to the soil has no place" was false in principle and in practice.[19]

For Riis, the real America most resembled Ribe. It was in the countryside that the values which best exemplified America were born and nourished. Here tightly-knit family life insured the individual's proper moral development; respect for hard work and the dignity of labor was taught; and love of God and nature inculcated respect for human life and all living things. By contrast the city was a babel of moral confusion.

In his nostalgia for the countryside, Riis was not alone. All over western Europe, as in the United States, people were migrating from the farm and village to the city. Many of them found the impersonal and unstable life of the city demoralizing. Those immigrants who settled in New York's tenement quarters were especially shocked by the dehumanizing deficiency of natural life. Thus Gregory Weinstein, a Russian-Jew who emigrated here in the 1880's, remembered that his enthusiasm for New York diminished as soon as he saw the tenements, saloons, and bordellos of the lower East Side. Depressed in spirit, he felt "terribly homesick for the beautiful green hills and valleys" of his native Vilna. Similarly, the novelist Michael Gold remembered his immigrant mother's joy when the family left its East Side tenement for a day's outing in Bronx Park:

19. Riis, *The Making of an American*, 423; Jacob A. Riis, "One Way Out," *Century Magazine*, LI (1895-96), 308.

"Ach, Gott!" she said, "I'm so happy in a forest! You American children don't know what it means! I am happy!"[20]

We can begin to understand now why Riis's star shone so brightly in the reform firmament of the 1890's. He himself was part of a great drama of human transplantation, and he expressed the deepest sentiments of his less vocal immigrant contemporaries. In a period of doubt and social unrest in this country, he reaffirmed those values which Americans had always believed were the foundation of national greatness. And Riis intensified his affirmations, his tributes to individualism and the countryside, with all the zeal and uncompromising dedication of the convert. In an era of pervasive nativism and troubled questioning of the free immigration policy, the former Danish immigrant stood out as an American among Americans. Riis's nationalism, his loyalty to his adopted country, were as deeply rooted in his character as his rural bias and his individualism. In a sense, Riis's Americanism was the keystone of his entire moral philosophy. Any man who pledged allegiance to God, whose life's work was directed by the code of rural virtues, and who took advantage of his country's freedom and opportunities to realize his maximum potentialities as an individual was simply being a good American.

Proud of his citizenship and grateful to America, Riis was determined that the heritage in which he shared should be transmitted intact to future generations. His hatred for the tenement was strongly conditioned by the belief that it retarded, if it did not preclude, the Americanization of the immigrant. Riis's sharpest criticisms were reserved for an immigrant group like the Chinese, who seemed most clannish and least inclined to adopt American speech, customs, and culture. The real problem of the tenements, in terms of the nation's long-range welfare, was this:

> One may find for the asking an Italian, a German, a
> French, African, Spanish, Bohemian, Russian, Scandinavian,

20. Gregory Weinstein, *The Ardent Eighties: Reminiscences of an Interesting Decade* (New York, 1928), 18; Michael Gold, *Jews Without Money* (New York, 1930), 155.

Jewish, and Chinese colony. Even the Arab, who peddles "holy earth" from the Battery as a direct importation from Jerusalem, has his exclusive preserves at the lower end of Washington Street. The one thing you shall vainly ask for in the chief city of America is a distinctively American community. There is none; certainly not among the tenements.[21]

His "clinching argument" against New York's Jewish ghetto was "it is clannish." Significantly, Riis entitled his autobiography *The Making of an American*. Unlike the native American critic of urban society, Riis could not take his Americanism for granted. He had to prove in deed and thought that he was worthy of his adopted country's hospitality. He had to distinguish himself in American eyes from those immigrants who remained foreigners all their lives — from the East Side Jews, for example, who stood "where the new day that dawned on Calvary left them standing, stubbornly refusing to see the light."[22]

[3]

"It seemed to me," Riis confided, "that a reporter's was the highest and noblest of all callings; no one could sift wrong from right as he, and punish the wrong."[23] It must be remembered that this apostle of Americanism was a reporter by profession, and one of the best. Riis's professional talents are peculiarly important to an understanding of his contemporary appeal and enduring fame.

Riis was a fine journalist whose sensibilities were those of a romantic poet. He remembered the annual fair at Ribe as an "enchanted land" of toys, trumpets, and honeycakes topped with an almond heart in the middle. Perhaps it was there that a wizard who possessed the secret of eternal youth cast his spell, insuring that Riis would never know the weariness and cynicism that comes with age and knowledge of evil. To the

21. Riis, *How the Other Half Lives*, 15.

22. Jacob A. Riis, "The Jews of New York," *Review of Reviews*, XIII (1896), 58; Riis, *How the Other Half Lives*, 83.

23. Riis, *The Making of an American*, 99.

day he died at the age of sixty-five, Riis remained the incorruptible idealist, certain that "on the brink of hell itself human nature is not wholly lost."[24] Even in the slum, Riis averred, "the spark of His image" resided in the hearts of men. Riis encountered more evidence of human depravity, suffering, and wreckage in a month than most men would confront in a lifetime. For all that, his faith remained unshaken that justice, truth, and love would eventually govern the affairs of men.

As Lincoln Steffens once said of him, "far deeper than any intellectual faculty lay his sympathy."[25] Riis's perception was that of the poet, not the scholar. Life was always fresh and wondrous for Riis because his powers of imagination and emotional response were inexhaustible. Even the slum, for all its faults, had one thing in its favor — "it was very human." Once Riis watched a group of children playing see-saw:

> The whole Irish contingent rode the plank, all at once, with screams of delight. A ragged little girl from the despised "Dago" colony watched them from the corner with hungry eyes. Big Jane, who was the leader by virtue of her thirteen years and her long reach, saw her and stopped the show.
>
> "Here, Mame," she said, pushing one of the smaller girls from the plank, "you get off an' let her ride. Her mother was stabbed yesterday."
>
> And the little Dago rode, and was made happy.[26]

This simple manifestation of human tenderness compensated for much of the meanness and viciousness Riis encountered. It contained the seed and promise of a better world; it was the spirit which would conquer the slum.

Riis's idealism, his poetic sensitivity, his capacity for emotional response, all converged in a passionate, ebullient love of life. And because he loved life, he hated whatever he believed was life-denying, like the slum. Here were no flowers, no trees, no natural growth at all; and very little human growth, either —

24. *Ibid.*, 261.
25. Steffens, "Jacob A. Riis," 422.
26. Jacob A. Riis, "The Passing of Cat Alley," *Century Magazine,* LVII (1898-99), 176.

merely the grim animal struggle for existence. People who toiled in the sweater's shop all their days and all their lives had lost their birthright, the capacity to appreciate the simple beauty and wonder of a child's laughter or of an ocean gently stirring beneath a sun-drenched sky. Thus Riis justified his work to God and man in terms of every human's right to happiness. "The saddest of all things," he told Richard Watson Gilder, "must be to go to one's grave with the feeling that in nothing one has been able to soothe or help the world's misery."[27]

An incorrigible romantic, Riis tended to view life as a kind of tournament in which the forces of good, like Danish knights of old, galloped forth to joust with the forces of evil. Against one knight, especially, the dragons of the slum, saloon, and political corruption, stood little chance. In his worship of Theodore Roosevelt, Riis displayed openly his sentimental idealism and suspended his faculties of critical judgment. Roosevelt was the personification of all the patriotic, manly, and human virtues which Riis admired:

> A man with red blood in his veins; a healthy patriot, with no clap-trap jingoism about him, but a rugged belief in America and its mission; an intense lover of country and flag; a vigorous optimist, a believer in men, who looks for the good in them and finds it. Practical in partisanship; loyal, trusting, and gentle as a friend; unselfish, modest as a woman, clean-handed and clean-hearted, and honest to the core. In the splendid vigor of his young manhood he is the knightliest figure in American politics today, the fittest exponent of his country's idea, and the model for its young sons who are coming to take up the task he set them.[28]

"I loved him from the day I first saw him," Riis unblushingly confided.[29] He found in Roosevelt a kind of superman who could do no wrong, and he needed this superman for reassurance. The romantic temperament is prone to create demi-gods

27. Jacob A. Riis to Richard W. Gilder, July 2, 1894, The Century Collection.

28. Jacob A. Riis, "Theodore Roosevelt," *Review of Reviews*, XXII (1900), 186.

29. Riis, *The Making of an American*, 328.

to assure itself that its beatific visions can and do materialize on earth. According to Riis, Roosevelt "nursed no ambitions; he built up no machine of his own. He was there to do his duty as it was given to him to see it. . . ."[30] In this judgment one sees the willful naïvete of a man who wanted to believe that somewhere morality and politics, virtue and power, were not incompatible. Although Tammany employed its power for evil purposes, Riis saw in Roosevelt a man who used power as an instrument of good. With someone like Roosevelt in the ranks, Riis could be certain that the promise of a better world was no idle dream.

Only a man like Riis could have written *How the Other Half Lives* or its sequel, *The Children of the Poor*, a book published in 1893 in which Riis revealed his monumental affection for the tenement young and outlined his program for their redemption through education, clubs, and exposure to nature. These books did not suggest the ponderous, aloof objectivity of the scholar, the righteous pomposity of the preacher, or the humorless, tiresome certitude of the reformer-pedagogue. Riis did present facts like the scholar, moralize like the preacher, and try to win converts like the reformer, but his infectious love of life and his vivid imagination combined to invigorate his words with a sparkle and vivacity always rare, but especially rare in the prose of reformers and preachers to wayward humanity. Riis brought the tenement slum to life. It became for his readers an immediate and felt experience, not simply an abstract and remote evil. No housing reformer, before or after, has equalled Riis's ability to make the slum a reality for those situated on a different plane of life.

Dramatic and anecdotal, Riis's style reflected his interest in human feelings and emotions. He did not bother much with statistics. Riis realized that one concrete illustration of the demoralizing effects of poverty would arouse the reader's compassion more swiftly and surely than statistics whose magnitude was beyond the power of mind to reduce to human terms. There was, for example, an ocean of human meaning condensed

30. Riis, *Theodore Roosevelt the Citizen*, 228.

in such a tragedy as had occurred in a seventh-ward tenement. A mother of six children had leaped to her death from a window because, as the neighbors said, she was "discouraged."[31] Although many before and after Riis described every conceivable feature of tenement life, he was the master. With the skill of an artist, he took stale and ordinary material and refashioned it into what seemed new, fresh, and original. When he applied such imagination and sensitivity to the commonplace, it seemed to be a revelation. Through Riis people not only came to hate the slum but, in a sense, discovered it for the first time.

[4]

Riis's predecessors had emphasized the dual purpose of housing reform. Better housing would, in the first place, contribute to the physical safety of both the poor and the community as a whole. There can be no quarrel with this assumption. The overcrowding, filth, and inferior sanitary facilities in the tenement obviously had an unfavorable effect upon health. Science and common sense confirmed this. But the housing reformer had also considered better housing as an instrument of social control. He observed that tenement neighborhoods, populated often by foreigners and their children, seemed to abound in vice, crime, and pauperism. He assumed, therefore, that the physical environment was at fault. The tenement must cause a deterioration of character, making the individual more susceptible to vice than he would have been in a different environment. Improve his housing, it followed, and you would influence his character for the better.

It is true that a statistical correlation could be drawn between poor housing on the one hand, and a resistance to Americanization or a low individual and neighborhood moral tone, on the other. It did not necessarily follow, however, that improved housing, in and of itself, would have socially desirable effects. The housing reformer never subjected to rigorous analysis his assumption that housing influenced character. He applied a

31. *Ibid.*, 36.

crude environmental determinism to the problem, underestimating the tenacious persistence in the individual of set habits and values.

Riis did not, in any clear and systematic fashion, analyze the relationship between housing and social structure. He accepted without much reflection the assumption that better housing would result in various social blessings. Often, however, Riis broke loose from this simple determinism. Almost unconsciously, he expanded the usual scope of housing reform to include the neighborhood in which the tenement was situated. Like the settlement worker, Riis realized that the tenement neighborhood contained many objectionable features which needed to be eliminated. More than previous housing reformers, he sensed that the tenement, the slum, was a way of life and not simply a problem of sub-standard housing. Thus socially effective housing reform would involve a reconstruction of the whole tenement environment and the customary life-organization of the inhabitants. Indeed, there was much in common between Riis and the settlement movement, striving since the late 1880's to improve neighborhood life through every channel of personal influence and environmental reform available to the middle-class humanitarian. In the Progressive era, the settlement was the profoundest embodiment of the ideal which inspired Riis, the ideal of community and human brotherhood expressed in a common Americanism. It concentrated, like Riis, upon the neighborhood as the unit of social reconstruction. The neighborhood ideal, as Riis observed, was "the heart of the settlement movement." The convictions which led Jane Addams to Halsted Street in Chicago and Lillian Wald to Henry Street in New York were exactly those which inspired Riis to declare war on the tenement and the slum.[32]

Everywhere in the tenement neighborhood, Riis saw the saloon, the poor man's social club. Its brightness and relaxed

32. Riis, *How the Other Half Lives*, 159, 163; Jacob A. Riis, *The Peril and Preservation of the Home* (Philadelphia, 1903), 187. Riis was highly conscious of the similarity of ideals and purposes between the settlements and himself. See *The Making of an American*, 316, and his personal tribute to the settlement movement, "What Settlements Stand For," *Outlook*, LXXXIX (1908), 69-72.

atmosphere contrasted sharply with the squalor and dinginess of the tenement. But if the saloon satisfied the worker's gregarious instinct, his need for companionship and sociability, it also encouraged him to squander his earnings on liquor while his family went without necessities. The saloon thus contributed to the decline of family life, a process presumably set in motion by the tenement. The saloon also taught a sorry brand of citizenship. Gangs of toughs, useful on election day, congregated there to be regaled by the same Tammany chieftains who sponsored their social clubs and protected them from the law when caught brawling or thieving. The saloon keeper, if not a precinct leader himself, was the friend of politicians. "The rumshop," Riis complained, "turns the political crank in New York." Perhaps worst of all, in Riis's estimation, was the saloon's effect upon the child. It not only solicited his patronage at an early age, initiating him into evil company and habits, but taught him contempt for law and order. Not "one child in a thousand, who brings his growler to be filled at the average New York bar," Riis protested, "is sent away empty-handed, if able to pay for what he wants."[33] What conclusion did the child draw, Riis wondered, as he watched his growler foam with beer in full view of the sign forbidding sale to minors?

As ubiquitous as the saloon in the tenement neighborhood was the street gang, the refuge of children who lacked any sense of identity and turned to their similarly confused peers for protection, security, and a code of values. Every corner had its gang of toughs, hostile to each other but united in their defiance of society.[34] What was the use of improving the tenement child's housing if the street gang waited outside, ready to initiate him into the jungle code of the pack. Riis realized that boys would form into gangs. His object was to direct this gregarious instinct into socially productive channels. Instead of an instigator of mischief and crime and the promoter of a distorted code of values, the street gang could be revamped into an organized force for good. But reform depended upon

33. Riis, *How the Other Half Lives*, 159, 163.
34. *Ibid.*, 164.

the alternatives to the saloon or the street, which were all society offered in the tenement neighborhood, and upon the interest taken in the moral development of the tenement child.

The East Side in the 1890's was in New York's great red light district.[35] Prostitution downtown was unabashedly open. An army of prostitutes, pimps, and madams plied their trade unmolested by the Tammany-ruled police: "On sunshiny days the whores sat on chairs along the sidewalks. They sprawled indolently, their legs taking up half the pavements. People stumbled over a gauntlet of whores' meaty legs," the novelist Michael Gold recalled. "The girls gossiped and chirped like a jungle of parrots. Some knitted shawls and stockings. Others hummed. Others chewed Russian sunflower seeds and monotonously spat out the shells."[36]

Although Riis, a proper Victorian gentleman reluctant to drag sex into the arena of public controversy, wrote little on the subject of tenement prostitution, his less squeamish contemporaries eagerly exposed it as a formidable evil in the lives of the poor. Frederick J. Shackleton, pastor of a Forsyth Street church, complained before the Mazet Committee in 1899 that solicitation was practiced from the stoops and windows of the tenements in his crowded neighborhood.[37] Edward J. Riordan, an investigator for this committee, reported that east of the Bowery he had frequently been "stopped by men and solicited to go into houses to meet girls." He singled out Allen, Chrystie, Rivington, Stanton, and Delancey Streets as especially vice-ridden. Edgar A. Whitney, another investigator, discovered that solicitation on the East Side was as impudent and aggressive as the less harmful kind practiced by the Jewish "pullers-in" of Baxter Street, clothing merchants who dragged reluctant passers-by off the streets and into their shops.[38]

35. It was unmolested except for the necessary protection money paid to politicians and police officers. Two state investigations in the 1890's, the Lexow Committee in 1894 and the Mazet Committee in 1899, documented the deeply-rooted police corruption in New York City.
36. Gold, *Jews Without Money*, 15.
37. Special Committee of the Assembly Appointed to Investigate the Public Offices and Departments of the City of New York and of the Counties Therein Included. Transmitted to the Legislature January 15, 1900, *Report*, II, 2001. Hereafter cited as Mazet Committee, *Report*.
38. *Ibid.*, 2028, 2029, 2002.

Children in such an environment learned about sex at a tender age; it was cheapened and degraded in their eyes. It took one veteran of the East Side jungle "years to learn that sex can be good as well as evil; more than the thing truck drivers bought for fifty cents on my street." While boys from better neighborhoods played cowboys and Indians at the age of five, Michael Gold and his tenement-spawned companions teased prostitutes: "Fifty cents a night! That's what you charge; fifty cents a night! Yah, yah, yah!"[39] Children were hired by proprietors of bordellos to distribute their cards. Others served as "lighthouses" or "watch-boys," running errands and guarding against possible surprise raids. "It is a fact," Riordan informed the Mazet Committee, that "young people on the east side are brought in daily and nightly contact with vice, and are obliged to live with it and see it, and are made familiar with it in every way."[40]

None of these things — prostitution, street gangs, saloons — were new to New York's tenement quarters. Reformers before Riis had noticed that squalid housing was usually coupled to a train of associated evils. The AICP, with its strong emphasis upon intemperance as a cause of poverty, always regretted the workers' easy access to saloons. Charles Loring Brace, who organized the Children's Aid Society in the 1850's, listed high among his objectives the removal of the child from the influence of the street and gang. None of the reformers, however, had linked all the disparate elements of tenement life together as the object for a general policy of neighborhood reconstruction. From housing reform they had expected social benefits which were not inherent in the simple act of modifying one defect in the environment of the immigrant and working poor.

Equally important, critics of tenement evils had not always considered alternatives to the vices they struggled to suppress. Riis, however, understood that the saloon and street gang served

39. Gold, *Jews Without Money*, 26, 17.

40. Mazet Committee, *Report*, II, 2029. Further information on the subject of prostitution in New York and the attitude of reformers can be found in *The Committee of Fifteen, The Social Evil, with Special Reference to Conditions Existing in the City of New York* (New York, 1902).

a functional purpose; they satisfied social needs and desires. The reformer could not abolish them unless he devised wholesome substitutes capable of fulfilling these same needs. In concrete terms, Riis's answer to the street gang was not the policeman's nightstick or the reform school, but rather the playground, boy's club, and public school.

The child was the key to neighborhood reconstruction. According to Riis, "The problem of the children is the problem of the State. As we mould the children of the toiling masses in our cities, so we shape the destiny of the State which they will rule in their turn, taking the reins from our hands." The community, for its own protection, had the solemn duty "to school the children first of all into good Americans, and next into useful citizens." Here was the answer to the troublesome riddle of Americanization and the reunification of the urban community. Since the child was "a creature of environment, of opportunity, as children are everywhere,"[41] it was only necessary to create for him a wholesome environment in which to mature.

Improved housing and the establishment of a neighborhood in which such institutions as the saloon, the house of prostitution, and the street gang were less influential would surely benefit immigrant parents as well as their children. But for all his optimism, for all his faith in the power of environment to shape individual habits and values, Riis realized that the adult was sometimes beyond redemption. Although "we can do almost anything with his boy," Riis pointed out, we could not always "do much for or with the old immigrant who comes to stay with us."[42] The old country, for better or worse, had already determined the main outlines of his personality. The child, by comparison, was putty ready for the hand of the social sculptor.

As Thomas and Znaniecki have explained, the immigrant child in the American city often exhibited a "condition of passive or active wildness in which behavior [was] not controlled by social customs and beliefs but directly conditioned by temperamental tendencies and swayed by momentary moods."

41. Jacob A. Riis, The Children of the Poor, (New York, 1893), 1, 8, 4.
42. Jacob A. Riis, "Special Needs of the Poor in New York," Forum, XIV (1892-93), 501.

Unwilling to organize his life around the scheme of values imported by his parents from abroad, but confused as to his identity and status in the American community, the immigrant child was frequently "a-moral"; the social objective was to expose him to "constructive influences which tend to develop in him a normal life-organization."[43] Although the authors of *The Polish Peasant in Europe and America* theoretically formulated the issue better than Riis ever did, he viewed the problem of the immigrant child in essentially the same light: guide the child's impulses into socially constructive channels, plant in his neighborhood attractive and wholesome counterinfluences to the saloon, street gang, and similar evils, and the tenement would surrender its power to produce moral and social decay.

By transmitting to the tenement child and adult a meaningful life-organization which would facilitate their acceptance of middle-class American values, Riis was striving, in the final analysis, to create a new system of primary group ties in the tenement neighborhood. The confusion of nationalities, religions, and cultural standards in tenement districts had discouraged, he believed, the birth of any sense of community. There was little to nurture social unity and cohesiveness. Apart from individual moral standards and the voluntary submission of the individual to the social norms of his ethnic group, there was no effective instrument of social control except for the law and policeman's club.

New York, of course, was not Ribe, Denmark, where Riis had experienced the powerful control exercised by the primary group over the individual and the security which it offered him in return for his obedience. New York was not the small town which was the only model of primary group control in the experience of native American reformers. The influence of the primary group is most effective in a small, self-contained community characterized by a high incidence of face-to-face relationships and a relative uniformity of ethnic origin and economic status. It depends less for its authority upon rational

43. Thomas and Znaniecki, *The Polish Peasant in Europe and America*, II, 1777, 1778.

persuasion, individual choice, and voluntary cooperation than upon an unreflective, spontaneous, and internalized sense of social solidarity. In this respect the attempt to establish a primary group ethos, a feeling of transcendent and universal community, in the heterogeneous and unstable tenement neighborhood was doomed to failure. In a more limited sense, however, the ideal of neighborhood reconstruction was sound. At very least, it implied a comprehensive and pragmatic assault upon the slum. No scheme which promised to improve the physical, moral, or social condition of the poor was foreign to its spirit. As Riis preached, the settlement practiced, reaching beyond the tenement in an effort to influence the total environment and personality of the poor.

The public school, in Riis's estimation, was one critical factor in the reconstruction of the tenement neighborhood. "When the fathers and mothers meet under the school roof as in their neighborhood house, and the children have their games, their clubs, and their dances there," Riis predicted, "there will no longer be a saloon question in politics; and that day the slum is beaten."[44] Thus the public school would serve the same function as the church in the medieval town, peasant village, or American hamlet — the visible symbol of the community's solidarity, the transmitter of its ideals and values. As the neighborhood social center, the school would shed light about American history, government, and customs to the immigrant and his child. A common bond of Americanism would link all those it reached.

Riis promoted a wide variety of educational reforms in this effort to make the school the focus of neighborhood unity. If the school repelled the child for any reason, it could hardly serve its exalted purpose. Thus Riis condemned the disgraceful physical appearance of the average city school. Much as he believed in the importance of education, he sympathized with the hookey-player who preferred to romp outdoors in the sun rather than incarcerate himself in the gloomy vaults of the existing public schools. Herds of rats in the Wooster Street

44. Jacob A. Riis, *The Battle with the Slum* (New York, 1902), 407.

school, Riis complained, shared the premises with the children. Like many others, this institution was poorly lit and ventilated. It was typical of the dirty, cramped, and cheerless quarters in which the immigrant child was expected to learn his American catechism.[45]

Along with an improvement and expansion in physical plant, Riis crusaded for an intensive use of school facilities. The forces of evil, such as the saloon and gambling syndicate, were perpetually in motion, exerting their baneful influence at all times. Why, then, was the school silent except for a few hours a day? This was no way to save the child from the streets. In the summertime, the streets were particularly alluring to tenement youth after a long, cooped-up winter, and Riis endorsed the establishment of summer vacation schools. Since the gang was "nothing but the genius for organization in our boys run wild," Riis asserted, why not put this talent to socially constructive ends by means of the school? Why not, in effect, organize public school children during the summer into a "great military body," ship them out of the city, and "make a real vacation of this for the boys who need it most by drilling them in camp?" And since the street gang was "hardest hit" by the responsible and well-supervised boy's club, the school could make a real contribution to neighborhood welfare by lending its building out of hours to such clubs.[46]

Riis warmly supported two innovations in curriculum to insure the school's all-inclusive influence over the child. One was the kindergarten, a moral as well as an educational experiment. Its function was to "rediscover . . . the natural feelings that the tenement had smothered." If not for its influence, the "love of the beautiful might slumber in those children forever."[47]

45. Jacob A. Riis, "Playgrounds for City Schools," *Century Magazine*, XLVIII (1894), 657. In connection with his work in educational reform, Riis strongly urged the establishment of special truant schools. He objected to the commitment of truants in reformatories, where they mixed with hardened juvenile criminals. He also advocated the creation of special juvenile courts. In each case, he wanted to insure that the erring, but potentially decent, child was not pushed by society into a life of crime.

46. Jacob A. Riis, "The Making of Thieves in New York," *Century Magazine*, XLIX (1894-95), 115; Riis, *The Children of the Poor*, 238.

47. *Ibid.*, 180.

The kindergarten shepherded the child in the dawn of his consciousness. By teaching him beauty and training his powers of self-expression at so early an age, it assisted in arousing his dissatisfaction with the ugly barbarism of the slums. He was then more likely to turn to the school, church, social settlement, and similar agencies devoted to his moral welfare to satisfy the yearnings aroused by the kindergarten.

In manual or vocational training Riis discovered a second curriculum innovation with manifold possibilities for influencing the child's future. The industrial school which taught boys a useful trade helped transform the tough street urchin into a respectable citizen. In the opinion of Joseph Lee, the prominent Massachusetts humanitarian for whose book on philanthropy Riis wrote an introduction, the industrial school made a civilized being out of a barbarian.[48] Vocational training, presumably, would allure the boy who saw no useful purpose in learning history, geography, and other academic subjects which had no relevance to his immediate experience. But this same boy, who perhaps had to lug heavy sacks of garments each day between his parents' tenement workshop and the manufacturer, could appreciate a school which promised to teach him a trade and equip him for a better life than that of his parents. And a boy with a respectable trade, in Riis's eyes, was a better candidate for good citizenship than an untrained boy.

Riis thought that training in home economics contained the answer for the needs of the tenement girl. It would perform wonders in keeping the tenement family together. "I am well persuaded," Riis declared with characteristic hyperbole, "that half of the drunkenness that makes so many homes miserable is at least encouraged, if not directly caused, by the mismanagement and bad cooking at home."[49]

As part of his crusade to rescue all children, Riis struggled to bring opportunities for wholesome play and recreation to the tenement districts. The park and playground, as well as the public school, were fundamental to the reconstruction of the

48. Joseph Lee, *Constructive and Preventive Philanthropy* (New York, 1902), 203.
49. Riis, *The Children of the Poor*, 197.

tenement neighborhood.[50] In his emphasis upon the need for neighborhood recreation facilities, Riis participated in a more general movement in the 1890's to direct, consciously and rationally, leisure activities. This movement grew out of the belief of middle-class reformers that the urban poor was being weaned on an unsavory diet. Gambling, low-grade melodrama, vaudeville, burlesque with its appetizing promise of "50 — Pairs of Rounded Limbs, Ruby Lips, Tantalizing Torsos — 50," beer-gardens, dance halls, and concert saloons, these were the staples of recreation. They satisfied, however, an important need in the life of the urban working class. The quest for pleasure was a natural response to sordid surroundings and long hours of dreary, unremunerative work.[51]

Recreation, play, and the constructive use of leisure time were not problems in the primary group environment of the peasant village in Europe or the American small town. In the peasant village, especially, play was an expression of community solidarity. It was closely integrated into religious, social, and economic life. Religious festivals, local ceremonies and pageants of one sort or another, celebrations of birth and marriage — in all these the family participated as a unit. Leisure was less a matter of individual taste and preference than an affirmation of family and communal solidarity. How different things were in the American industrial city where leisure activity was both individualized and commercialized. Far from being an expression of solidarity, play was, on the contrary, an expression of dis-integration:

> The East Side, for children, was a world plunged in eternal war. It was suicide to walk into the next block. Each block was a separate nation, and when a strange boy appeared, the patriots swarmed.

50. On the history and significance of the play movement in the 1890's and after consult the following: Henry S. Curtis, *The Play Movement and Its Significance* (New York, 1917); Clarence E. Rainwater, *The Play Movement in the United States: A Study of Community Recreation* (Chicago, 1922); Charles M. Robinson, "Improvement in City Life: Philanthropic Progress," *Atlantic Monthly*, LXXXIII (1899), 533-36.

51. The quote from a temporary burlesque advertisement is found in Foster Rhea Dulles, *America Learns to Play: A History of Popular Recreation, 1607-1940* (New York, 1940), 217, 212.

"What streeter?" was demanded, furiously.

"Chrystie Street," was the trembling reply. Bang! This was the signal for a mass assault on the unlucky foreigner, with sticks, stones, fists and feet.[52]

There was no guarantee, of course, that slum children or their parents would take advantage of parks, playgrounds, clubhouses, and other facilities provided for their use. They might be used in the wrong way. As we realize today, a park can be as perfect a setting for juvenile gang warfare or mugging as for wholesome play. "To suggest," furthermore, "that a boy will not be delinquent because he plays ball is no more valid than to say that he will not play ball because he is delinquent. He may do either, neither, or both."[53] This does not imply, however, that putting parks or playgrounds where none had existed would do harm, or fail to do good. The tenement inhabitant sought diversion from the monotony of his work and the depressing squalor of his home. He was not likely to travel outside of his neighborhood to satisfy his yearning. At the very least, Riis believed, he should be given the opportunity for wholesome diversion and not have to resort to the saloon or dance hall.

The movement to reconstruct the tenement neighborhood by directing the leisure of the poor sparkled with ideas and suggestions. Some of Riis's contemporaries concentrated on the adult. The Committee of Fifty for the Investigation of the Liquor Problem, a leader in the struggle for adult recreation in tenement districts, recommended that the city build "large plain buildings" in different parts of the city to serve as club-houses[54] in which the immigrant worker could satisfy his social needs without resort to the liquor and unsavory company of the saloon. Such organizations as The People's University Extension Society of New York, and the Educational Alliance, hoped to elevate the moral and aesthetic standards of the poor by stimu-

52. Gold, *Jews Without Money*, 42-43.
53. Henry D. McKay, "The Neighborhood and Child Conduct," in Paul K. Hatt and Albert J. Reiss, Jr., eds., *Cities and Society: The Revised Reader in Urban Sociology* (Glencoe, Ill., 1957), 822.
54. Raymond Calkins, *Substitutes for the Saloon* (New York, 1901), 72-73.

lating their intellects and instinct for beauty. They might then turn more often to the city's libraries, museums, and art galleries, and less frequently to the concert saloon and vaudeville show.

Although Riis heartily endorsed any and all such proposals to guide the adult's leisure time into socially constructive channels, his interest in recreation was predominantly a reflection of his ceaseless effort to capture the mind and emotions of the child. "In the matter of healthy play," Riis complained, "the school-boy in New York does not have a chance. Any village boy is better off than he." Play was the child's safety valve. Unfortunately, "with the landlord in the yard and the policeman on the street sitting on his safety valve and holding it down," the child was "bound to explode." The community which made no provision for allowing the child to release his excess energies through harmless play was criminally negligent. It encouraged the mischief and delinquency of the street gang, and the commercial exploitation of the young. The community was obligated to provide alternatives to those agencies which pandered to the lowest sensual instincts of the child. "Under the rough burr" of the tenement child lay "undeveloped qualities of good and of usefulness." The right kind of play would help draw them out. The wrong kind would simply smooth the path to the reformatory and prison. As a disciple of Froebel, whom he described as "the great kindergartner who gave us the best legacy of the nineteenth century to its successor," Riis agreed that play was the true occupation of the child, through which he first perceived moral relations.[55]

Riis, as we have seen, hated the tenement partly because he loved the green purity of nature. It was not surprising, therefore, that he combined his passion for the outdoors with his belief in the redeeming potentialities of wholesome play. Thus he enthusiastically advertised and promoted the *Tribune* Fresh Air Fund, the summer excursions sponsored by churches, settle-

55. Riis, "Playgrounds for City Schools," 659; Jacob A. Riis, *A Ten Years' War: An Account of the Battle with the Slum in New York* (New York, 1900), 147; Riis, *The Children of the Poor*, 64; Jacob A. Riis, *The Peril and Preservation of the Home*, 166, 167; Riis, *The Children of the Poor*, Ch. X.

ments or charities, and every other such attempt to bring the slum child into contact with nature. A splendid vision came to Riis, which he set forth in almost apocalyptic terms:

> And then if you were to ask me to point to the goal we are striving after, where we shall be quite safe, where the slum cannot come, I should lay before you a map of the city and put my finger upon the islands that lie in the East River, stretching their green length five miles or more from Fiftieth street or below clear up into Hell Gate to the mouth of the Sound. And I should tell you that on the day when we shall have grown civic sense and spirit robust enough to set them apart as the people's playground forever, on that day we shall be beyond the reach of the slum and of slum politics for good and all.[56]

Riis worked as hard to bring nature to the tenement world of brick, asphalt, and concrete as he did to bring the tenement child to nature. He wanted to see small parks built where antiquated tenements took their toll in human life and suffering.[57] These would be lungs for the poor, oases of fresh air, flowers, trees, and grass for mothers with babies, and children whose only playground had been the congested streets. Riis expected miracles from these parks, from the contact between nature and the tenement child: "Down in the worst little ruffian's soul there is, after all, a tender spot not yet pre-empted by the slum. And Mother Nature touches it at once. They are chums on the minute."[58] The school and the park, joining forces to touch the head and the heart of the tenement child, were surely the means to bring light into dark places.

Riis had another vision. Why not attach a park-playground

56. Jacob A. Riis, "The Island Playgrounds of the Future," *Charities*, XI (1903), 205.

57. For Riis's story of the long struggle to raze Mulberry Bend and build a park in its place see his article "The Clearing of Mulberry Bend: The Story of the Rise and Fall of a Typical New York Slum," *Review of Reviews*, XII (1895), 172-78. The Bend, located in the Italian quarter of the lower East Side, was detested by Riis as the symbol of all the degradation of slum life.

58. Riis, *The Children of the Poor*, 173. Similarly: "I have seen an armful of daisies keep the peace of a block better than a policeman and his club, seen instincts awaken under their gentle appeal, whose very existence the soil in which they grew made seem a mockery." *How the Other Half Lives*, 136.

to every school? If we did this in New York, then children would undoubtedly "be attracted to a school that was identified with their playground. Truancy would cease."[59] Here was a real community center which would put the street gang out of business. It would constitute a kind of neighborhood commons, a visible symbol of unity transcending ethnic and religious differences. If the school became, as Riis hoped, a social and intellectual beacon for adults as well as children, it would help restore the family cohesiveness which the tenement had wrecked. The school, park, playground — these were the tools which would civilize the child, Americanize the immigrant, reconstruct the tenement neighborhood, and reduce the importance of the policeman's night stick as an instrument of social control. In Riis's eyes, no greater challenge confronted the housing or social reformer than the creation of new primary group relationships based on the neighborhood in geography and a common Americanism in spirit.

59. Riis, "Playgrounds for City Schools," 665.

4.   The Tenement House Committee of 1894

It is discreditable that so many of us should cherish personal ease and private success above the public weal. . . .

RICHARD WATSON GILDER,
Civic Patriotism, 1894

[1]

"I want to arouse neighborhood interest and neighborhood pride, to link the neighbors to one spot that will hold them long enough to take root and stop them from moving. Something of the kind must be done or we perish." Riis directed these words to a group of "visitors" for the Charity Organization Society of New York. He explained to them the importance of "having the public schools made neighborhood centers," and the need of insuring "the children's right to play." He spoke of the pathetic "hunger for the beautiful, the aesthetic starvation of the tenement Mollie wanting red shoes rather than a square meal." Hers was the "cry of the soul that is perishing in the slum."[1]

Riis, so emotionally and intellectually linked to the settlement movement of the period, was unusual among housing reformers. The professional "housers" to whom the Progressive era gave birth — individuals like Lawrence Veiller, E. R. L. Gould, Carol Aronovici, Bleecker Marquette, Bernard J. Newman, John Ihlder, James Ford, and Emily W. Dinwiddie — did not usually share his intense commitment to neighborhood reconstruction. Closer in spirit, perhaps, were the lay figures especially identified with housing reform — Albion Fellows Bacon, Robert W. de

1. *Charities,* VII (1901), 48.

Forest, Felix Adler, James B. Reynolds, Alfred T. White, and Richard Watson Gilder. The part-time lay reformers, including the host of settlement workers, moved from housing to charity and social work, child labor, good government, recreation, and other causes with great facility.

Whatever the scope of their interests, both laymen and professionals shared one common assumption — that better housing was a key to social control, as well as improved health and physical well-being. The typical housing reformer concentrated his energies overwhelmingly upon the tenement with its structural and sanitary defects, striving to establish minimum standards by law, and hoping thereby to save the child, preserve the worker's family from disintegration and to educate the immigrant *imperium in imperio* into good American citizenship. Neither the lay nor professional housing reformer of the Progressive era was so naïve as to assume that the physical and social needs of the immigrant, working-class population could be satisfied by improved housing alone. Thus de Forest, as president of the Charity Organization Society of New York, was involved in a multitude of philanthropic efforts, and Alfred T. White served as president of the Brooklyn Bureau of Charities for many years. Even the professional housing reformer like Veiller moved beyond housing into court reform, tuberculosis control, and recreation. However, neither the professional nor lay housing reformer ever really analyzed the elusive relationship between housing and social control, or suggested that improved housing might have limitations as an effective instrument of social control.

[2]

The anatomy of early Progressive housing reform is discerned most clearly in the shape of two commissions, those of 1894 and 1900. The purpose of these commissions, authorized by the state legislature and appointed by the governor, was to investigate tenement conditions. Their recommendations would then serve as a basis for amendment of the tenement code. The two commissions were modeled after the one which had been created in 1884. The greater achievements of the later commissions, particularly that of 1900, can be traced in part to the social and economic crisis of the 1890's. Better housing seemed urgent, a prerequisite to the establishment of unity and stability in the urban community. Their success, however, was also related to the vigorous and transfigured public health movement which emerged after 1890. The years between 1890 and 1910 have been described as "the golden age of public health."[2] During this period municipal and state boards of health began applying the recent revolutionary discoveries in bacteriology to the prevention and cure of disease, medical education was vastly improved, and medical research reached a high level of organization. Housing reform had a large stake in this medical progress.

As Lawrence Veiller, secretary to the Tenement House Commission of 1900, explained, the housing and public health movements had much in common. They were both concerned with essentially the same problems: "ventilation, sewage disposal, water supply, disposal of wastes, insect-borne disease, personal hygiene, the spread of communicable disease and even public health education."[3] For the first time housing reformers did not have to explain the high incidence of tenement disease and mortality on the basis of some vague connection between physical health and the squalor of the tenement. Thanks to bacteriology, reformers could demonstrate beyond question the relationship between the tenement environment and physical debilitation. At the same time municipal boards of health could exercise their powers more effectively than ever before. If indifference or opposition to housing reform had been excusable in the prebacteriological era on the grounds of ignorance, this

2. C.-E. A. Winslow, *The Evolution and Significance of the Modern Public Health Campaign* (New Haven, 1923), 36. Two biographies useful for understanding developments in public health and medicine in the latter nineteenth century are C.-E. A. Winslow, *The Life of Hermann M. Biggs: Physician and Statesman of the Public Health* (Philadelphia, 1929); and Simon Flexner and James Thomas Flexner, *William Henry Welch and the Heroic Age of American Medicine* (New York, 1941).

3. Lawrence Veiller, "Housing as a Factor in Health Progress in the Past Fifty Years," in Mazÿck P. Ravenel, ed., *A Half Century of Public Health* (New York, 1921), 324.

was no longer possible. The tendency of housing reformers to concentrate upon the sanitary shortcomings of the tenement environment — to equate sanitary control with social control — was in part an outgrowth of the dramatic achievements in bacteriology and preventive medicine. Not only were the sanitary defects strikingly apparent, but reformers could criticize them with the assurance and comfort of scientific certainty. For these reasons it is necessary to explore the public health movement before turning to the Tenement House Committee of 1894.

Although the germ theory of disease had been advanced as early as the seventeenth century, it was two hundred years before Pasteur and Koch in the 1870's proved conclusively that specific micro-organisms were responsible for specific diseases. In the next two decades discovery of the bacteriological origins of many of man's most ancient scourges followed in rapid succession: typhoid, leprosy, and malaria in 1880; tuberculosis in 1882; cholera in 1883; diphtheria and tetanus in 1884; plague in 1894; dysentery in 1898. The American public quickly accepted the novel and rather exciting idea that the human body was a favored host of armies of tiny living organisms. Indeed, the imaginative appeal of the germ theory may explain why, according to one authority, it at first "gained acceptance from laymen . . . more quickly than from the medical profession."[4]

The bacteriological revolution occurred at a critical juncture for preventive medicine. Sanitarians and boards of health had accomplished much before 1890 in educating the public to the importance of personal and municipal cleanliness. Partly as a result of their efforts, urban mortality rates had declined. In New York, for example, a death rate of 32.19 per thousand for the decade 1856-65 had dropped to 26.32 in the years 1876-85. In most American cities mortality declined from an average of

4. Howard D. Kramer, "The Germ Theory and the Early Public Health Program in the United States," *Bulletin of the History of Medicine*, XXII (1948), 241. Kramer points out, however, that many of the younger physicians, such as Hermann M. Biggs and William H. Welch, immediately accepted "the full import of the new discoveries." *Ibid.*, 242.

25 to 40 per thousand in 1860 to the more respectable figure of 16 to 26 per thousand in 1880. One important reason for this downward trend was the diminished incidence of such epidemic diseases as smallpox, yellow fever, typhoid, and typhus.[5]

There were limits, however, to the usefulness of the personal and environmental cleanliness which sanitarians emphasized before 1890. Preventive medicine remained in a primitive stage until it realized the importance of the personal factor in contagion and the spread of disease. The modern city could not function efficiently in the absence of sanitary control; but sanitary control could not attain its maximum efficiency until the role of the infected individual in spreading disease was understood. After 1890 preventive medicine was metamorphosed as sanitarians and public health officials shifted their interest from environment to the manner by which disease was transferred from one individual to another. For our purposes, the most important developments in the new era of public health were the establishment of diagnostic laboratories by city and state boards of health and the well-organized campaign to educate the public in the fundamentals of modern hygiene.

Although the health boards of Massachusetts, Michigan, and Providence, Rhode Island, had established research laboratories in the late 1880's, New York City's Board of Health was the first to establish a diagnostic laboratory in the modern sense. As a result of a cholera scare in 1892, a Division of Bacteriology and Disinfection was added to the Board. The following year this division undertook the clinical diagnosis of suspected diphtheria cases. In 1894 the New York *Herald* organized a public subscription fund to be applied to the manufacture of diphtheria antitoxin for distribution among the poor. The *Herald* suggested that the Board of Health spend the money collected for this benevolent purpose. The Board accepted the

5. Board of Health of the Health Department of the City of New York, *Annual Report*, 1896, 14; Kramer, "The Germ Theory and the Early Public Health Program in the United States," 235; George Rosen, *A History of Public Health*, 338-39.

offer and in January 1895 began to supply the city's hospitals with antitoxin.[6]

Nothing better illustrates the parallel progress in housing reform and preventive medicine than the Board of Health's drive against tuberculosis, a savage executioner of the tenement population. In November 1893, the Board requested Dr. Hermann N. Biggs, head of the new Bacteriological Division, to prepare a report on tuberculosis. On the grounds that the disease was both preventable and communicable, transmitted primarily through dried sputum floating in the air as dust,[7] Biggs recommended several remedial measures. The most important of these included a campaign of public education and the examination of sputum by the Bacteriological Division. The Board, in approving Bigg's suggestions, noted that its "first object . . . was to attract attention to the infectious nature of tuberculosis and to point out the measures necessary to guard against the infection."[8] Circulars were printed in several languages and distributed to every tenement in the city.

Supplementing the diagnostic work of municipal boards of health were the laboratories of state health departments. By 1914 every state with two exceptions had established such a laboratory. Indeed, by the outbreak of World War I, laboratory research into the origin, transmission, and prevention of disease had reached an impressive level of organization. Founded between 1899 and 1917 were the laboratory sections of the American Public Health Association, the Association of American Pathologists and Bacteriologists, the American Association of Immunologists, and numerous professional journals.[9] By 1901 medical research had achieved sufficient stature to become an

6. Board of Health of the Health Department of the City of New York, *Annual Report*, 1894, 17; Charles F. Bolduan, "Over a Century of Health Administration in New York City," Department of Health of the City of New York, *Monograph Series No. 13*, Mar. 1916, 26.

7. It is recognized today that tuberculosis is mainly transmitted by droplets from infected persons.

8. Board of Health of the Health Department of New York, *Annual Report*, 1893, 29.

9. Frederic P. Gorham, "The History of Bacteriology and Its Contribution to Public Health Work," in Ravenel, ed., *A Half Century of Public Health*, 92-93.

outlet for the funds of philanthropists. The Rockefeller Institute was founded in that year and opened its first laboratory in 1904.

As pathological research and the diagnostic laboratory received increasing attention in preventive medicine, sanitarians and health officials labored to acquaint the public with the fruits of their discoveries. Referring to tuberculosis, Dr. Biggs asserted that "all the suffering and death consequent upon the prevalence of this disease are, in view of modern scientific knowledge, largely preventable by the careful observation of simple, well-understood and easily applied measures of cleanliness, disinfection and isolation." The importance of educational work was "incalculable in widely disseminating popular and scientific information with regard to the results of the latest studies in infectious diseases."[10] The New York Health Department after 1890 included in its educational work the preparation of pamphlets in various languages, designed particularly for the immigrant poor. These short and simple brochures discussed such topics as infant feeding, the transmission of infectious diseases, and the care of consumptives. In 1906 the Board of Health initiated a program of free stereopticon lectures in city parks on health subjects, which were later supplemented by open-air moving pictures. In 1914 a Bureau of Health Education was created to coordinate the Board's numerous educational services.

The Health Department had established a "Summer Corps" of physicians in 1876, whose duty it was to visit tenement districts and care for sick children. Two decades later, in 1897, a team of 150 medical inspectors was appointed in order to examine public school children for evidence of infectious disease. The addition of seventeen trained nurses in 1902 strengthened the program. Finally, in 1908, a separate Division of Child Hygiene was created which took over the work of the summer corps and school inspection. The nurses and physicians of this division entered into close contact with tenement children and their parents, using the opportunity to disseminate principles

10. Hermann M. Biggs, "Preventive Medicine in the City of New York," *The Address in Public Medicine* (delivered at the 65th annual meeting of the British Medical Association in Montreal, Canada, Sept., 1897), 12, 21.

of modern hygiene among those most in need of advice. The
increasing attention paid to the health and welfare of the young
was reflected in mortality rates. In New York the infant death
rate dropped from 273 per thousand live births in 1885 to 94
in 1915.[11]

The diagnostic research laboratory and the extensive, well-
organized program of public health education just discussed
were two outstanding contributions of the early bacteriological
era to preventive medicine. Sanitarians and health officials now
grasped the implications of the personal factor in contagion, in
contrast to dirt, refuse, sewer gas, and similarly unpleasant, but
not necessarily lethal, features of the environment. Charles V.
Chapin, a distinguished sanitarian of the time, summarized the
difference between the pre- and post-bacteriological eras of
preventive medicine when he observed that "work which prevented the passing of excretory effluvia from one human being
to another was real health work, and of course the oldtime
health officers did much of it, though they wasted infinite time
in removing dead cats and ash piles and in searching for sewer
gas."[12]

The Progressive housing reformer benefited greatly from the
vigorous public health movement which bacteriology had
launched. It supported his contention that the overcrowding,
the primitive waste disposal facilities, and the inadequate lighting and ventilation of tenements took a heavy toll in life and
health. If the accomplishments of housing reformers after 1890
could be traced in part to public fear — fear of the slum's threat
to the health and well-being of the entire city — they were also
grounded in a more realistic understanding of the origin and
transmission of such common tenement diseases as diphtheria,
pneumonia, tuberculosis, and the various diarrheal afflictions.

[3]

The Tenement House Committee of 1894 owed its origin to
a series of articles on tenement conditions which had appeared

11. Charles V. Chapin, "History of State and Municipal Control of Disease,"
in Ravenel, ed., *A Half Century of Public Health*, 151.
12. *Ibid.*, 140.

in the *Press* and to the personal efforts of Edward Marshall, Sunday editor of the *Press*, to draw the attention of the state legislature to New York's housing problem. Appropriately, Dr. Cyrus Edson, sanitary superintendent of the New York Board of Health, was one of the seven men appointed to the Committee. He was joined by two lawyers, Roger Foster and John P. Schuchman; William D'H Washington, a civil engineer; George B. Post, an architect; and Solomon Moses of the United Hebrew Charities. The Committee chose Marshall as its secretary.[13]

The Committee members held their first official meeting on May 12, 1894. Their report to the legislature, presented the following January, represented the most thorough study ever made of tenement life in New York. In the course of its investigation, the Committee touched on all phases of the subject — sanitary conditions, overcrowding, educational opportunities, model tenements, rentals, the sweating system, fire hazards, lack of recreational facilities. It held numerous public hearings before which landlords, real estate agents, social workers, health officials, and others interested in the housing question testified. The committee's careful and comprehensive analysis resulted in a valuable civic education for New York. For a while the housing problem became a front page news story.

Richard Watson Gilder served as chairman. This frail magazine editor and man-of-letters is not often remembered today as a tenement reformer. Yet from 1894 until his death in 1909 Gilder persistently struggled to improve the housing conditions of the poor. He was the son of a Methodist minister, and from his father, William Henry Gilder, Richard had inherited a deeply rooted sense of moral obligation.[14] The elder Gilder,

13. Veiller, "Tenement House Reform in New York City, 1834-1890," 105.
14. Richard Watson Gilder was first introduced to the housing problem by his father: "The tenement-house population is discovered by different people at different times. I discovered the tenement-house population before the Civil War, when I was taken by my saintly and now sainted father into the old Five Points and was shown things that no tenement-house commissioner, certainly none of 1900 — or 1901 — can now see in this city. Sub-cellars occupied by the refuse of humanity; Old Cow Bay; scenes such as exist in the pictures that Dante makes, but not now in reality, certainly, in this city." New York State Conference of Charities and Correction, *Proceedings*, 1901 (published in the *Thirty-fifth Annual Report* of the New York State Board of Charities, II, 459).

who served as the chaplain of a New York regiment during the Civil War, died of smallpox contracted in an army hospital. As chairman of the Tenement Committee, Gilder did not hesitate to draw attention to sanitary abuses in tenements owned by the wealthy Trinity Church, a congregation of his own affiliation. Like most tenement reformers of the Progressive era, Gilder was spurred to action by an irrepressible urge to see justice done and the community's welfare protected. The struggle against evil was even more important than victory. What counted was that *somebody* had to uphold ideals; otherwise, "things get to be more and more selfish, sink to a lower and lower plane."[15] Though Gilder was referring specifically to his enlistment in the crusade for good government, his words illuminate equally well his motivation as a housing reformer. Because most men were busy advancing their private, selfish interests, someone had to protect the interests of the community as a whole. Civic responsibility was the highest expression of individual morality.

Under Gilder's leadership, the Committee of 1894 focused attention upon three features of the tenement system: the high incidence of disease and mortality resulting from structural and sanitary defects of the average tenement; overcrowding in tenement homes and streets; the absence of parks and playgrounds in tenement neighborhoods. The large majority of bills prepared by the Committee related to questions of light and ventilation, sanitation, and fire protection. The measures included a 70 per cent limitation on lot coverage (90 per cent for corner lots) in the construction of future tenements, as well as a window opening to the outer air in each room. The Committee also demanded the removal of wallpaper from rooms in existing tenements and the prohibition of its use in future tenements on the grounds that such paper, often piled layers thick, collected dirt. Similarly, the Committee recommended that the use of tenements as lodging houses, stables, or rag storage depots be prohibited, since such uses also accumulated

15. Rosamond Gilder, ed., *Letters of Richard Watson Gilder* (Boston, 1916), 326-27.

filth. The Committee was shocked to discover that only 306 persons out of a total of 255,033, whose living conditions were carefully examined by its investigating staff, had access to bathtubs in their homes. This situation it described as "a disgrace to the city and to the civilization of the nineteenth century." Cleanliness, the Committee observed, was the "watchword of sanitary science, and the keynote of the modern advice in aseptic surgery." The scarcity of bathtubs was morally as well as physically reprehensible, for "the cultivation of the habit of personal cleanliness [has] a favorable effect, also, upon character; tending to self-respect and decency of life." Although the city maintained several free river "floating baths," these were useful only in summer and even then were inconvenient. But the Committee neither prepared a bill on the subject of baths nor requested the legislature to require the installation of baths in tenements. Impressed by the operation of indoor bathhouses by such private organizations as the AICP and the Baron de Hirsch Fund, as well as by European municipalities, the Committee simply recommended to the city that it construct bathhouses which would offer the poor, at moderate prices, "every kind of bath desirable." The Committee's action was rather mild, considering the deficiency of bathing facilities in tenement neighborhoods and their alleged importance in preserving health and moral respectability. Nothing resulted except for Mayor Strong's appointment of a committee including William G. Hamilton, vice-president of the AICP; Dr. Moreau Morris, a member of the Tenement House Commission of 1884; and William H. Tolman, secretary of the City Vigilance League and general secretary of the AICP, to investigate the bath question. Although this committee suggested six possible sites, the city procrastinated and by 1900 not one bathhouse had been completed.[16]

16. Tenement House Committee of 1894, *Report* (Albany, 1895), 49; *Report on Public Baths and Public Comfort Stations* (Being a Supplementary Report to the Inquiries into the Tenement House Question in the City of New York, Pursuant to Chapter 479 of the Laws of 1894, by the Mayor's Committee of New York City, transmitted to the Legislature April 9, 1897). New York State in 1892 had passed a law permitting any city, village, or town to erect bathhouses.

Although the Committee was also outraged by the lack of adequate tenement toilet facilities, it achieved little more than in the case of baths. T. F. Murray, one of the inspectors, reported that he had seen a young girl in a Charlton Street tenement approach a water closet with a pail in her hands. Unable to enter the closet without soiling her feet, she simply "threw the contents into the closet, and the excrement went all over the walls." An examination of 3,984 tenements, containing 33,485 separate dwelling units and a population of 121,323, revealed that only 51 of them contained private toilets. In most of the houses (3,392), they were located in the yard; in 541 they were found in the basement or halls. The average population for each water closet was 7.62.[17] The Committee, however, did not recommend the mandatory installation of separate water closets in each apartment, but rather that each water closet have a window opening to the outside. To meet the need for clean, antiseptic toilet facilities, the Committee suggested that the municipality construct public lavatories, once again allowing builders and landlords to evade their responsibilities.

A combination of congestion and flimsy construction resulted in great injury and loss of life from fire in tenement districts. The Committee found that although fewer than one-third of New York's dwellings were tenements, more than half the city's fires occurred in them. It prepared a series of bills to combat the fire hazard, including the enforcement of existing laws which required the fireproofing of the first floor of tenements to provide a buffer between upper stories and cellars, where many of the fires originated; the location of dumbwaiters, elevators, or lifts upon exterior walls if their enclosures were not fireproofed; the use of solid partitions between apartments; and fireproof staircases. The Committee believed that such measures would serve the purpose and not prove inordinately expensive.

None of the structural or sanitary changes proposed by the Gilder Committee seriously affected the dumb-bell pattern of construction or the 25 x 100 foot lot. In this sense the Com-

17. Tenement House Committee of 1894, *Report*, 510, 114, 115.

mittee wrestled with superficialities, striving to abolish the baneful effects of the dumb-bell while leaving it essentially intact. There was one interesting exception to the Committee's general reluctance to violate property rights. The Board of Health theoretically had the power to vacate and condemn as public nuisances unsanitary or dilapidated dwellings. It rarely exercised its authority, however, because there was no provision for funds by which to compensate the owner. The Committee turned to England for guidance in this problem. The Torrens Acts (1868-82) had authorized English municipalities to demolish buildings, singly or in small groups, which were deemed hazards to health or public safety. Similarly, the Cross Acts (1875-82) permitted the clearance of large slum areas. These measures, along with the Laboring Classes Lodging Houses Act inspired by Lord Shaftesbury in 1851, were consolidated in the Housing of the Working Classes Acts of 1885 and 1890. The Shaftesbury measure, which authorized the Public Works Loan Commissioners to lend funds to municipalities or private building associations (thus supplementing purely slum clearance schemes), did not appeal to the Committee and most other American reformers wedded to a strictly private enterprise resolution of the housing question. Influenced by the slum clearance and compensation procedures incorporated in the Cross and Torrens Acts, the Committee did urge that "power be given to the Board of Health to institute condemnation proceedings for the destruction of buildings which are so unsanitary as to be unfit for human habitation; with provision for reasonable compensation to the owners in case of such destruction."[18]

The New York State Legislature enacted the slum clearance measure suggested by the Commission in 1895, and the Board of Health swung into action the following year when it condemned eighty-seven buildings. With one exception these were all rear tenements.[19] Over 2,000 of them constituted some of

18. *Ibid.*, 63.
19. Board of Health of the Health Department of the City of New York, *Annual Report*, 1896, 38-39. The next year 8 more rear houses were vacated and condemned. By the end of 1897, 55 of these buildings had been destroyed, 17 were remodeled to the satisfaction of the Board of Health and reoccupied, 5 were remodeled but not used for habitation, and no action was taken on 17. Board of Health of the Health Department of the City of New York, *Annual Report*, 1897, 15-17.

the oldest tenements in the city, and they were decrepit, dirty, and deadly. In the opinion of the *Times*, which heartily commended the Board's action, "these rotten hives of poverty, vice, and misery have reeked with physical and moral disease and spread their infection to swell the rate of death and degrade the quality of life about them long enough."[20]

The condemnation law was less important in itself than as a premonition of things to come. When a conservative and moderate reformer like Gilder was prepared to recommend the expropriation of property to protect the health and welfare of the community, it was clear that the days of the dumb-bell were numbered. It would never be easy to overcome the combined opposition of builders and landlords or the hesitant conservatism of the state legislature, but a direct assault upon the dumb-bell was inevitable. The housing movement needed only the right leadership to overcome its obstacles.

[4]

Perhaps no feature of tenement life was more apparent or more objectionable to reformers than the extraordinary overcrowding. New York City in 1894, comprising Manhattan and part of the Bronx, contained a total estimated population of 1,957,452. Among European cities this total was exceeded only by that of Paris and of London. New York's density of population per acre, 76.0, was surpassed only by Paris, Berlin, Cologne, Liverpool, and Glasgow. However, New York's density of 143.2 per acre below the Harlem River (Manhattan Island) was the greatest in the world. A certain district of the eleventh ward was among the most crowded spots on earth with a density per acre of 986.4 in 1894. The closest approximation the Commission could discover was the Koombarwara district of Bombay, bursting with a density of 759.66 persons per acre in 1881. The most congested wards in Manhattan — the seventh, tenth, eleventh, thirteenth and seventeenth — ranged in density from 366.8 to 701.9 persons per acre.[21]

20. New York *Times*, July 16, 1896, 4.
21. Tenement House Committee of 1894, *Report*, 256, 257, 266-72.

Witnesses before the Commission complained frequently of small tenement apartments crowded to the ceiling with families and single lodgers. Robert Graham, of the Church Temperance Society, recalled one of these, a three-room apartment in the Italian quarter, shared by two families and four male lodgers, totaling fifteen persons. Adah S. Woolfolk, a resident at the College Settlement on Rivington Street, once found eleven people in two rooms on the ground floor of a rear tenement. These were extreme examples of a common condition, which intensified all the sanitary and structural defects of the average tenement, and, in the opinion of the Commission, also had serious moral consequences. It produced a "condition of nervous tension; interfering with the separateness and sacredness of home life; leading to the promiscuous mixing of all ages and sexes in a single room — thus breaking down the barriers of modesty and conducing to the corruption of the young, and occasionally to revolting crimes."[22]

To relieve congestion, the Committee recommended the mandatory enforcement of the statute requiring in tenement apartments a minimum of 400 cubic feet of air for each adult and 200 for each child under twelve, but did not consider the possible consequences of such a law if enforced. Much of the overcrowding in tenement apartments resulted from the practice of accepting boarders and lodgers to supplement family income, and especially to help meet the monthly rent bill. Rents consumed about 25 per cent of a family's earnings, a large proportion of an income totaling only a few hundred dollars a year. Of course the ratio of rent to income varied greatly from family to family, neighborhood to neighborhood, and the estimate of 25 per cent is a very rough one. Certain figures presented to the Commission, however, suggest that it is a reasonable estimate. An investigation of 2,425 houses revealed that the average rent for each apartment was $9.91 a month, while the average income for all the occupants was $9.04 a week. The number of rooms averaged 2.4. An investigation

22. *Ibid.*, 424, 435, 13, 70.

by Adah S. Woolfolk of 600 families for the College Settlements Association confirmed these figures. Miss Woolfolk found that the rent for one room averaged $4.24; two rooms, $8.08; three rooms, $10.75; four rooms, $14.46, and she calculated that these rents averaged 27 per cent of total monthly earnings per family. Notice also that the Commission's average of $9.91 a month for 2.4 rooms ranged between the rents listed by Miss Woolfolk for apartments of two and three rooms.[23]

Although the immigrant earned more in America than in Europe, the cost of living, including housing, was much higher. M. E. Ravage, for example, a Rumanian Jew who migrated here in 1900, complained that "the prices of things in America were extortionate." In Vaslui, his native village, people may have lived in houses that were "low and made of mud," but they were "individual and sufficient, and the yard was spacious and green in summer, filled with trees and flowers to delight the senses." Ravage estimated that the monthly rental for an apartment in a Rivington Street tenement equalled a year's rent in Vaslui.[24] The lodger problem, then, was the natural outgrowth of the high cost of living in America. Indeed, Adah S. Woolfolk found that a kind of "cooperative plan of housekeeping prevailed" among the Italian families she investigated. Several families lived together, "paying their rent and purchasing their supplies in common; in this way they were able to have a larger amount of food and ampler quarters — usually three rooms — for a smaller expenditure of money by the individual family. . . ."[25]

It is apparent that if the Board of Health really enforced the laws against overcrowding, many immigrant families would have suffered a serious loss of income and been hard pressed to pay their rent. Objectively, from the point of view of health, comfort, and perhaps morality, the Committee was justified in demanding that the law prohibit overcrowding in tenement apartments. Yet from the point of view of the immi-

23. *Ibid.*, 209, 210, 433, 434.
24. M. E. Ravage, *An American in the Making: The Life Story of an Immigrant* (New York, 1917), 82, 83.
25. Tenement House Committee of 1894, *Report*, 434.

grant any restriction of his right to accommodate boarders seemed a cruel imposition. The best interests of the immigrant and the community, as the housing reformer defined them, did not always coincide with the immigrant's definition of those same interests.

A second difficulty arose in connection with the enforcement of laws prohibiting overcrowding. People who were driven onto the street had to find accommodations. Whether such people were lodgers, occupants of rear tenements condemned by the Board of Health, or occupants of tenements expropriated to make room for parks, they had to live somewhere. Objectively, once again, it seemed both right and necessary to insure family privacy, build parks, and tear down rear tenements. On the other hand, the problem of relocation, to which the Committee gave little thought, lurked behind such reforms. Any kind of dwelling was better than none; and if the dispossessed simply crowded into tenements elsewhere in the neighborhood, the net gain was negligible. Since restrictive legislation would not build houses, the housing reformer had to be careful that the fruits of his labors did not create as many problems as they solved. The immigrant needed parks and privacy, to be sure, but he needed a place to live as well.

The immigrant needed a job also. Although the Committee recommended nothing on the subject of the tenement sweatshop system, which involved the manufacture of clothes and other articles in dirty, hot, cramped tenement apartments, Edward Marshall, in a supplementary report, condemned the "misery-breeding possibilities" of sweatshop manufacture. Housing reformers, generally, were always striving to reduce the importance of the sweatshop in the tenement economy, and shackle it with various sanitary and licensing restrictions. Here, again, a conflict of interests arose between the reformers and those whom they sought to benefit.

In the opinion of a congressional investigating committee "a large proportion . . . of all the clothing worn by the majority of our people is made under conditions not merely revolting to humanity and decency, but such as to endanger the health of the wearer."[26] The situation, no doubt, was far from ideal for either the operative or the consumer. The latter did not wish to purchase a garment which exposed him to contagion, while no Russian Jew or Italian immigrant preferred, early on a hot summer morning, to incarcerate himself in a room "crowded with scantily-clothed, dull-faced men and women sewing upon heavy woolen coats and trousers."[27] The immigrant, however, accepted whatever work was available. The long hours and low pay of the sweatshop were preferable to the even more rigorous hardships of unemployment. The housing reformer did not always consider the plight of the ignorant, unskilled worker barred from the sweatshop by licensing or sanitary restrictions and unable to find an alternative source of income.

Such institutions as the boarder and sweatshop had become integral features of the social and economic structure of the immigrant community, accepted by the immigrant and viewed as unavoidable concessions to a hostile, new environment. They were, in the final analysis, a stage in the Americanization process. Like Tammany, another undesirable institution in the eyes of the reformers, the boarder and sweatshop helped the immigrant to survive and adapt to American life.

The Tenement House Committee of 1894 unhesitatingly condemned the overcrowding, the boarder's intrusion upon familial privacy, and sweatshop conditions; but preoccupied with the sanitary pathology of the tenement system — the inadequate toilet and bathing facilities, the absence of light and ventilation, the oppressive congestion — it lost sight of the tenement neighborhood as a complex system of cultural, economic, and social relationships. The Committee did acknowledge that "the difficulties of the tenement-house question are augmented by the extraordinary agglomeration of nationalities, the novelty of these people to their surroundings, and the strain of acclima-

26. Committee on Manufactures on the Sweating System, *Report*, 52nd Congress, 2nd Session, House Report No. 2309 (1893), xxii.

27. Helen Moore, "Tenement Neighborhood Idea — University Settlement," in Frances A. Goodale, ed., *The Literature of Philanthropy* (New York, 1893), 37.

tization."[28] It recognized less clearly that the integration of these people into American life depended less upon immediate sanitary controls (some of which resulted in economic hardships) than upon a long-range, gradual series of adjustments which would increase the frequency of their exposure to the life and thought of the American community.

For many immigrants the American community was not a reality but a kind of brooding omnipresence, remote, distant, and incomprehensible. "Of that greater and remoter world in which the native resides," M. E. Ravage related, "we immigrants are for a long time hardly aware. What rare flashes of it do come within range of our blurred vision reveal a planet so alien and far removed from our experience that they strike us as merely comical or fantastic — a set of phenomena so odd that we can only smile over them but never be greatly concerned with them."[29] Thomas and Znaniecki have noted that in the case of the Polish peasant, both first and second generation, "the controlling, standardizing and organizing role of the American state and society . . . [was] almost negligible." The average Polish immigrant did not "participate directly and individually in American life except through business relations."[30] Indeed, Thomas and Znaniecki suggest that the principal controlling influence over the individual was not even the immediate neighborhood, but rather the Polish-American community. Thus the immigrant adapted as best he could to American conditions, even if it meant the sweatshop, the tenement, and indeterminate allegiance to his ethnic group.

The Committee's concern over the deficiency of park and recreation facilities in tenement districts was its principal contribution to neighborhood reconstruction. Gilder and his associates hoped to enrich the life of the tenement dweller by introducing such rare treasures in the tenement neighborhood as fresh air, grass, and playgrounds. The Committee pointed out that "during the public hearings no suggestion more frequently recurred than that in favor of small parks, and of play-

28. Tenement House Committee of 1894, *Report*, 10.
29. Ravage, *An American in the Making*, 61.
30. Thomas and Znaniecki, *The Polish Peasant in Europe and America*, II, 1477.

grounds for children." It complained that although the area of the city below 14th Street was 2,528 acres and the population 707,520, there were only 64.654 acres of park, 2.55 per cent of the entire area. The Committee recommended the construction of at least two parks in the lower East Side and the completion of three more, including Riis's pet project at Mulberry Bend. Upon the advice of Riis and Dr. Roger Tracy of the Board of Health, the Committee also recommended and prepared a bill providing for the attachment of a "good and sufficient playground" to every public school erected in the future. As far as any "unhousing of the population by the destruction of buildings for park purposes" was concerned, the Committee observed simply that "whatever harm might come from this is more than offset by the benefits."[31]

[5]

Although the Gilder Committee made no specific recommendations on the subject of model tenements, it examined those currently in operation and found them satisfactory in every respect. According to the Committee they reduced death rates, raised the level of "morality and self respect" of the tenants, favorably influenced the surrounding neighborhood, and paid "fair profits" to investors. In approving model tenements, the Committee reflected the view of almost every contemporary housing reformer.

Mention has already been made of Alfred T. White's Improved Dwellings Company and the Astral Apartments, both in Brooklyn; the Improved Dwellings Association; and the Tenement House Building Company. Aside from a handful of other scattered experiments such as the Cutting Buildings on 14th Street and Avenue A, there were few other model tenements in the New York area by the mid-90's. The interest aroused in the tenement problem by the Gilder Committee, however, soon resulted in the most ambitious model tenement scheme ever attempted.

31. Tenement House Committee of 1894, *Report*, 41, 42, 43, 45.

In March of 1896 the Better Dwellings Committee of the AICP sponsored a conference whose object was the "inauguration of such a plan as shall commend itself to the best judgment of the experts in housing — in all probability, the formation of some kind of building company."[32] As a result of the conference a Committee on Improved Housing was formed which decided to work independently of the AICP. The officers of the Committee, soon known as the Improved Housing Council, included Richard Watson Gilder, chairman; W. Bayard Cutting, president of the Improved Dwellings Association, vicechairman; and William H. Tolman, general agent for the AICP, secretary. The Council sponsored an architectural competition, requesting plans suited to a 200 x 400 lot. It did not, significantly, repeat the same mistake as the *Plumber and Sanitary Engineer*, trying to reconcile the health and comfort of tenants with the 25 x 100 lot.[33] After a series of plans had been submitted and judged, the Council decided to form a company to carry out the best design, and on July 6, 1896, the City and Suburban Homes Company was born.

Most of the directors and officers of the new company were wealthy philanthropists who had already invested in model tenements or served on the governing boards of model tenement corporations. Samuel D. Babcock, Cornelius Vanderbilt, D. O. Mills, W. Bayard Cutting, and his brother Robert Fulton Cutting, president of the AICP, were all connected with the Improved Dwellings Association. Alfred T. White added his distinguished name to the roster. Other directors included the banker, Isaac N. Seligman; Charles S. Smith, ex-president of the New York Chamber of Commerce; George W. Young, president of the United States Mortgage and Trust Company; John D. Crimmins, a director of the Tenement House Building Company; and Joseph S. Auerbach, a well-known lawyer. The model tenement, clearly, was one important channel through which the wealthy businessmen of New York participated in

32. New York *Times*, Mar. 4, 1896, 2.
33. The plans were judged by a committee consisting of E. R. L. Gould; W. H. Folsom of the AICP; and A. W. Longfellow, Jr., a Boston architect and designer of model tenements in Boston.

housing reform. They provided the money, while the leadership and moral force was provided by charity organizations like the AICP and Charity Organization Society; religious leaders such as Felix Adler and W. S. Rainsford; and conscientious citizens like Jacob Riis, Richard Watson Gilder, and E. R. L. Gould.

Elgin Ralston Lovell Gould was elected president of the City and Suburban Homes Company, a position held until his death in 1915. After 1896 Gould grabbed the torch long held by White and became one of the nation's most persistent publicists for model tenements. Gould was born in Ontario, Canada, in 1860. He received his Ph.D. from Johns Hopkins (where he was a classmate of Woodrow Wilson) for his study of local government in Pennsylvania. After becoming an American citizen in 1885, Gould moved on to a brilliant career as a political scientist and expert in municipal affairs. He taught at Hopkins, the University of Chicago, and Columbia. Seth Low appointed him City Chamberlain of New York in 1902, and Governor Hughes called upon him in 1907 to serve as vice-chairman of the Commission to Revise the New York City Charter.

Between 1887 and 1892 Gould did considerable research for the United States Department of Labor, spending much time in Europe. This research laid the foundation for his reputation as an authority on the housing problem. The eighth special report of the Commissioner of Labor (1895) was Gould's massive opus, *The Housing of the Working People*, a detailed, scholarly analysis of housing reform in Europe and America which concentrated upon the financing and achievements of all model tenements in operation. Gould's conclusion, the thesis of his research which he reiterated the rest of his life, was that the "proper housing of the great masses of working people can be furnished on a satisfactory commercial basis."[34]

Gould viewed tenement reform as a contribution to social as well as sanitary control; as we have seen, his attitude was shared by most other housing reformers. The tenement, Gould

34. Gould, *The Housing of the Working People*, 18.

complained, was a standing menace to "the family, to morality, to the public health, and to civic integrity."[35] The home was the "character unit of society," and when there was "little or no opportunity for the free play of influences which make for health, happiness, and virtue, we must expect social degeneration and decay."[36]

Gould's conception of the social utility of improved housing illustrates perfectly the tendency of the reformer to confuse social control with sanitary control. Although Gould occasionally spoke of the importance of parks in the tenement neighborhood and the need to rescue young boys and girls who were being "poisoned by the philosophy of the streets,"[37] he never systematized his random observations about the general environment into a coherent policy of neighborhood reconstruction. He tended, in practice, to isolate the tenement from its neighborhood, from the vast array of influences which determined the value system of the immigrant poor and their children, and which would continue to operate despite any change in the quality of their housing. To modify radically, for example, the heritage which the immigrant carried to America — surely one of the most important influences determining the quality of his adjustment to American life — involved much more than better housing. As one immigrant observed, "the alien who comes here from Europe is not the raw material that Americans suppose him to be." He has an "Old World soul," which conflicts with America from the moment he lands.[38]

Gould's philosophy of housing reform was reflected faithfully in the policy and operations of the company which he led for nineteen years. It launched its activities in December 1896 with an authorized capital stock of one million dollars and a firm commitment to the principle of "investment philan-

35. Quoted in New York *Times,* Feb. 23, 1894, 10.
36. E. R. L. Gould, "The Housing Problem in Great Cities," *Quarterly Journal of Economics,* XIV (1899-1900), 378.
37. E. R. L. Gould, "The Housing Problem," *Municipal Affairs,* III (1899), 111; and "Park Areas and Open Spaces in Cities," American Statistical Association, *Publications,* I (1888-89), 49-61.
38. Ravage, *An American in the Making,* 60, 61.

thropy." Dividends were limited to 5 per cent, any additional profits going into a reserve fund or into expansion. The company promised to erect its dwellings in accordance with high sanitary standards.

It is well to emphasize once again that "investment philanthropy" was not viewed as charity. Housing reformers universally agreed that housing was a business, that reform could succeed only by the application of business principles, and that model tenements represented nothing but business investments tempered by justice. In paying prevailing neighborhood rents but getting good housing in return, tenants were not recipients of charity but only of the justice to which they were entitled.

Gould, like Riis, White, and Gilder, was strictly in the entrepreneurial tradition on questions of housing finance. He argued that there was nothing "in foreign experience with municipal housing of working people to render its repetition with us either desirable or attractive." It was "bad principle and worse policy" for municipalities "to spend public money competing with private enterprise in housing the masses."[39] The major responsibility of the state was to "provide a well-conceived tenement-house sanitary and building code."[40] In this respect, Gould faithfully adhered to the classic conception of the nineteenth-century state—a state obligated to protect health, safety, and morals by establishing certain limits beyond which individuals could not trespass in pursuit of private gain, but bound otherwise not to interfere in the social and economic order. Thus Gould would have the state set standards below which no housing could fall, but leave actual provision of the housing to market forces.

This entrepreneurial tradition which Gould reflected had always been the dominant one in housing reform. Reformers assumed that a program of model tenements and restrictive legislation was sufficient to insure a supply of good housing. The state did not have to enter the business directly. Exceptions to this tradition were few and far between. Felix Adler had

39. E. R. L. Gould, "The Only Cure for Slums," *Forum*, XIX (1895), 498.
40. Gould, "The Housing Problem in Great Cities," 385.

wisely, but futilely, recommended to the Gilder Committee that the municipality purchase suburban land to lease to individuals or companies who would provide good low-income housing. His recommendation and prophesy were in advance of their time: "The chief point to which I have desired to call attention is that now is the time to act. So favorable an opportunity will never occur again. The Greater New-York will soon become a reality. Land in the surrounding districts, still held at a comparatively low valuation, will soon and steadily advance."[41] Gould himself favored the construction of carefully supervised municipal lodging houses to care for the social stratum which included "the drunkard, the incorrigible, the criminal, the immoral and utterly useless."[42] These were the outcasts of society, however, the diseased elements of the social organism that the state justifiably might segregate.

Committed to an entrepreneurial and business-like solution to the housing problem, Gould excluded such incorrigibles from the sanctuary of the model tenement. Also excluded was a slightly higher social stratum—the "casual worker," "irregular rent payer," "shiftless laborer," and all those who had "grown deeply in debt and lost heart."[43] These were poor economic risks best handled, Gould suggested, by the Octavia Hill method of "friendly rent collection." Octavia Hill, an Englishwoman, had purchased some London slum property in the 1860's with John Ruskin's assistance. She remodeled the premises and became an advisor and friend to the tenants, listening sympathetically to their problems while insisting upon prompt rent payments, sobriety, and moral respectability. As Miss Hill's operations expanded, she could not handle the work alone and began training agents in her principles of friendly rent collection. The agents who managed her properties were expected to treat tenants with businesslike firmness tempered by kindness and justice. Miss Hill exerted a profound influence over the London and American charity organization societies, particularly in the

41. Quoted in New York *Times*, Dec. 3, 1894, 10.
42. Gould, "The Housing Problem," 116.
43. *Ibid.*, 115.

development of friendly visiting or volunteer personal service to the poor.

The best known exemplar of friendly rent collection in this country before 1896 was Ellen Collins, highly praised for her work in Manhattan's squalid fourth ward. Miss Collins, whose father had helped organize the AICP in the 1840's, had been active in Civil War relief and in the 1870's became a visitor for the New York State Board of Charities. In 1880 she invested more than $20,000 in the purchase and restoration of three tenements in the vicinity of Water and Roosevelt Streets. She did away with dance halls and saloons on her property, prohibited liquor, and introduced such amenities as a sewing school for girls, and yards planted with flowers and grass. Miss Collins set no limits to the potentialities of benevolent land-lordism in influencing the character of the poor, provided that the daily supervision of the property was entrusted to a "resi-dent agent, who is intelligent, honorable and efficient, who can apply the owner's ideas to the habits of the tenants, and whose own mode of life will serve as an object lesson. . . ."[44] In 1903 she sold the houses, along with four adjoining ones she had subsequently bought, convinced that efficient manage-ment of renovated tenement property insured dividends to the landlord, justice to the poor, and guidance to the ignorant or demoralized.

Sixteen years after Ellen Collins began her work, an ambitious experiment in friendly rent collecting was launched by the Octavia Hill Association of Philadelphia. Limiting dividends to 4 per cent (later 4½ per cent), the Association bought five houses during its first year of operation, and by 1917 owned 179 houses containing 244 families. It also served as agent for 244 houses with 460 families. The Association purchased property which was run-down, but reasonable in price and not beyond repair, transferring management to its agents, "both paid workers and volunteers . . . trained in all the details of business management as well as in the personal friendly side of

44. Tenement House Committee of 1894, *Report*, 136. See also "The 'Butter-milk House,' an Oasis in the Cherry Hill District," *Charities*, XII (1904), 868-70.

their relations to the people." Although the Association had been created primarily to implement Octavia Hill's principles of friendly rent collection, it actually became a versatile instrument of housing betterment in Philadelphia. It not only sponsored the organization of a Philadelphia Housing Commission in 1909, but worked to secure and enforce housing legislation. In 1914 the Association succumbed to the lure of the model tenement, forming a subsidiary Philadelphia Model Housing Company which erected thirty-two, two-story homes the following year.

Trinity Church became a surprising addition to the ranks of benevolent landlordism after 1909. The vestry property committee requested Emily W. Dinwiddie of the COS Tenement House Committee to survey their holdings. On the basis of her report, they appointed her supervisor of the property. With Miss Dinwiddie's assistance, Trinity lost its reputation as one of the largest and most irresponsible landlords in New York. The Church refused to renew leases on tenements which had been poorly managed and tore down many of the worst buildings.

Although Riis, White, and other housing reformers lauded the Octavia Hill method, its effectiveness, like the model tenement's, was limited by a deficiency of investment philanthropists. Its advocates, however, championed it as a third front of housing reform. Remedial legislation prevented the construction of intolerably bad housing while model tenements insured good accommodation at reasonable rentals. The Octavia Hill method guarded the welfare of those who could not afford model tenements but had to live in that numerically preponderant category which Gould characterized as "tenement houses already built, not irremediably insanitary in their construction, [but] measuring up to standards which are being outlived."[45]

Gould hired Blanche Geary, who in London had absorbed

45. Gould, "The Housing Problem in Great Cities," 392. For other expressions of opinion on the Octavia Hill method consult: Lawrence Veiller, "The Housing Problem in American Cities," American Academy of Political and Social Science, *Annals*, XXV (1905), 257; Alfred T. White, "Better Homes for Workingmen," 371-72; Jacob A. Riis, *How the Other Half Lives*, 218-19.

the Octavia Hill principles of enlightened management, to collect rents from tenants of the City and Suburban Homes Company. He noted that objections were sometimes raised to her weekly visits, but only when "the tenant has something to conceal, an unkempt apartment or some other infraction of the rules."[46] It is difficult to say exactly how much tenants resented such paternalism, but it was possibly more than Gould willingly admitted. As an ideal, the Octavia Hill method was exemplary; it answered the challenge of critics of housing reform who complained that the poor would only use their bathtubs for coal, bannisters for firewood, and plumbing for bludgeons. The ignorant Sicilian or Polish peasant — who leaped across centuries in time when he moved from his native village to a complex, industrial society — had to be educated to the responsibilities now demanded of him. In this sense, the Octavia Hill method indicated an understanding that sanitary control was inadequate to the attainment of social and moral objectives. The immigrant would not automatically respond to a change in environment in precisely the manner which the reformer desired; he had to be taught the responses which were expected of him. Even so, there was no guarantee that he would think or act as the reformer hoped. The Octavia Hill method was a useful instrument of social control, but only if applied with understanding, intelligence, and discretion.

The social stratum for whom Gould really intended the model tenement was the temperate, steadily employed wage earner. Gould welcomed as tenants those dependable and reliable "waiters, dressmakers, laborers, carpenters, women day-workers," who could afford to pay the average $.93 a room per week which the City and Suburban Homes Company charged.[47] The Company's first two ventures, the Alfred Corning Clark Estate on the West Side, and another unit on the East Side, opened in 1898 and 1900. Apartments rented to

46. Gould, "The Housing Problem," 124.

47. *Ibid.*, 124; Francis R. Cope, Jr., "Tenement House Reform: Its Practical Results in the 'Battle Row' District, New York," *American Journal of Sociology*, VII (1901-02), 349.

those whose incomes ranged between $300 and $800 a year.[48]
Like Alfred T. White, the Company sought to bestow maximum
comfort and safety commensurate with a profit: broad central
courts; apartments two rooms deep to guarantee light and
ventilation; fireproofed staircases, stairwells, and partitions;
steam heating (except in the Clark buildings); private water-
closets; stationary washtubs; and gas appliances.[49] On the
other hand, few apartments contained private bathtubs and
rooms were small: about 7½ by 12 feet for bedrooms and
7 by 15 feet for parlors.

Under Gould's leadership the City and Suburban Homes
Company prospered. Its Manhattan property in 1916, the year
after his death, included the 372 apartments of the Clark Estate
on the West Side, three developments on the East Side totaling
2,401 apartments, a Junior League Hotel for women, and the
Tuskegee and Hampton for Negroes. The latter two developments located on the West Side contained 174 apartments. The
Company's tenements accommodated more than 11,000 people
and represented an investment of five and a half million dollars.
Gross rents exceeded $525,000 a year, and 4 per cent dividends
distributed in 1916 totaled $130,000. In order to protect its
mammoth investment, proving that model tenements paid, and
to demonstrate that "improved dwellings are the best guarantee
of civilization," the Company applied itself diligently to problems of supervision and management. Anxious to set an example
for tenants, it kept courts and interior portions of buildings

48. At $.93 a room, a two-room apartment would cost $96.72 for a year. This
would be almost 30 per cent of the income of a family earning $300 a year. It
would certainly have been difficult for a family earning less than $300 to
afford a two-room apartment, let alone any of the Company's larger three- and
four-room apartments. A four-room apartment, at $.93 a room, would cost
$193.44 a year. This would be about 25 per cent of an income totaling $800
a year.

49. Gould, "The Housing Problem," 127. Also Cope, "Tenement House
Reform," 349. Gould, however, did not think that model tenements should be
made "too attractive," because of the danger that "parsimonious members
amongst the better-off elements of wage-earners will be sure to become tenants
and thus monopolize advantages intended for the very poor," E. R. L. Gould,
"The Economics of Improved Housing," pamphlet reprinted from the *Yale
Review*, V (May 1896), 17.

impeccably neat, and promptly took charge of necessary maintenance and repair work. Not content with "mere cleanliness," the Company worked toward "super-cleanliness."

The City and Suburban Homes Company did not rely exclusively upon the power of example to influence tenants, but took positive measures to "bite into their consciousness" its standards of upkeep and personal deportment. From Miss Geary's rent collecting evolved a corps of women agents, who visited apartments personally to collect weekly rents in advance. These women examined the condition of apartments and pondered whether particular tenants were "desirable" or not. Sometimes they advised tenants on personal problems and assisted them in finding employment. Whatever tenants may have thought of the Company's women rent collectors and close supervision, they apparently considered their accommodations a bargain for the price. Vacancy rates were low — only one out of 2,947 apartments in 1916 and "literally . . . shoals of applicants."

Although Gould considered the Manhattan houses a vast improvement over the average commercial tenement, they were not, he believed, the "acme of achievement." At best, they were an intermediate stage for the better paid worker between the "promiscuous and common life of the ordinary tenement and the dignified, well-ordered life of the detached home." The wage-earner or salaried employee in the $800-$1500 bracket — "mechanics, letter-carriers, policemen, firemen, clerks, bookkeepers" — deserved more than a tenement in crowded Manhattan.[50] The housing reformer accepted the tenement as a fact of life only grudgingly and reluctantly. His ideal was the privacy of the single-family detached home, in contrast to the "promiscuity in human beehives, rendering independence and isolation of the family impossible."[51] To encourage suburban settlement, the Company poured its capital into a Brooklyn "Homewood" project. It viewed Homewood as a contribution to the relief of congestion in Manhattan, congestion which had created the tenement in the first place.

Homewood was a 530-acre tract in the New Utrecht district

50. E. R. L. Gould, "Homewood — A Model Suburban Settlement," *Review of Reviews*, XVI (1897), 43, 47.
51. New York *Times*, Feb. 18, 1900, 23.

of Brooklyn, located between Ovington Avenue and 74th Street. The Company planned to build and dispose of cottages on liberal payment terms. The typical cottage was a two-story brick and timber structure including a porch and gables to "add quaintness." It was situated on a 30 x 100 foot lot and cost about $3,810.[52] Imposing its own zoning restrictions, the Company barred saloons, factories, tenements, and flat-roofed buildings. As a conscientious realtor, the Company not only supplied homes but city gas and water, trees, hedges, sidewalks, and macadamized streets. By 1916 the little community of 250 homes represented an investment of more than $700,000.

Gould realized that one company could not singlehandedly decentralize New York's population, relieving its congestion by attracting workers to outlying boroughs. Thus he ardently urged a well-planned municipal transit system to direct the tide of settlement. Cheap, convenient transportation might stimulate the establishment of other Homewoods. "Rapid transit," Gould argued, "is the most important of all factors in improving the housing of a city's population. Firstly, because it extends the habitable area; and, secondly, by this extension helps to offset the consequences of rapidly rising values within or near congested districts."[53] When Gould testified before the Gilder Committee, he suggested that improved rapid transit was "one of the sources you must look to here in New York for help, perhaps the principal source." The Committee, greatly concerned with the problem of overcrowding, welcomed Gould's advice and recommended that "rapid transit facilities be pushed forward as vigorously as possible."[54] Jacob Riis, the champion of suburban life, paid high tribute to the Homewood experiment. It stood for "the way out that must eventually win the fight. That is the track that must be followed, and will be when we have found in rapid transit the key to the solution of our present perplexities."[55]

52. Gould, "Homewood," 44; Percy Griffin, "Model Cottages at Homewood," *Municipal Affairs*, III (1899), 132-35.
53. New York *Times*, May 8, 1896, 3.
54. Tenement House Committee of 1894, *Report*, 367, 75.
55. Riis, *A Ten Years' War*, 87.

In the meanwhile several decades of model tenement agitation, climaxed by the formation of the City and Suburban Homes Company in 1896, had resulted in disappointingly little construction. As even the staunchest defenders of model tenements admitted, commercial tenements were still more profitable. Dividends of 6 per cent to model tenement investors in either the United States or Europe were unusual. The average dividend was 4 or 5 per cent, and sometimes dropped as low as 2 per cent.[56] In contrast, returns from ordinary commercial tenements ranged between 5 and 10 per cent, often much higher.[57] The model tenement, moreover, involved a heavy initial capital outlay and represented a stable investment, neither of which was suited to the small speculative builder who dominated the low-income housing market. Tenement house construction around 1900 was essentially a short-run speculative operation. Tenements were usually erected in rows of three or more by men who had borrowed the necessary working capital, and whose objective was to finish and sell out as quickly as possible. They could thus transfer the mortgage obligations to the purchaser and leave him to battle with the Health Department in case any violations of the tenement code were discovered. The builder, in short, was not an investor but a speculator, betting on the chance that the difference between his costs and selling price would net him several thousand dollars for a few months' work.[58]

Ordinary tenement lots on the lower East Side varied in price between $9,000 and $24,000, on the upper East Side between $5,000 and $9,500. Construction costs for a tenement, including interest, ranged between $16,000 and $26,000 in these

56. Gould, *The Housing of the Working People*, 429-31.

57. Edward Marshall, "New York Tenements," *North American Review*, CLVII (1893), 755; Tenement House Committee of 1894, *Report*, 52, 204; E. R. L. Gould, "Financial Aspects of Recent Tenement House Operations in New York," in De Forest and Veiller, eds., *Tenement House Reform in New York City*, I, 359-61. Profitability was usually calculated on the basis of the equity investment.

58. Lawrence Veiller, "The Speculative Building of Tenement Houses," in *ibid.*, 367-82.

same areas.[59] Such costs were not trivial, but they could be met by the small entrepreneurs who invested in tenement property because of the relatively modest equity required. Many of these petty capitalists were immigrants who had scraped together enough for the equity on a tenement, but hardly commanded access to the kind of capital necessary for a model tenement. The New York *Times*, after a survey in 1896, concluded that "the tenements and the rear tenements in this city are very largely, almost entirely, owned by people of moderate means in the 'middle classes' of the community." Half the rear tenements were "owned by individuals, both men and women, who themselves live in their miserable premises." The *Times* published the names of the owners of all the rear tenements in the city, and judging from these names many of the owners were German, Irish, Jewish, and Italian immigrants or their descendants. A later survey of property distribution on the lower East Side revealed that for a sample parcel of holdings in January 1900 less than $500,000 in value, 72.8 per cent were owned by individuals, in contrast to "estates, corporations and other combinations."[60]

Gould, the Gilder Committee, and others could proclaim the value of model tenements all they wished, but no amount of rhetoric could modify the speculative structure of the housing market or force wealthy individuals and corporations, on any large scale, to channel their capital from more lucrative fields of investment into tenement "investment philanthropy."

[6]

The New York *Times*, referring to the "awakened interest in tenement-house reform in this city," as evidenced by the formation of the City and Suburban Homes Company, credited

59. Gould, "Financial Aspects of Recent Tenement House Operations," 360-61; New York *Times*, June 2, 1902, 8.
60. New York *Times*, Feb. 24, 1896, 2; Leo Grebler, *Housing Market Behavior in a Declining Area: Long-term Changes in Inventory and Utilization of Housing on New York's Lower East Side* (New York, 1952), 97.

the fermentation to the "exhaustive investigation in 1894 by the Legislative Tenement House Commission."[61] Many of the Gilder Committee's recommendations were enacted into law. Since the Committee, however, had proposed nothing which fundamentally altered the quality of the average tenement or affected the routine of life in the tenement neighborhood, its historical significance lies elsewhere. The Gilder Committee performed a valuable educational service, focusing much attention upon the housing problem. Its report of more than 600 pages was a rich source book from which reformers could draw to document their case against the slums. In contrast to any private individual, the state legislature was obligated to take heed of the Committee investigations, criticisms, and recommendations. What this particular Committee had left undone, perhaps another might accomplish. A state commission to reform the tenements was a weapon which could be used again.

The facts unearthed by the Committee in the course of its hearings and investigations aroused much public indignation against the squalor and sanitary defects of the tenements. Probably the most dramatic display of this indignation stormed around Trinity Church (not yet redeemed by Emily Dinwiddie). The Gilder Committee brought to public attention the fact that Trinity, one of the largest landowners in the city and the largest single owner of tenement property, was enriching its treasury with rents from several hundred dilapidated disease-traps — mostly situated on the West Side, in the fifth, eighth, and ninth wards.[62]

President Wilson of the Board of Health complained publicly that many of Trinity's tenements were "old and rickety," and that the death rate in them for the previous five years was one-third higher than for the rest of the city.[63] The Committee revealed that Trinity had refused to obey the 1887 law requiring the installation of water on every tenement floor. It is not

61. New York *Times,* Nov. 22, 1896, 9.
62. Tenement House Committee of 1894, *Report,* 536-45; New York *Times,* Dec. 11, 1894, 3. The *Times* featured a series of articles on Trinity's tenements through the month of December.
63. New York *Times,* Dec. 14, 1894, 2.

surprising that such exposures incensed public opinion.[64] The wealthiest church in America was not only an un-Christian and uncharitable landlord, but a stubborn offender against a "public sentiment fully enlightened by scientific sanitation and aroused by University Settlement Work and the Tenement House Commission."[65]

If a respectable corporation like Trinity was willing to defy public opinion in order to preserve its income from unsavory tenements, what could be expected from landlords who made less claim to Christian virtue? They, too, would need the power of law to force them to fulfill their obligations to their tenants and society. In general, the unfavorable publicity directed against Trinity served to advertise the Committee's work to the public and impress upon it the urgent necessity for restrictive legislation. The climate of opinion favorable to reform which Trinity had inadvertently helped to create in 1894 and 1895 was still serviceable five years later when reformers were ready to tackle the dumb-bell directly.

64. *Ibid.*, Mar. 6, 1895, 4.
65. *Ibid.*, Dec. 14, 1894, 4.

5. | Lawrence Veiller and the New York Tenement House Commission of 1900

> There was a rumor that Mr. Veiller was a visionary Ruskinite. It was reported that he did not believe in interest and profits; that he had actually rented a safe deposit box in which to keep his savings rather than invest them and so become a participant in the capitalist system.
>
> EDWARD T. DEVINE,
> *When Social Work Was Young*

[1]

Soon after the Gilder Committee had completed its work, a dramatic series of events occurred which profoundly altered the structure of the housing problem in New York. A charter for Greater New York was drawn up, adopted in 1897, and put into effect on January 1, 1898. It contained a provision calling for the appointment by the municipal assembly of a commission to revise the city's building code. The commission, whose work would affect the vast population and territory of five boroughs, was established in January 1899. Its labors gave birth to an unsatisfactory building code — and to the initial triumphs of Lawrence Veiller. One of the least known but most important municipal reformers of the Progressive era, Veiller almost single-handedly abolished the dumb-bell tenement as a form of construction after 1901. More than any one individual, he shaped the thinking and practical evolution of the housing movement in New York and the nation between 1898 and 1917. Organizer and first deputy commissioner of the New York City Tenement House Department from 1902-04, secretary and director for many years of the Tenement House Committee of the Charity Organization Society (COS), organizer and director of the National Housing Association after 1910, the author of several influential books, Veiller transformed the housing movement from a well meaning but sporadic and ineffectual pastime of a few moral-minded individuals into a disciplined campaign. He first revealed his unparalleled qualities for leadership as secretary of the New York Tenement House Commission of 1900, which he created and whipped into the most successful instrument of reform in the history of housing movements in America. As the architect and craftsman of the national housing crusade during the Progressive era, Veiller displayed those same qualities which made him the keystone of the Tenement Commission of 1900 — a genius for organization and administration, tireless dedication, political shrewdness, and, above all, a mastery of his subject which awed even his most bitter adversaries.

[2]

Convinced at an early age that better housing for the poor was the solution to many other social problems, Veiller in 1898 suggested to the AICP and the State Charities Aid Association that they help in forming a permanent tenement house society. Neither group was interested in Veiller's proposal, so he turned to Robert W. de Forest, president of the COS.[1] Veiller informed de Forest that his projected society would "secure the enforcement of the existing laws relating to tenement-houses"; "present united opposition to bad legislation arising either at Albany or in the Municipal Assembly and affecting the tenement-house question"; "obtain such new and

1. Lawrence Veiller, Reminiscences, Columbia Oral History Project, 9. All citations in this and the next chapter are drawn from the copy in possession of Mr. Veiller at the time it was used by the author.

remedial legislation as may be necessary"; and make a "general study of the tenement-house question."[2] Veiller argued convincingly that the new society might influence the work of the forthcoming building code commission. The COS did not act until December 1898, when it decided not to form an independent society as Veiller had originally suggested, but a committee within the COS.[3]

Frederick W. Holls, a lawyer, was appointed chairman of the new Tenement House Committee. It also included George B. Post, an architect who had served on the Gilder Committee; Richard Watson Gilder; Felix Adler, founder of the Ethical Culture Society and a member of the first state appointed Tenement House Commission in 1884; E. R. L. Gould; I. N. Phelps Stokes and Ernest Flagg, both architects long interested in tenement improvement; Edward T. Devine, general secretary of the COS; Constant A. Andrews, chairman of the AICP Department of Dwellings;[4] John Vinton Dahlgren, a former attorney for the Building Department in New York; and Robert W. de Forest, president of the COS. Veiller was appointed secretary and executive officer. The COS Tenement House Committee, though its membership changed over the years, consistently guided the housing reform movement in New York for the next two decades. Staffed by outstanding authorities on the housing problem, it represented a triumph for organization and *expertise* in housing reform — the maturity of a trend toward organization and efficiency which, by 1900, had already manifested itself in many areas of American political and economic life. In this connection, the Committee served as a permanent pressure group, a lobbyist for housing

2. Draft, dated Apr. 26, 1898, of a proposal "to establish a permanent Tenement House Commission or Society, as a new philanthropic body," Veiller MSS. Also Lilian Brandt, *The Charity Organization Society of the City of New York, 1882-1907: History, Account of Present Activities* (New York, 1907), 45.

3. Charity Organization Society (COS), *Seventeenth Annual Report*, 1898-99, 41.

4. The AICP Department of Dwellings had evolved out of a tenement house committee established by the Association in the 1870's. In 1885 this committee merged with the Sanitary Reform Society to form the AICP's Sanitary Department, and later, its Department of Dwellings.

reform which defended the interests of the unorganized and comparatively powerless tenants. Its success was largely the consequence of the initiative, originality, and dedication of its founder and executive officer, Lawrence Veiller.

Compared to Veiller, such well known housing reformers as Alfred T. White, Richard Watson Gilder, and Jacob Riis were amateurs whose influence, essentially, was rooted in their personal prestige rather than in any organized, permanent pressure group. They were not amateurs because their knowledge of tenement conditions or their interest in the subject was that of a dilettante, but in the sense that housing reform for them was an avocation and a moral responsibility, not a full-time paying vocation. Veiller, by contrast, was a professional reformer who usually worked through some organization to mould public opinion and impose his will upon recalcitrant legislators. He relied for success less upon moral suasion than upon his ability to manipulate men and events. Like any true professional, he knew his subject thoroughly. Veiller was an expert legislative draftsman and political in-fighter, and in his grasp of structural technicalities he was the peer of any architect or builder.

Veiller's distinguished career was initially launched at the expense of the municipal building code commission, appointed in January 1899. He drafted a series of recommendations which were presented to it in the name of the COS Tenement House Committee. These proposed, among other things, that no air shaft should measure less than 150 square feet in area, that non-fireproof tenements should be limited to six stories in height, that every tenement should be provided with at least one bath-tub or shower, that the walls of future tenements should extend three feet six inches above the roof on all sides to permit their use as children's playgrounds, that no wooden buildings should be allowed on the same lot as a tenement.[5] When the building

5. Brochure, dated May 6, 1899, inviting recipient to attend a conference sponsored by the COS Tenement House Committee, Veiller MSS. Also Lawrence Veiller, "New York's New Building Code as Affecting Tenement-House Reform," *Charities Review*, IX (1899-1900), 388-91; COS, *Seventeenth Annual Report*, 1898-99, 45.

code commission delivered its report to the municipal legislature in September 1899, Veiller and the COS were appalled. They found not only that their suggestions had been ignored, but that the commission had moved the building code a "distinct step backward."

The commission's revised code permitted tenements to reach eight stories in height, if the first two floors were fireproofed. The old law had allowed six stories. The new code permitted the construction of wooden dumb-waiter shafts, a serious fire hazard. It authorized the construction of wooden tenements habitable by six families. The old code had limited occupancy to three families. The commission, in the opinion of its critics, had permitted too much discretion to the Buildings Department in applying the law.

Veiller complained that the commission was almost entirely composed of spokesmen for the building interests. There was "no representative on this commission of the tenement house interest." He pointed out that the COS recommendations which the commission had ignored had been endorsed by the New York chapter of the American Institute of Architects, the Architectural League, the "leading architects of the city," "all the tenement house reform people," and "all the charitable societies."[6] Veiller and the COS Tenement House Committee led the opposition to the new code in the hearings before the municipal legislature in September-October 1899.[7] They were joined by municipal reform organizations such as the City Club and the Social Reform Club. Within the legislature, Republicans and representatives of the Citizens' Union "denounced the code as a job and a fraud upon the people." This opposition was in vain. The code, according to the New York Times, was "rushed

6. Mazet Committee, Report, III, 3457, 3462, 3463. Numerous other witnesses before the Mazet Committee criticized the new code. These included James M. MacGregor, a former superintendent of buildings in New York; James B. Reynolds, headworker at University Settlement; Albert S. MacGregor, Robert W. Gibson and Ernest Flagg, all architects. Also, New York Times, Sept. 10, 1899, 15.

7. H. W. Desmond, editor of the Real Estate Record and Guide, complained that "criticism of the code . . . is the special product of the Charity Organization Society." New York Times, Dec. 10, 1899, 25.

through the Municipal Assembly by order of Richard Croker."[8] The council followed suit and the measure was signed by Mayor Van Wyck in October.

Thoroughly disgruntled, the COS decided to strike back. Veiller directed a counter-offensive aimed at creating a wave of reform sentiment powerful enough to induce the state legislature to step in and undo the work of the municipal authorities. As part of his campaign of protestation and education, Veiller organized for the COS Tenement House Committee its famous tenement exhibition of February 1900. The unique idea for a social exhibition had entered Veiller's mind as early as 1898.[9] He had begun work on the project even before the building code commission had delivered its report in September 1899. Assisted by I. N. Phelps Stokes, Veiller "worked about 16 hours a day for months" to prepare the exhibit whose general purpose, as he later explained, was to prove that in New York "the working-man is housed worse than in any other city in the civilized world, notwithstanding the fact that he pays more money for such accommodations than is paid elsewhere."[10]

Visitors to the Sherry Building at 404 Fifth Avenue, where the exhibit was located, were greeted by an array of maps, charts, tables, photographs, diagrams, and cardboard models designed to acquaint them with all phases of the tenement problem in New York. Material pertaining to tenement conditions in Europe and other American cities was also included for comparative purposes. One of the most widely discussed features of Veiller's pioneering social exhibit was the cardboard

8. New York *Times*, Oct. 26, 1899, 4, Sept. 13, 1899, 14, Sept. 23, 1899, 5, Oct. 11, 1899, 14, Oct. 15, 1899, 16.

9. In his April 26, 1898, draft of a proposal to establish a permanent tenement house society, Veiller had suggested the making of a model of a block showing the existing conditions. Veiller MSS. On March 22, 1899, I. N. Phelps Stokes suggested the possibility of a tenement exhibition before a meeting of the COS Tenement House Committee. On April 11, Veiller and Stokes submitted to the Committee a tentative plan for such an exhibition. COS Tenement House Committee, Minutes, Mar. 22, 1899, Apr. 11, 1899.

10. Veiller, Reminiscences, 13; Veiller, "Tenement House Reform in New York City, 1834-1900," 115. Veiller found Stokes of great service in preparing the exhibit. He generally respected Stokes's advice and considered him one of the pillars of tenement reform. Lawrence Veiller to author, Interview, July 13, 1959.

model of an entire tenement block, the one bounded by Chrystie, Forsyth, Canal, and Bayard Streets. The block contained 39 tenements groaning under the weight of 2,781 inhabitants. These people shared only 264 water closets; they did not have access to a single stationary bathtub. Only forty apartments were furnished with hot running water. Thirty-two cases of tuberculosis had been recorded on the block within the past five years, as well as 660 applications for aid to two private charities alone. Such conditions illustrated what Veiller had in mind when he referred to New York as "the City of Living Death."

A second impressive feature of the exhibit were the disease and poverty maps prepared by Veiller. Arranged in two parallel series, these maps listed every tenement block in the city, giving the "street number of each building, the height, number of stories, also the amount of land covered, the shape of the building, and the small amount of land left vacant for light and air."[11] Each black dot on the poverty maps represented five families who had applied for charity within the past five years, and hardly a tenement in the city was free from at least one dot. Each black dot on the disease maps indicated one case of tuberculosis within the past five years. Once again, nearly every tenement had at least one tuberculosis dot. Some contained as many as twelve.[12]

After the exhibit closed in March 1900, having been attended by 10,000 persons, it went on tour to other American cities

11. Veiller, Reminiscences, 15.

12. Creating these disease and poverty maps was one of Veiller's most difficult tasks. Because it would have been too expensive to have surveys made of the tenement districts, Veiller had linen tracings made of the insurance or real estate maps which "every insurance man and realtor was using every day in his business." These were done in drawing ink, and then black prints were made from them. Then each building had to be colored individually and the dots stamped. Veiller later donated these maps to the New York Historical Society.

For additional details on the exhibit, consult: Veiller, Reminiscences, 11-19; COS, *Seventeenth Annual Report*, 1898-99, 47-48; Lawrence Veiller, "Tenement House Reform," American Academy of Political and Social Science, *Annals*, XV (1900), 138-41; Lawrence Veiller, "The Tenement-House Exhibition of 1899," *Charities Review*, X (1900-01), 19-27; Lawrence Veiller, "Tenement House Reform in New York City," 111, 16; New York *Times*, Feb. 10, 1900, 7.

and to the Paris Exposition. It was acclaimed as "one of the greatest contributions, if not the greatest, ever made in this or any other country to a proper understanding of the subject of the housing of the poor." According to Jacob Riis, it inaugurated a new era of tenement reform, one which would not cease until "decent living conditions have become the rule rather than the exception." The Reverend W. T. Elsing, pastor of the DeWitt Memorial Church on Rivington Street in New York's lower East Side, wrote Veiller that "if you die tomorrow you have done a great life work."[13] In all the exhibit was vivid testimony to Veiller's originality and understanding of the strategic importance of moulding a sympathetic public opinion.

Governor Theodore Roosevelt, who had attended the exhibit, was so impressed by Veiller's handiwork (especially the disease and poverty maps) that he told Robert W. de Forest afterward, "Tell me what you want and I will help you get it."[14] Roosevelt, of course, was no stranger to the housing problem. As a member of the New York State Legislature in the 1880's he had struggled to abolish tenement cigar manufacture. During his term as Police Commissioner of New York City (1895-97), Roosevelt had been close to Jacob Riis. For two years, Roosevelt admitted, Riis had been his "main prop and comfort."[15] According to Roosevelt, Riis and he "looked at life and its problems from substantially the same standpoint."[16] On no issue did the two men agree more forcibly than the unfortunate social consequences of the tenements. Like Riis, Roosevelt championed what a later generation would call the American way of life; and Riis had proved to Roosevelt's satisfaction that the tenement slum was incompatible with good American citizenship. At a speech delivered at the COS exhibit, Roosevelt advised his

13. Lillian W. Betts, "The Tenement-House Exhibit," Outlook, LXIV (1900), 589; Jacob A. Riis, "The Tenement House Exhibition," Harper's Weekly, XLIV (Feb. 3, 1900), 104; W. T. Elsing to Lawrence Veiller, Feb. 21, 1900, Veiller MSS.

14. Veiller, Reminiscences, 20.

15. Theodore Roosevelt to Jacob A. Riis, Apr. 18, 1897, Riis MSS. "When I went to the Police Department it was on your book that I had built, and it was on you yourself that I continued to build." Theodore Roosevelt to Jacob A. Riis, Oct. 25, 1897, Riis MSS.

16. Theodore Roosevelt, An Autobiography (New York, 1914), 174.

audience to "go and look through the charts downstairs, which show the centres of disease and poverty, and remember that it is there that the greatest number of votes are cast." In the governor's opinion, tenement reform represented "an effort to cut at the root of the diseases which eat at the body social and the body politic."[17]

Assured of Roosevelt's support, Veiller and de Forest decided that a state tenement commission would best serve the interests of reform. Roosevelt acquiesced and Veiller quickly prepared a bill for the state legislature early in 1900 authorizing the appointment of such a commission. At this point began Veiller's initiation into the subtleties of Albany politics. He learned that "the building 'ring' in New York and the corrupt Tammany officials in the Building Department especially, were violently opposed to any such legislation." They feared exposure, according to Veiller, of their inefficient enforcement of the building laws. Unable to get his bill out of the assembly committee to which it had been referred, Veiller bombarded Roosevelt with pleas for help. Finally, an exasperated governor implored Jotham P. Allds, chairman of the committee: "Can't you see Mr. Veiller about that Tenement House Commission? O Lord! I wish it could pass!"[18]

After considerable delay, Veiller and Roosevelt succeeded in prying the bill from the committee and winning its approval in the lower house. It was then placed on the senate calendar. At this point, Veiller explained, the Tammany leadership maneuvered to defeat the measure indirectly by delaying action until the closing days of the session. By doing this they could exploit a provision in the state constitution which required that all special laws pertaining to cities of the first class (250,000 or more) had to be approved by the mayor within fifteen days or, if disapproved, reconsidered and passed by the legislature over his veto. Because Veiller's bill applied only to New York City it would have to go to Mayor Van Wyck, and if it did not reach him more than fifteen days before the end of the

17. New York *Times*, Feb. 11, 1900, 6.
18. Veiller, Reminiscences, 21; Theodore Roosevelt to Jotham P. Allds, undated, Veiller MSS.

session he could kill it by merely withholding his approval. And when the legislative session entered the fifteen-day period prior to adjournment without final senate passage of the tenement bill, it seemed that Tammany had defeated the novice reformer.[19]

Confronted with an apparently hopeless situation, Veiller now exhibited the political adroitness which would typify his housing work. He abruptly switched his bill from the category of "special" legislation applying to New York City alone to the category of "general" legislation for cities of the first class. In this form it would go directly to the governor, instead of to the mayor, for approval. Redrafting its provisions to make it apply to Buffalo as well as New York City, Veiller asked his friends in the Buffalo Charity Organization Society to prepare a "spontaneous" demand on the Buffalo senators to support the revised bill. The response was favorable, and when the original measure was taken up in the senate one of the senators from Buffalo offered an amendment, prepared by Veiller, which struck out the words "New York City" and substituted "cities of the first class" (which included only New York and Buffalo at the time).[20] The senate adopted the amendment, and the amended bill, providing for the creation of the New York State Tenement House Commission of 1900, was approved by both houses of the legislature and signed by Governor Roosevelt. The governor soon named the fifteen members of the new Commission, which appointed Veiller as its secretary.[21]

19. Veiller, Reminiscences, 23-24.
20. Ibid., 24-26.
21. The two Buffalo members of the Commission were William A. Douglas, a lawyer, and Williams Lansing, an architect. The thirteen New York members included Otto M. Eidlitz and Myles Tierney, both builders, and Alfred T. White of model tenement fame; Charles S. Brown, a real estate agent and broker who substituted for E. R. L. Gould when Gould declined his appointment; the architects I. N. Phelps Stokes and Raymond T. Almirall; Paul D. Cravath, a lawyer who served for several years as chairman of the COS Tenement House Committee; F. Norton Goddard, a merchant and the only member of the Commission unwilling to sign the final report, because it was too "moderate" in its recommendations; James B. Reynolds, headworker at University Settlement; Dr. George B. Fowler, former Health Commissioner of New York City; Hugh J. Bonner, former chief of the New York Fire Department; William J. O'Brien, a union official in the building trades; and Robert W. deForest, who was elected chairman.

Phelps Stokes's skills as an architect and de Forest's skills as a diplomat were especially useful to the Commission. Lawrence Veiller to author, Interview, July 13, 1959.

[3]

Born in Elizabeth, New Jersey, in 1872, Veiller was educated at City College in New York. He became interested in social problems after studying the social critics of Victorian England, notably Ruskin and Carlyle.[22] Upon receiving his B.A. in 1890, Veiller immersed himself in the life of the immigrant and working-class poor in that greatest of laboratories — the tenement quarters of New York. His experience with the East Side Relief Work Committee during the Depression of 1893 convinced him, "at the mature age of 20 years, that the improvement of the homes of the people was the starting point of everything."[23] A job as plan examiner in the Buildings Department during the Strong administration (1895-97) gave him valuable experience in the technical phase of the tenement problem.

Veiller was a short and stocky man with a beard. His manner was brisk and alert; he was quick to grasp the essence and details of a problem. He had little patience with those who used philanthropy to further their own personal interests — as a means to increase business or social contacts. Similarly, he had no use for those who meant well but did not measure up to his own exacting standards of proficiency. In typically blunt fashion, Veiller once informed the social workers at a National Conference of Charities and Correction that they knew little about housing, or other reform specialties.[24] When the august and respected Richard Watson Gilder asked the twenty-two year old Veiller if he cared to serve on the staff of the Tenement Committee of 1894, he firmly rejected the honor because he did not wish to associate himself with Edward Marshall, the Committee's secretary. In Veiller's opinion, Marshall had committed the unpardonable sin; he was not a sincere reformer but a sensationalist who used reform as a lever to raise the circulation of his paper.[25] Although Veiller was an abrupt and aggres-

22. Lawrence Veiller to author, Interview, July 13, 1959.
23. Veiller, Reminiscences, 3.
24. Lawrence Veiller, "The National Housing Association," in the National Conference of Charities and Correction, *Proceedings*, 1910, 225.
25. Lawrence Veiller to author, Interview, July 13, 1959; Richard Watson Gilder to Lawrence Veiller, June 11, 1894, Richard Watson Gilder Collection.

sive individual, supremely self-confident and fully conscious of his abilities, he disliked publicity and preferred to work shielded from the public gaze.[26]

If Veiller often sacrificed tact in favor of honesty, he could sooth the wounded vanity of adversaries by the exercise of a sharp wit and flashes of captivating charm. One contemporary remembered him as "interesting and fun occasionally."[27] Veiller was the technician of housing reform, but he was not a narrow and parochial man. His professional interests included, besides housing, city planning, tuberculosis control, and court reform. In 1913 Veiller was appointed to the Advisory Committee on the Height, Size and Arrangement of Buildings of the Board of Estimate and Apportionment of New York City. Although he did not sign the Committee's report because he desired more stringent restrictions upon the amount of lot space a building could occupy, its work served as the basis for New York's first zoning ordinance, adopted in 1916. Veiller contributed several papers to the National Conference on City Planning (organized in 1909) and helped found the American City Planning Institute. In 1921 he prepared for the United States Department of Commerce its influential Standard Zoning Law.

As director of the COS Department for the Improvement of Social Conditions after 1907, Veiller guided the Society's tuberculosis and court work. The COS established its special tuberculosis committee in 1902, when Veiller left the Society for several years, but he took charge of the work from 1907 until the committee's dissolution in 1919. One of his first contributions was the preparation of a tuberculosis exhibit which won acclaim at the International Tuberculosis Congress held in Washington in 1908; it was displayed the following year at the Museum of Natural History. Under Veiller's leadership, the committee successfully sponsored special educational campaigns in the Italian quarters of the city, the establishment of

26. The author is indebted to Miss Frances Perkins for some clues to Veiller's character, Interview, June 11, 1959. Also, Lawson Purdy, Reminiscences, Columbia Oral History Project, 10; William Jay Schieffelin, *ibid.*, 32; William H. Allen, *ibid.*, 150-51.

27. Robert S. Binkerd, Reminiscences, Columbia Oral History Project, 36.

municipal hospitals for care of tuberculosis patients, the formation of an Association of Tuberculosis Clinics, the creation of "fresh-air classes" for "pre-tubercular" school children as well as educational exhibits in the public schools, and medical examinations for industrial workers.

After the COS organized a special committee on criminal courts in 1910, Veiller supplemented his housing and tuberculosis work with efforts to reform the Magistrates' or Police Courts, which frequently dealt with the tenement population.[28] In his spare time, Veiller found relaxation in Renaissance painting, Oriental art, and the study of English culture.[29]

Veiller did not posit much faith in the inherent virtue of his fellow men. He was something of a cynic in contrast to many Progressive reformers, who shared the idealist's belief in the perfectibility of the human race and the inevitability of progress, in the power of reason and good will to win converts to the side of righteousness. More than Jacob Riis, certainly, Veiller conceived of a universe in which power regulated human affairs more decisively than love, Christian brotherhood, or the milk of human kindness. Significantly, he frowned upon the amount of time and energy which reformers invested in promoting model tenements. He favored restrictive legislation which represented not an appeal to man's altruism and spirit of self-sacrifice, but the application of state power to enforce justice. In Veiller's opinion, every human being had a "God-given right to light and air." If certain groups, notably builders and landlords, served their own interests by depriving people of this right, then it was "unquestionably the duty of the state" to match its interests and power against theirs.[30]

Veiller's participation in the housing movement, however, involved more than the addition to its ranks of a tough-minded realist, an expert manipulator of public opinion, a legislative draftsman, and an organizer and strategist of pressure groups. Neither his realism nor his administrative responsibilities damp-

28. Veiller describes his court work at length in his unpublished Reminiscences.
29. Lawrence Veiller to author, Interview, Aug. 1, 1959.
30. Veiller, "The Housing Problem in American Cities," 257.

ened a deeply-rooted moral sensibility. He may have lacked the bubbling optimism and winsome personal warmth of a reformer like Riis, but he was no less committed to better housing in the name of justice and the well-being of the community. Unlike those politicians or bureaucrats who enjoy power as an end in itself, Veiller regarded power as the means to the attainment of fundamentally moral ends.

Like Riis, Veiller revolted against housing conditions which degraded the individual, thwarted his moral and physical growth, and unleashed his worst animal instincts. The tenement environment, he protested, bred sickness and death, crime, immorality, drunkenness, and family demoralization.[31] What one kind of environment had created, another could undo; it was fully within the community's power to improve the housing of the poor and thus change the quality of their lives. If the community failed through indifference or ignorance it was, in effect, directly responsible for the consequences. In this sense — his belief in the right of every individual to a decent home environment whatever his social or financial status — Veiller did reflect in full measure the humanitarian idealism which erupted in the Progressive era. He was not so tough-minded or so perfect an administrator that he could not feel personally responsible for the welfare of those human beings helpless in the face of community neglect and "greed on the part of those who desire to secure for themselves an undue profit."[32]

Although an Episcopalian by heritage, Veiller's humanitarianism did not spring from any religious fervor. He was a secular reformer who believed that the attainment of individual moral integrity and the fulfillment of one's social responsibilities were religion enough.[33] Veiller's solicitude for the condition of the poor did not arise out of any conception of Christian love due to all men, but from a disciplined moral individualism. Society owed every man at least the opportunity to realize

31. Veiller, "Tenement House Reform," 138-39.
32. Veiller, "The Housing Problem in American Cities," 250.
33. Lawrence Veiller to author, Interview, Aug. 20, 1959.

his potentialities, unhandicapped by a degrading environment which stacked the odds against him.

Veiller's humanitarianism was closely linked to a conviction that tenement reform was a key to the problem of social control. Like many others, Veiller feared that industrialism, immigration, and urbanism had created deep ethnic and class rifts in American life. According to Veiller, the great city had arisen in connection with the "change from agricultural to industrial life." Housing reform was basic to an alleviation of the "evils attendant upon that development."[34]

If an exclusively American population was packed into the serried tenements hoarding every foot of space in the district east of Broadway and south of 14th Street, the problem of social control would have been difficult enough. The presence of the immigrant, however, made it appalling in magnitude. Clearly, an environment which discouraged the nurture of first-class human beings could not produce first-class citizens. The tenement obstructed the reunification of an urban community in which the native middle class lived physically, socially, and culturally in a world apart from the immigrant, working-class population.

Veiller realized that the transition from the European peasant village to a modern urban civilization involved a restructuring of the personality so drastic that it frequently resulted in utter demoralization. He turned to the suburbs and countryside as an alternative to urban settlement, an alternative which promised to ease the pain of adaptation to American life. There was not the "slightest reason," he argued, "why the greater part of our tremendous foreign population, which has come from rural peasant life in Europe, should not continue in similar rural peasant life in this country — in fact, there is every reason why it should."[35] In broadest terms, Veiller's real solution to the housing problem was urban decentralization.

He did not think that dispersion of the urban population should apply only to the immigrant. The "bad effect upon the

34. Veiller, "The Housing Problem in American Cities," 248.
35. *Ibid.*, 265-66.

community of a congregate form of living" applied as much
to the native American. So far as Veiller was concerned,
"Waldorf-Astorias at one end of the town" were as responsible
as tenements at the other "in their destruction of civic spirit
and the responsibilities of citizenship." The preservation of
democratic institutions depended upon "an organized effort
to distribute the population and set the tendency back to rural
or semi-rural communities."[36]

Veiller's objection to the tenement as a way of life was
grounded in the traditional conservative "stake in society"
theory. The property-owning taxpayer was more likely to take
an intelligent interest in the affairs of his community than the
rootless cliff dweller. A man who owned his own home had
every incentive "to work industriously, to be economical and
thrifty, to take an interest in public affairs." By contrast, what
incentive was there for the man in a two- or three-room cubicle
lofted high above the earth to "develop a sense of civic responsibility or patriotism?"[37] Veiller realized, however, that urban
decentralization was a long range ideal. In the meanwhile,
immediate and drastic action was necessary to protect those
who lived in the city.

[4]

The Tenement House Commission of 1900 was largely Veiller's
creation. He was appointed its secretary in April and soon
became its guiding spirit. Veiller drew up the plan for the
Commission's work, and took charge of its investigations and
the preparation of most of its special reports.[38] He wrote
most of its *Report* and its proposed tenement house code, an
extraordinarily difficult task requiring expert legal and technical knowledge.[39] He prepared himself for this feat by com-
piling a detailed history of all the tenement house legislation
applicable to New York. Finally, Veiller originated the idea for

36. *Ibid.*, 255, 265.
37. *Ibid.*, 255.
38. *Charities*, VII (1901), 540. See draft dated June 1900 of Veiller's "personal views as to the work to be done by the Tenement House Commission."
Veiller MSS.
39. Veiller, Reminiscences, 32.

a separate Tenement House Department to enforce his new code, and then piloted the Commission's bills through the state legislature.

The Commission discovered more than 80,000 tenements in existence throughout the five boroughs in 1900. Of these more than half, 42,700, were in Manhattan alone. The 80,000 tenements housed a population of 2,372,070, of which no fewer than 1,585,000 lived in Manhattan.[40] The Commission could neither abolish all existing tenements nor abolish the tenement outright as a mode of habitation in the future. It could, however, make existing and future tenements safer, cleaner, and more comfortable.

Veiller, we will remember, had recommended to the municipal building code commission in 1899 that it prohibit air shafts less than 150 square feet in area, and he brought to the Tenement Commission his determination that the dumb-bell, as it had existed since 1879, must be proscribed. He was supported by the Commission, which agreed that the dumb-bell contributed greatly toward making the housing of New York workers worse than in any city of America. In the Commission's opinion, "the greatest evil of the present day" was the absence of light and air in the average tenement apartment; in short, the dumb-bell air shaft. C. A. Mohr, an inspector for the Commission, explained that tenement bedrooms could be slept in anytime for "they exceed the Arctic zone in having night 365 days in the year."[41]

The Commission complained that this eternal darkness contributed to the spread of tuberculosis, a scourge which had "become practically epidemic in this city." One of the eight public hearings of the Commission was devoted entirely to the relationship between tenement conditions and the "White Plague." It heard many physicians blame the tenement, "especially with regard to light and air," for the high incidence of

40. Detailed statistics concerning the New York tenements in 1900 were compiled for the Commission by Veiller. They can be found in his chapter, "A Statistical Study of New York's Tenement House," in De Forest and Veiller, eds., *The Tenement House Problem*, I, 191-240.

41. C. A. Mohr, "Tenement Evils as Seen by an Inspector," in *ibid.*, 436.

tuberculosis, costing over 8,000 deaths a year.[42] The Commission learned that if the incidence of tuberculosis was plotted over a period of time, it was found to concentrate most heavily in neighborhoods and blocks where sanitary conditions were poorest. On a single block on Cherry Street alone, the Health Department recorded 102 cases of tuberculosis between 1894-99.[43] Dr. John Pryor, the Health Commissioner of Buffalo and a witness before the Commission, later wrote that the dark, crowded tenement was the "natural breeding place" of tuberculosis, whereas sunlight and fresh air were its greatest enemies.[44]

Impressed by such testimony, the Commission recommended the prohibition of the narrow dumb-bell shaft in future tenements. Veiller's revised code replaced it by a court which varied in size depending upon the height of the building, but which, under no circumstances, could measure less than four feet six inches in width. There was no possibility now that the undeveloped northern portions of Manhattan or the other boroughs would suffer the ravages of the dumb-bell after 1901. Its prohibition was a major triumph for the Commission of 1900.

The Commission was responsible for two other decisive reforms. Veiller's code required the installation of a separate water closet in each apartment of future tenements (and most builders found it to their advantage to install a separate, attached bathtub as well). The provision of private bathroom facilities represented an improvement long overdue in New York's multiple dwellings. The Tenement House Law of 1901 also included stringent fire-protection measures. It limited the height of future non-fireproof tenements to five stories (except for buildings forty feet or more in width, which could legally reach six stories or sixty-seven feet), and re-enacted previous laws requiring the fireproofing of halls and stairs as well as the floor above the cellar in tenements five stories or more in height.

42. De Forest and Veiller, "The Tenement House Problem (Being the general report of the Commission)," in *ibid.*, 12, 13. Hereafter referred to as "The Tenement House Problem."
43. Hermann M. Biggs, "Tuberculosis and the Tenement House Problem," in *ibid.*, 449.
44. John H. Pryor, "The Tenement and Tuberculosis," *Charities Review*, X (1900-01), 443.

The Tenement Law of 1901, in addition, specified in detail the location and construction of fire escapes.

Veiller's code required important changes in existing tenements. Landlords had to install a window in the wall of any windowless interior rooms, linking it to adjoining windowed rooms, as well as replace all school sinks (sewer-connected privies) and privy vaults with "individual water-closets of durable non-absorbable material." Other required improvements included the provision of satisfactory fire escapes, the lighting of dark hallways by substituting glass panels for wood in certain doors on each floor, and the waterproofing of cellar floors.

The Commission was responsible for many other measures concerning the fireproofing, sanitation and ventilation of tenements. Its work, on the whole, affected the tenements more fundamentally than anything since the 1860's, when the establishment of the Metropolitan Board of Health and the Tenement House Law of 1867 marked the beginnings of municipal sanitary control. Indeed, the Commission inaugurated a new era in housing, as New York tenements after 1901 were known as "new law" in contrast to those erected under the less stringent provisions of the "old law." Veiller, however, always regarded the Tenement House Law of 1901 as a compromise, not an ideal, and even expressed a wistful desire that "the city might be purified by fire, and that whole sections might be thus destroyed."[45]

The Commission's code was firmly supported by Governor Odell, who had succeeded Roosevelt.[46] The only real opposition, in the hearings before legislative committees and the chief executive, came from speculative builders whose protests, in the words of a local newspaper, "could not count for much with any fair-minded hearer."[47] Within the legislature, however, the

45. Veiller, "The Housing Problem in American Cities," 249.

46. Veiller, Reminiscences, 33-34; New York Herald Tribune, Feb. 26, 1901, 14, Mar. 27, 1901, 3.

47. New York Evening Post, Apr. 11, 1901, 4. Also New York Times, Apr. 11, 1901, 5; New York Herald Tribune, Apr. 10, 1901, 6. The builders were supported in their opposition, of course, by the owners of old law tenements who were required to make several alterations of their property at their own expense.

code faced a major crisis which Veiller subdued by a combination of threat and compromise.

Veiller's code required all new fire escapes to consist of open iron platforms connected by stairs on the outside of each apartment. These would replace the vertical ladders with which many tenements were provided. Veiller, however, learned that certain "powerful up-State political leaders" were interested in a company which manufactured steel rope-ladders and intended to block the whole tenement bill unless it permitted the use of these rope. ladders.[48] Distressed at the thought of men, women, and children climbing down ladders "swinging against the side of the building 60 feet in the air," Veiller contacted Senator Greene, who was handling the amendment, and advised him as follows: "Senator, if you want the law changed so as to permit these flimsy steel rope-ladders as the sole fire escapes for the thousands of people, old people, women and children in New York City who live in 6-story tenement houses, you and your friends can go straight to hell and I will open up this proposition to the whole State and tell the State just who is back of this business, and what it means."[49]

Having thrown Greene on the defensive, Veiller offered to compromise the issue. He would accept an amendment authorizing the use of the rope-ladders on three-story buildings not containing more than three families. The Tenement Law of 1901 was saved when Greene agreed to Veiller's proposal. Like any good politician, Veiller knew that compromise, at least on details, could not be avoided.

[5]

Although the Tenement House Commission of 1900 established a sub-committee on the "Moral and Social Influence of Tenement House Life," it subordinated neighborhood reconstruction to sanitary control. In outlining the Commission's work, Veiller informed de Forest that he appreciated the importance of social investigations, but felt that the Commission had "distinct limi-

48. Veiller, Reminiscences, 46-47.
49. *Ibid.*, 49-50.

tations as to what it can accomplish in the way of legislation."
He did not think it "feasible" to flood the state legislature with
bills or possible for the Commission to legislate the social
problems of tenement life out of existence.[50]

Though Veiller was a more skillful and effective housing
reformer than Jacob Riis, far more adept in technical problems
and administration, he adhered to a narrower conception of
the housing reformer's responsibilities. For Riis's broad social
and humanitarian point of view, Veiller substituted the expert's
concern for technical proficiency. In Veiller's opinion, the
ability to draft a workable housing law, push it through the
legislature, and insure its proper enforcement, was infinitely
more useful than any amount of social theorizing. Riis was
particularly interested in what Thomas and Znaniecki have
described as the "production of new schemes of behavior and
new institutions" to replace those which had disintegrated and
which could no longer give purpose and direction to the individual or social group.[51]

In contrast to this positive approach to the problem of
neighborhood reconstruction, the Commission, under Veiller's
direction, stressed the repression or eradication of socially undesirable habits and institutions which prevailed in tenement
districts. It expressed some interest in parks and schools, but
was less concerned with creating new value systems than with
hindering the operation of the old. The Commission, for example, complained that gambling played too conspicuous a
role in the life of the poor.[52] It singled out the policy racket,
a numbers game, as the chief offender. Not only men, but
women and children patronized the policy shop. Women became "fiends," selling their household possessions and children's

50. Draft dated June 1900 of Veiller's "personal views as to the work to be
done by the Tenement House Commission," Veiller MSS.
51. According to the same authors, "the immigrant — or more exactly, the
uneducated and socially non-constructive immigrant — feels himself here in a
human wilderness, with nobody and nothing but his physical strength to rely
upon, just as if he were in a wild forest or prairie." Thomas and Znaniecki,
The Polish Peasant in Europe and America, II, 1774.
52. A sensitive interpretation of the immigrant's participation in games of
chance can be found in Oscar Handlin, *The Uprooted, the Epic Story of the
Great Migrations that Made the American People* (Boston, 1952), 160-62.

clothes to acquire betting capital. The Commission urged upon the legislature that "every means to be taken to stamp out and eradicate this serious menace to the welfare of the community."[53]

More insidious than gambling was the omnipresent, unabashedly open prostitution in tenement neighborhoods. In the eyes of the Commission, this tenement-centered prostitution had to be quashed, regardless of public policy toward prostitution in other districts. There could be no "difference of opinion regarding the enforced mingling in the same house of old and young with prostitutes and their procurers."[54]

The objection of housing reformers to tenement prostitution was an outgrowth of their intense concern for the welfare of the tenement family in general, the tenement child in particular. The social evil was a corrupting influence over both. "If only the young boys and girls could be kept from prostitution," one critic asserted, "the worst and most lamentable features of the whole question would be removed. There is no sadder picture than a young girl selling her body, or a young boy purchasing it, before he or she has become fully aware of the consequences of such an act."[55] The Tenement Commission, "profoundly impressed" by the familiarity of the young with vice, their acceptance of prostitution as a normal feature of everyday life, complained that "when dissolute women enter a tenement house their first effort is to make friends with the children." In prostitutes' rooms, children "beheld sights from which they should be protected." The Commission observed that prostitutes hired families to do their cooking and laundry or perform other services for pay, thus securing their silence or friendship.[56] The Committee of Fifteen, organized in December 1900 to support the Commission's drive against tenement prostitution and to suppress the "Raines-Law Hotels" (saloon-centered prostitution), agreed that two opinions could not exist "as to the necessity of protecting children of tender years from close contact

53. F. Norton Goddard, "Policy — A Tenement House Evil," in De Forest and Veiller, eds., *The Tenement House Problem*, II, 27; De Forest and Veiller, "The Tenement House Problem," 53.
54. *Ibid.*, 52.
55. "Municipalities and Vice," *Municipal Affairs*, IV (1900), 706.
56. De Forest and Veiller, "The Tenement House Problem," 51.

with depravity." The cry of parents "when they ask merely for the opportunity of bringing up their children in an atmosphere free from the pollution of the most degrading forms of moral evil" must be heard and respected.[57]

Lillian Wald, founder of the Henry Street Settlement, confirmed the sweeping indictments made by the Tenement Commission and the Committee of Fifteen. She, too, protested that prostitution in the lower East Side was omnipresent. Walking down Allen to Grand Street one evening, she noticed that every house contained "bedecked, unfortunate creatures, who tried by a peculiar hissing noise to draw the attention of the men." Under the "El" children were playing a hissing game in imitation of the women, while "babies sat on the stoops, playing with the business cards of the houses."[58]

The state legislature enacted the Commission's bill designed to discourage tenement prostitution by punishing landlords and prostitutes with unusual severity. The measure provided a maximum six-month prison term for prostitutes and a $1,000 fine for landlords who knowingly rented their premises for immoral purposes. The law was striking testimony to the reformer's concern for the moral welfare of the tenement child.

[6]

One of the striking characteristics of Progressive social reform was its tendency toward "nationalization." A few local or state reform organizations would investigate and publicize an evil and perhaps prod their state legislatures into enacting corrective legislation. Soon other communities would discover that the

57. Letter from the Committee of Fifteen to Governor Odell, in *Charities*, VI (1901), 266. In 1902 the Committee of Fifteen published a summary of its investigations and conclusions. The Committee of Fifteen, *The Social Evil with Special Reference to Conditions Existing in the City of New York*. The New York *Times*, in praising the work of the Committee, commented that the purity "of the moral and social atmosphere in which children are compelled to live" was more important even than light and air. New York *Times*, Oct. 9, 1901, 8.

58. Lillian D. Wald to Dr. Abbott E. Kittredge, Oct. 29, 1903, Lillian D. Wald MSS. Archbishop Corrigan of New York was another who condemned the prevalent vice and its influence upon children in tenement neighborhoods, New York *Herald Tribune*, Mar. 27, 1901, 3.

evil was in their midst also. In time the inevitable national organization formed, and state after state appointed investigating commissions. Child labor regulation, the regulation of women's working hours, the establishment of minimum wage boards, workmen's compensation, prostitution control and sex hygiene, the idea of the consumers' league, and widows' pensions were a few of the reform ideas which leaped across states with startling rapidity in the years before World War I. Housing was no exception.

The extraordinary achievements of the COS Tenement House Committee between 1898 and 1901 resulted, for the first time, in the development of a national housing movement. Through Lawrence Veiller, in particular, New York's struggle for better housing became the fountainhead for the national crusade. In the two decades after 1898, Veiller labored to create housing movements in cities where none had existed, and to provide central leadership for the ever-expanding corps of housing reform partisans. During the Progressive era he became not only New York City's, but the nation's, outstanding housing expert.

Not every city had tenements, but nearly all had slums inherited from the free-wheeling expansion of the nineteenth century. Veiller surveyed the housing situation in most leading American cities for the Tenement House Commission of 1900. He found "bad housing conditions" almost everywhere, but only a few cities with a serious tenement problem. In Boston, one of these cities, tenements fronting on narrow alleys and streets had sprung up in the North and West Ends; but few were more than four stories high, and they did not cover so large a percentage of the lot as the New York variety. Boston had taken some housing action in the 1890's, prior to the dramatic success of the New York State Tenement House Commission of 1900. Following a tenement investigation by the Massachusetts Bureau of Statistics of Labor in 1891, a tenement house law was enacted in 1892 which prohibited non-fireproof tenements. The law was superseded in 1899 by a measure which limited non-fireproof tenements to sixty-five feet in height and prohibited a building from exceeding in height a multiple of two and one-half times the widest street it faced. Veiller singled out Cincinnati, with a population of 325,000, as another tenement city. Here many workers lived in large brick tenements as well as "ramshackle, dilapidated buildings," and "picturesque house-boats." Finally, Veiller described Hartford, Connecticut, as a city with the worst housing conditions of any for its size (80,000). Many families lived in what were originally one-family buildings converted into tenements, and in tenements being erected along the lines of the New York dumb-bell.

Except for New York and some sections of Boston, Cincinnati, and Hartford, the multi-story tenement was exceptional. In Chicago, for example, workers lived in one- or two-story houses, but these were often wooden and lacked proper drainage. Chicago, moreover, suffered the blight of the rear house. A City Homes Association was formed in 1899 to work for reform legislation. Buffalo, like Chicago, was relatively free of high-rise tenements, most workers inhabiting one- and two-story dwellings. The Buffalo Charity Organization Society, through its Committee on Sanitary Conditions in the Homes of the Poor, struggled for housing legislation in the 1890's. Following a housing investigation in 1892 inspired by an imminent cholera epidemic, the Committee drafted a housing ordinance approved by the city council in 1893.

Organized reform action had also developed in Philadelphia before 1900. The state legislature enacted a housing code for the city in 1895 and the Octavia Hill Association was formed the following year. In Philadelphia, few homes exceeded two stories in height or accommodated more than two families. However, many workingmen's homes were dilapidated and without good drainage facilities. Like Philadelphia, neither Baltimore nor Washington had a tenement problem, but homes in both cities often fronted on narrow alleys hidden from public view. Dirt and refuse accumulated in these passageways, and many of the homes lacked adequate water or sewer connections.

Pittsburgh had not developed a tenement system, but Veiller

found that conditions were deteriorating in this industrial community with its large foreign population. Congestion aggravated the housing problem in some areas of the city, cellar habitation was on the rise, and a wooden shanty town sprawled along the outskirts of the metropolis. Pittsburgh harbored a few large wooden tenements, comprising some of the city's worst housing, but the small house prevailed as in the remaining communities surveyed by Veiller: Cleveland, San Francisco, New Orleans, Detroit, Milwaukee, Louisville, Minneapolis, Providence (although tenements accommodating eight or more families had begun to appear), St. Paul, Rochester, Denver, Toledo, Columbus, Syracuse, and Nashville. Kansas City, although free of tenements, had many dilapidated shanties and cellar dwellings. Many workers owned their own homes in all these communities.[59]

Except for New York, Pennsylvania was the only state to enact a housing law before 1900. The other cities had to depend upon local building and health ordinances, and most of them had decreed some such ordinances in the 1880's and 1890's. These dealt with the same problems of light, air, ventilation, sanitation, fire-protection and construction as the New York State measures. Enforcement, usually delegated to building or health departments, was spotty. Veiller hoped other cities and states would adopt restrictive housing codes with standards high enough to reclaim existing slums and prevent others from developing. He also preferred that other cities maintain their single-family or small-house pattern. Thus Veiller discouraged any literal adoption of the New York law, whose details represented a compromise with the established tenement structure, congestion, and land values.

As early as 1899, Veiller had expressed an interest in national housing conditions. In May of that year he suggested to the secretary of the National Conference of Charities and Correction that the housing problem be considered at the next annual meeting. He referred to the work of the COS Tenement House Committee, offering any necessary advice and aid. At the same time he sent a questionnaire to different cities hoping to arouse their interest in housing. Following the achievements of the Tenement House Commission of 1900, requests for information and assistance poured into the office of the Committee. It became, for all practical purposes, a national housing bureau.[60]

By the end of 1903 it was possible to refer to a national housing reform movement. In Boston, the mayor had appointed a tenement house commission. An investigation of Jersey City's tenements by Mary B. Sayles was followed by a meeting at Whittier House Social Settlement resulting in the organization of the Tenement-house Improvement League and the appointment of a state commission. The Charity Organization Societies of Buffalo and Hartford had begun systematic efforts to improve housing codes and their enforcement. In Cincinnati the Associated Charities acted as a clearinghouse transmitting information on unsanitary housing conditions to the board of health. A model tenement company was organized in Pittsburgh, while housing reform was promoted by the women's clubs of the city and Kingsley House, a settlement. The Associated Charities of Syracuse had appointed a committee on housing responsible for the preparation of tenement house laws. The Civic League of the Woman's Institute in Yonkers borrowed materials from the New York COS tenement house exhibit for the edification of local citizens, sponsored a general meeting addressed by Lawrence Veiller, and labored to persuade the mayor and council to enact a housing ordinance. In Cleveland the Chamber of Commerce appointed a committee to investigate housing conditions.

Other cities rose to the challenge in the next three years. The COS Tenement House Committee was swamped with visitors and letters of inquiry. Housing studies were underway in Baltimore, St. Louis and Chicago. Kansas City appointed a tenement house commission. San Francisco, Portland, Maine, Philadelphia, Los Angeles, Washington, D. C., and New Orleans enacted

60. Veiller, Reminiscences, 87, 88.

housing codes or had their slums investigated by citizens' committees. "With most of these movements and with others as well," the New York Tenement House Committee cooperated.[61] Much of this activity resulted in permanent organization. By 1912, thirty-eight cities claimed a housing association or committee. In addition state organizations were active in Indiana and Massachusetts.[62]

Given his penchant for organization and centralized responsibility, it is not surprising that Veiller soon decided to impose order upon this lively but uncoordinated national housing movement. In 1907 he suggested to de Forest, a trustee of the Russell Sage Foundation, that the foundation sponsor a national housing association. Two years later Veiller renewed his proposal. He pointed out that many cities had awakened to their housing problem, that "there had been practically no time in the last 10 years when we had not taken an active part in advising and guiding these cities." It was necessary, Veiller concluded, "to tie all these movements together through the creation of a national organization." The National Housing Association was born in 1910 when the directors of the Russell Sage Foundation agreed to finance the project. De Forest became its first president, Veiller its director.[63]

Despite a limited staff and budget, Veiller succeeded in making the Association a vigorous instrument of reform. Housing reformers gathered at its annual meetings to compare notes and map strategy. The Association published a large number of pamphlets designed for popular consumption, as well as a quarterly entitled *Housing Betterment* and bound volumes of the annual conference *Proceedings*. Veiller personally wrote or edited much of this material.

The Association's principal function was to advise cities

61. COS, *Twenty-fourth Annual Report*, 1905-06, 67-68.
62. *Housing Betterment*, I (Feb. 1912), 1-3.
63. Veiller, Reminiscences, 88-90; Lawrence Veiller to Robert W. de Forest, July 29, 1909, Veiller MSS. For a statement of the Association's initial organization, purposes, and leadership, consult Veiller's article, "The National Housing Association: A New Organization 'To Improve Housing Conditions Both Urban and Suburban in Every Practicable Way,'" *Survey*, XXIII (1909-10), 841-48.

which desired better housing conditions, but lacked experience in dealing with so technical a problem. After 1910 Veiller was constantly on the move, "visiting various cities at the request of people . . . who had prepared housing laws and wished to submit them to the acid test of [his] consideration."[64] He was assisted in this work by John Ihlder, field secretary of the Association. Virtually all the state and local housing codes in the two decades after 1900 were influenced by Veiller's work. Either Veiller assisted directly in their formulation, or they were adapted from the New York Tenement House Law of 1901, or from Veiller's two books: a *Model Tenement House Law* (1910), and a *Model Housing Law* (1914). A third volume, *Housing Reform* (1910), explained the techniques of organizing a reform movement. In these books, Veiller summarized the essence of the New York experience, hoping to save other cities from unnecessary errors and to simplify their task. The *Model Housing Law* applied not simply to tenements but to one- and two-family homes as well. Veiller wrote it because most cities, as we have seen, did not house their workers in the five- and six-story brick tenements so familiar to New York.

New Jersey was the first state to benefit from the interest in housing reform ignited by the Tenement House Commission of 1900. A state-wide measure was enacted in 1904 which followed the New York law in most respects. Connecticut's law of 1905 was adapted from the New York code also, but applied only to new construction. In Wisconsin a state law enacted in 1907 was declared unconstitutional, but was succeeded by another measure in 1909 which applied only to first-class cities (Milwaukee). In the same year Indiana, thanks to the efforts of Albion Fellows Bacon, passed a housing code whose provisions were similar to the New York law.

Following the publication of a *Model Tenement House Law* in 1910, five states (Kentucky, 1910; Massachusetts, 1912, 1913; Indiana, 1913, 1917; Pennsylvania, 1913; California, 1917) enacted housing codes along the lines sketched by Veiller. The

64. Veiller, Reminiscences, 107.

state codes of Michigan (1917), Minnesota (1917), and Iowa (1919) were drawn from the *Model Housing Law*. The Michigan legislation, an almost verbatim reproduction of the model law, was described by Edith Elmer Wood as "the most advanced state-wide law yet passed." By 1920, about twenty cities had enacted new housing codes while twenty more had inserted housing provisions in their building and health ordinances. Virtually all of these cities — which included Syracuse, St. Paul, Grand Rapids, Duluth, Berkeley, Cleveland, Columbus, Lansing, Portland, Oregon, and Salem, Massachusetts — adapted their codes from the New York law or Veiller's model laws.[65]

Of course Veiller and his associates were not always successful in the struggle for better housing. Opposition from real estate interests or their spokesmen in the state legislatures sometimes proved too powerful to vanquish. One notable defeat came in New York when Veiller tried to push through a housing law applicable to the six second-class cities of the state — Albany, Schenectady, Syracuse, Troy, Utica and Yonkers. It is worth examining this episode in detail for it illuminates the political dynamics of housing reform.

Representatives of the six cities in 1912 requested the National Housing Association to prepare a law for them. Veiller drafted the legislation and accepted the burdensome task of steering it through the state legislature. He contacted Al Smith, speaker of the Democratic - controlled assembly. Smith, to Veiller's pleasant surprise, needed little urging. The future governor would be happy to sponsor the measure because "the Legislature has been giving New York City a hell of a plastering for many years with tenement laws, and I shall be glad to see the up-State [Republican] cities get a little of the same treatment."[66] The senate enacted the bill with little opposition; after

65. On Veiller's influence on housing legislation between 1904-20, consult: Edith Elmer Wood, *The Housing of the Unskilled Wage Earner: America's Next Problem* (New York, 1919), 80-90; Ford H. MacGregor, *Tenement House Legislation, State and Local* (Madison, Wis., 1909), 10 ff.; Lawrence Veiller, *A Model Housing Law* (Russell Sage Foundation: New York, 1920), rev. ed., v-vi; James Ford, "The Enforcement of Housing Legislation," *Political Science Quarterly*, XLII (1927), 549-50.

66. Veiller, Reminiscences, 102.

some delay it passed the assembly and was signed by Governor Sulzer.

By 1914, however, the opposition had sufficiently recovered from Veiller's legislative blitzkrieg to organize their forces and exert pressure upon the Albany statesmen. Two bills were introduced at the beginning of the legislative session in January 1914: one to repeal the housing law, the other to appoint a commission to investigate conditions in the cities affected. Once again Veiller took arms against "the slum landlords, builders, real estate interests all united in a well-organized campaign to secure the passage of these two measures." Although the bill was not repealed, the legislature appointed a sub-committee to visit the cities. The hostility to the housing law expressed at public hearings by real estate men persuaded the legislature to suspend its operation until February 1915. For appearance's sake, a commission was appointed to investigate conditions in the upstate cities. In February the law was repealed for good. For Veiller, always conscious of the importance of organization in enacting and protecting housing legislation, the moral was clear; he pinned the defeat upon the failure of the law's sympathizers to give it "the attention that is necessary if a law of this kind is to be maintained in its integrity."[67]

Difficult as it was to enact housing legislation, the experience of the code for New York's second-class cities suggests that it was even more difficult to protect it against amendment or nullification. The builder resented housing legislation which he feared would raise costs and thus restrict sales. He was joined in his opposition by associated interests — banks and loan companies which financed real estate operations, suppliers of materials, real estate traders — all of whom had a stake in an active housing market. And, of course, landlords always resisted legislation which raised their maintenance costs. As Veiller recognized, only the counter-pressure of vigilant reform groups could protect the housing legislation. The unorganized consumer was helpless.

67. *Ibid.*, 106. On the abortive second-class city housing law see also *Housing Betterment*, III (Apr., 1914), 3-5, IV (June, 1915), 23.

Veiller's contemporaries appreciated the technical skills which he applied to the task of improving the nation's housing. Time and again his associates in the gruelling struggle for better housing expressed their awareness of his indispensable contributions. Although Jacob Riis is the name most people associate today with Progressive housing reform, there is no doubt that Veiller was the pivotal figure after 1898. Riis was the prophet, the moralist, who had aroused the consciences of men in the 1890's. Thereafter, Veiller's technical proficiency, political resourcefulness, and administrative abilities transformed conscience into legislation.

Riis himself in 1910 revealed to Veiller his "full appreciation of the great things you have done for tenement house reform — things which hardly any other man could have done."[68] In the same spirit Albion Fellows Bacon acknowledged her special debt of gratitude. Veiller had made "two missionary journeys" to Indiana and "saved us from shipwreck and disaster."[69] The governor of Michigan, in recommending the enactment of a housing code for that state in 1915, referred specifically to Veiller in his legislative message: "I suggest that this Legislature enact a housing law of State-wide application. 'A Model Housing Law' by Lawrence Veiller, Secretary of the National Housing Association, furnishes a scientific basis for this much needed law."[70]

Veiller, America's first professional housing reformer, not only changed the course of New York City's housing development, but influenced the housing history of states and cities throughout the nation in the two decades after 1900. Although the quality and enforcement of the codes adopted as a result of his efforts varied from place to place, Veiller left as a permanent legacy to the nation the principle of a community's right to high minimum standards of restrictive housing legislation. In March 1917, after Minnesota had enacted a housing code,

68. Jacob A. Riis to Lawrence Veiller, Mar. 14, 1910, Veiller MSS.
69. Albion Fellows Bacon, "How to Get Housing Reform," National Conference of Charities and Correction, *Proceedings*, 1911, 320.
70. Veiller, Reminiscences, 108.

the secretary of the Minneapolis Civic and Commerce Association informed de Forest of Veiller's contribution:

> Mr. Veiller made two special trips to Minneapolis for the purpose of helping us fight through and maintain the provisions of the Bill which were being attacked by various interests. During the four or five days spent in Minneapolis on each trip, he worked almost continuously night and day. . . . While the code was originally based upon the "Model Housing Law" which proved from the beginning a tremendous help, it was the presence of Mr. Veiller on the ground here for several days that really resulted in the approval of the bill by the various organizations behind it and in the action taken by the Legislature.[71]

Here was a succinct summary of how Veiller transmitted his legacy.

71. A. M. Sheldon to Robert W. de Forest, Apr. 16, 1917, Veiller MSS.

The Age of Veiller

In the old days I used to see Lawrence Veiller with mixed emotions. I was never a great admirer of Lawrence Veiller. Perhaps I should have been. It wasn't so much on court work that I saw him but he seemed to me the quintessence of what as a Socialist I didn't like — the certain type of reformer in the Charity Organization Society.

NORMAN THOMAS,
Reminiscences

[1]

Although restrictive legislation was the key to Veiller's reform philosophy, a basic corollary was the need for effective enforcement machinery. Not content simply to write a new tenement code in 1901, Veiller wanted to insure that the municipality could force men to obey it. As early as 1898, when he was trying to convince the COS of the desirability of a tenement house society, Veiller displayed an interest in the question of enforcement. Anyone familiar with the housing situation in New York knew that enforcement was egregiously lax. Jacob Riis, for example, complained to Richard Watson Gilder that he found the stairs in new tenements always constructed of wood, although the law required slow-burning or fire-proof material. "What we need in New York," Riis proclaimed, "is a club which shall not be stuffed, to clear the field with."[1]

Veiller informed de Forest and his associates that the Building and Health Departments had been hopelessly inept in enforcing the tenement laws. He particularly condemned the tendency of the Building Department to approve plans for tenements

1. Jacob A. Riis to Richard Watson Gilder, undated, Jacob A. Riis MSS.

occupying 75 per cent of the lot, when the law stipulated a maximum coverage of 65 per cent. Later, as secretary of the Tenement House Commission, Veiller prepared a report upon the "Non-Enforcement of the Tenement House Laws in New Buildings." He discovered only fifteen out of 333 tenements under construction in Manhattan which did not violate the law in some respect, and none in the Bronx, Brooklyn, or Queens.

The Commission's report, which Veiller wrote, ascribed the failure to enforce the tenement code to the shortage of inspectors in the Health Department, as well as the confusing division of responsibility among the Health, Building, Police, and Fire Departments. Veiller observed that the sixty-one inspectors of the Health Department could not possibly cope with the 82,652 tenements of Greater New York. The law providing for semiannual inspection had become a dead letter. The various departments shifted their responsibilities from one to another. None maintained a separate tenement bureau.

Some builders took advantage of the feeble code enforcement to dupe the purchaser. Before tenement construction could begin, plans had to be filed with and approved by the Building Department. After construction had started, there was no way to insure that the approved plans were being honored unless the Building Department inspected the work at frequent intervals, forcing the builder to eliminate violations. Since such inspection was rarely the case, builders often sold tenements to purchasers who assumed that the property had satisfied all legal requirements. Any repairs subsequently ordered by the Board of Health, which had charge of the completed structure, had to be made at the expense of the owner.[2]

In Veiller's opinion, the Commission had wasted its time unless it established the machinery to insure that builders and landlords obeyed his new code. Thus he urged the formation of a separate tenement house department. He applied to enforcement the same idea that lay behind his formation of the COS Tenement House Committee — centralization of responsibility in the hands of trained experts.

2. Lawrence Veiller, "The Non-Enforcement of the Tenement House Laws in New Buildings," in de Forest and Veiller, eds., *The Tenement House Problem*, I, 241-57.

At a meeting of the COS Tenement House Committee on February 17, 1900, Veiller first presented his scheme "for the creation of a permanent State Board of Tenement House Commissioners, which should have entire supervision and control of all tenement houses in cities of the first class."[3] He repeated the suggestion to the Tenement House Commission of 1900, explaining in a letter to Chairman de Forest that "the failure to solve the tenement house problem in New York has been due largely to the fact that there has not been any one special body vested with the sole responsibility and duty of looking after the tenement houses. . . ."[4] In October 1900, Veiller prepared an outline of a Tenement House Department for the Commission, which preferred to make it a city rather than a state agency, as Veiller originally suggested.[5] After the New York legislature incorporated the Tenement House Department into the city's charter, Veiller obligingly prepared its budget for the Board of Estimate.[6] From conception to completion, the New York City Tenement House Department was a tribute to Veiller's inexhaustible talent for organization.

Seth Low, elected mayor of New York in 1901, had to appoint a commissioner to head the department that was scheduled to begin operations when Low took office in January 1902. Although Veiller was the logical candidate, Low was reluctant to appoint him, as was de Forest to recommend him. According to Veiller, Low considered him too radical, a potential embarrassment to his administration.[7] Similarly, de Forest seems to have detected traces of radicalism in the junior member of the COS hierarchy; although loath to accept the job himself, he would not recommend Veiller.[8] In time, this taint of radicalism

3. Minutes of the Meetings of the Tenement House Committee, Feb. 17, 1900. Hereafter referred to as Tenement House Committee, Minutes.
4. Lawrence Veiller to Robert W. de Forest, June 1900, Veiller MSS.
5. Lawrence Veiller to Robert W. de Forest, Oct. 17, 1900, Veiller MSS. This letter consists of a detailed outline of Veiller's projected Tenement House Department.
6. Otto T. Bannard to John C. Clark, Nov. 20, 1901, Veiller MSS. In this same letter Bannard, vice-president of the COS, acknowledged that Veiller's initiative had sparked "the whole of the recent tenement house reform movement."
7. Veiller, Reminiscences, 39.
8. Edward T. Devine to Robert W. de Forest, Nov. 7, 1901, Veiller MSS.

would fade. During his youth men mistook Veiller's brash self-confidence and uncompromising independence for ideological unorthodoxy. In the eyes of builders and landlords, the man emerged out of nowhere as a storm trooper of reform. As one contemporary later observed, Veiller's "mere presence at a hearing was wont to cause panic among conservative real estate interests."[9] These real estate interests would settle down once they realized that Veiller was no foe of the profit system. His aggressiveness and enormous fund of technical knowledge probably frightened them more than any radical ideas he may have expressed. It was distressing to encounter a reformer whom they could not intimidate.

De Forest's lack of confidence disturbed Veiller. He was "deeply disappointed" by de Forest's "luke-warm and passive attitude." Under no circumstances would he consent to serve in a subordinate capacity, except under de Forest. "I cannot see," Veiller informed the president of the COS, "that I am called upon to tie my own hands; to help another, perhaps, to mar the work which thus far I have successfully carried on."[10] Josephine Shaw Lowell, "the conscience of the Charity Organization Society," finally resolved the impasse when she persuaded de Forest to accept the job.[11]

Press and public hailed de Forest's appointment as ideal.[12] A lifelong New Yorker whose roots stretched back to colonial Huguenot ancestry, de Forest was one of New York's most distinguished civic leaders; without him no committee for civic betterment was complete. A lawyer by profession, he served as counsel and director to a score of banks, railroads, and insurance companies. He supplemented this work with an incredible array

9. Louis H. Pink, *The New Day in Housing* (New York, 1928), 96.

10. Lawrence Veiller to Robert W. de Forest, Nov. 23, 1901, Veiller MSS. Veiller bluntly informed de Forest that a successful administration of the new Department depended upon either de Forest's assuming the office or actively advocating Veiller's appointment.

11. Veiller, Reminiscences, 40. After de Forest had been appointed Commissioner, Josephine Shaw Lowell wrote Low that she was "especially rejoiced," Josephine Shaw Lowell to Seth Low, Dec. 18, 1901, Seth Low MSS.

12. *Charities*, VII (1901), 534-35.

of philanthropic pursuits. As president of the COS, de Forest encouraged the growth of scientific, professional social work. He helped found the New York School of Social Work and occupied the presidency of the Russell Sage Foundation for many years. He held high posts in the Welfare Council of New York, the State Charities Aid Association, and the New York Conference of Charities and Correction.

Like his friend Theodore Roosevelt, de Forest was a New York aristocrat sensitive to the social responsibilities which his position imposed. Although his wealth, ancestry, and refined tastes precluded any real contact with, or understanding of, the poor, de Forest did possess a large measure of *noblesse oblige:* the fortunate were obliged to share their intellectual and moral resources with the poor, to devote their time and money to insuring social and economic justice for all classes.

President of the COS, a member of its Tenement House Committee, chairman of the Tenement House Commission of 1900, first commissioner of the New York Tenement House Department, president of the National Housing Association which Veiller in fact organized and directed, de Forest received much public acclaim as a housing reformer. Despite his myriad other business and philanthropic interests, de Forest actually did find time to participate in sessions of the COS Tenement House Committee, hasten to Albany to promote housing legislation, and deliver lectures on housing. His prestige was an invaluable asset to Veiller, who had neither de Forest's personal influence nor his tact. It is no discredit to de Forest, however, to observe that housing reformers and social workers, if not the public, realized that Veiller was the driving force behind the Progressive housing movement.[13]

De Forest was only the nominal chief of the Tenement House Department, but Veiller, whom he appointed as his first deputy commissioner, was the real power. Indeed, de Forest publicly admitted that he would not have accepted the post unless Veiller consented to serve as his deputy; privately, he informed Veiller

13. Frances Perkins to author, Interview, June 11, 1959.

that he would have to do "the major part of the work." [14] Veiller proceeded to organize the Department from top to bottom, outlining the duties of each bureau and individual, from the commissioner down to the most obscure clerk. This was a superb administrative tour-de-force, done with such finesse that the Department functioned for many years essentially as Veiller had established it. He created three key divisions — Buildings, Inspection, and Records. The first was responsible for inspecting plans of projected tenements as well as their examination in the course of construction. The Inspection division had supervision over completed tenements, thus assuming the former duties of the Board of Health. Veiller, with his fetish for precision and facts, set up the special Records division to compile encyclopedic information relating to the tenements and their population. Finally, he ensured that the Tenement House Department possessed the power to license tenements, thus preventing unethical builders from dumping structural violations in the hands of unwary purchasers. After 1902 no tenement could be occupied until the builder had received a license from the Department certifying that the house had met all legal requirements. [15]

The Veiller-de Forest regime did not outlast the Low administration, 1902-3. Both men resigned after George B. McClellan, Jr., assumed the mayorality in 1904. They neither wished to serve under a Tammany regime nor expected that Tammany wished to retain their services. McClellan appointed as commissioner a politician by the name of T. C. F. Crain, who had been

14. *Charities,* VII (1901), 533; Veiller, Reminiscences, 40. A letter from de Forest to Veiller is revealing on this point concerning the real head of the Department: "Just a line to let you know that the Tenement House Department is pulling through, and that we expect soon to demonstrate that we can get along without you. I don't mean that it is easy, or that some things are not being neglected, or that some things are not going the wrong way. But it undoubtedly is a good thing in some aspects to have me and the rest obliged to run the scheme without you." Robert W. de Forest to Lawrence Veiller, Sept. 13, 1902, Veiller MSS. At the time Veiller was vacationing in New Hampshire.

15. For a full account of the organization of the Tenement House Department, consult Tenement House Department of the City of New York, *First Report,* Jan. 1, 1902-July 1, 1903 (2 Vols.). Veiller wrote most of this detailed summary of the Department's work and organization as well as the existing tenement situation in New York. Lawrence Veiller to author, Interview, July 13, 1959.

recommended by Tammany boss Charles F. Murphy.[16] Under Crain the Department nearly collapsed in less than a year. Veil,-ler, however, did not intend to permit Crain to nullify his years of hard work.

Upon leaving the Tenement House Department, Veiller was asked by the trustees of the City Club to become secretary of their organization. In the next two years he revived this some-what moribund association, leading it into a variety of struggles for civic betterment. Among other things, he labored for im-proved police regulation of street traffic, a four year term for New York's mayor, relief from push-cart congestion in Man-hattan's thoroughfares, rapid transit expansion, and the protec-tion of the city from franchise grabbers. All the while he kept a watchful eye over affairs of the Tenement House Department.

Veiller had agreed to join the City Club on condition that the trustees allow him to participate in the deliberations of the COS Tenement House Committee. Only a few months after Crain had taken office in July 1904, Veiller expressed before the Com-mittee his dissatisfaction with the new administration. He com-plained that Crain had discontinued the policy of vacating unfit tenements, that nothing was being done to alter old tenements under the provisions of the Law of 1901, and that corruption was hampering the Department's efficiency and prestige. He reiterated his charges in December. Although the Committee declined to act as a body, it authorized Veiller to take any nec-essary steps to remove Crain.[17]

Veiller prepared a lengthy memorandum for the benefit of Mayor McClellan. He charged that under Crain the Tenement House Department had squandered public funds by appointing useless inspectors, had failed to make a systematic inspection of tenements, protect tenants against fire, or prevent the use of cel-lars for living purposes. In December 1904, when he informally

16. Crain had asked Murphy for the appointment. Except for his corporation counsel, secretary, police, street-cleaning, health and tax board commissioners, McClellan accepted all of Murphy's candidates for municipal office after he succeeded Seth Low as Mayor in 1904. Harold C. Syrett, ed., *The Gentleman and the Tiger: The Autobiography of George B. McClellan, Jr.* (Philadelphia, 1956), 183.

17. Tenement House Committee, Minutes, July 7, Dec. 1, 7, 1904.

presented these accusations to McClellan, Veiller suggested that the mayor check their accuracy against departmental records. After that McClellan might accompany him on a tour of inspection of the slums, a sojourn which the crafty reformer knew was always good for a shock. The day of inspection soon arrived; Veiller deliberately led McClellan, as their first stop, to one of the most miserable tenements he knew: "We went down into the sub-cellar which was quite dark. I deliberately let Mayor McClellan get into the sewage up to his shoetops and the peppery Mayor was then quite ready to remove Crain." [18]

The adroitness in handling Crain's dismissal proved that although Veiller was intransigeant at times, he was not rash. Veiller realized that if he publicized his charges against Crain before consulting McClellan, he would have made an enemy of the mayor of New York. Though Veiller was quite rigid in defending the principles behind his tenement legislation, he was flexible and opportunistic when it came to details. As a political strategist, he could be direct or devious, depending on the situation. Thus he purposely complicated sections of the Tenement House Law of 1901 in order to bore and confuse legislators.[19]

Crain's two successors as Tenement Department commissioners were both honest and reasonably able men. Edmond J. Butler, who served through 1909, had been active in COS affairs and in the Catholic charity, the St. Vincent de Paul Society. John J. Murphy, commissioner from 1910 to 1917, had been associated with municipal reform as an officer of the Citizens' Union. The Department had many shortcomings under the Butler-Murphy administrations, but it never sank so low as under Crain. Veiller acted as an unofficial adviser to the Department, helping it to interpret and enforce the housing code he had written.

[2]

Enforcing the Tenement House Law of 1901 was no simple task. Veiller compared the job of cleaning New York's 82,000

18. Veiller, Reminiscences, 66. On Veiller's removal of Crain, consult also Lawson Purdy, Reminiscences, Columbia Oral History Project, 36.
19. Lawrence Veiller to author, Interview, Aug. 20, 1959.

tenements to the "cleansing of the Augean stables." During the
Veiller-de Forest years, a pioneering zeal pervaded the Department's work. Even those same "wise virgins" who staffed the
settlements, charities, and social reform organizations of the Progressive era enlisted in the ranks. The Tenement House Department was a new field of adventure, another opportunity to
exercise the benevolent instinct. By 1903 ten women inspectors
were employed, while the Department could draw from a supplementary eligible list of sixty. Most of these women were
college educated. They found romance and excitement in defective plumbing, vermin-filled bedrooms, and cracked plaster. The
job of tenement inspector fulfilled their yearning to "know life
at its barest and hardest, to grapple with cold physical facts, to
stand on a common footing with those who have had no special
advantages or opportunities." [20]

In time, of course, the novelty of the new Department diminished. It became another municipal agency with routine problems of administration and chronic defects of operation and
organization. Many obstacles hampered its efficiency, and it
ushered in no golden age of glistening, whitewashed tenements.
Yet it did succeed in cleaning up thousands of old-law tenements
and supervising the construction of thousands of new-law buildings. On balance, the idea of a separate housing department paid
off in terms of a cleaner and healthier New York.

In July 1903, the Department totaled 385 employees, of whom
166 occupied the critically important post of inspector. By 1916
the number of employees had increased to 588, of whom 207
were inspectors. At the same time, however, the number of tenements in Greater New York had grown from approximately
82,000 to 104,000 (of which 26,000 were new-law). The number and quality of employees were never wholly adequate to the
job of enforcing the tenement law. Turnover was excessive.
Commissioner Butler, for example, complained frequently of

20. Mary B. Sayles, "The Work of a Woman Tenement-House Inspector,"
Outlook, LXXV (1903), 121. Another of the women inspectors told of her
"distinct pleasure in getting to the bottom of the difficulty in an involved case
of bad plumbing." Emily W. Dinwiddie, "Women Tenement Inspectors in
New York," American Academy of Political and Social Science, *Annals*, XXII
(1903), 396.

the inability of the Department to attract and hold good men.[21] Salaries were too low. Chief inspectors in 1903 earned from $1,800 to $3,000, supervising inspectors, $1,500. The salary for the arduous job of ordinary district inspector was $1,200. Between 1905 and 1907 no less than 50 per cent of the total staff of the Department transferred, resigned, or were dismissed. The "evil" had reached such a dimension that Butler refused to consent to further transfers. Low pay was a persistent problem, not only with the New York City Tenement House Department, but with code enforcement agencies throughout the country. As late as 1927, James Ford reported that the average salary for a housing inspector was only $2,000.[22]

The Department's chronic shortage of manpower was reflected in an inability to inspect tenements at regular intervals. The law stipulated a monthly inspection of tenements whose average rentals totaled $25.00 or less. This provision was not enforced. There were hardly enough inspectors to investigate the thousands of complaints which poured each year into the offices of the Department. These complaints received first priority, followed by re-inspections of tenements which had violations registered against them. If a district inspector had time after caring for complaints and re-inspections, he would devote it to inspection. Veiller, however, had described systematic inspection as the "keynote of successful administration."

Re-inspections consumed an inordinate amount of time. In the year ending June 30, 1908, over 58 per cent of the inspection force's time had been devoted to re-inspections.[23] In many cases violations stretched back for years. Indeed, the frequent inability of the Department to enforce the law promptly, if at all, must be added to turnover and understaffing as a persistent snag in its work.

Uncooperative tenants and landlords represented one source of delay, particularly in the case of minor violations. Possessing

21. Tenement House Department, *Third Report*, 1906, 33-34, *Fourth Report*, 1907-08, 19-20.
22. James Ford, "The Enforcement of Housing Legislation," 555.
23. Bureau of Municipal Research, *Tenement House Administration: Steps Taken to Locate and to Solve Problems of Enforcing the Tenement House Law* (New York, 1909), 10.

a full quota of serious structural and sanitary offenses, the Department was reluctant to press court action for relatively trivial violations. Thus the stipulation of the code requiring landlords to file their names with the Department went unenforced.[24] Although the law required the night lighting of tenement halls, Commissioner Butler complained that the force at his disposal was hardly sufficient to follow up citizens' complaints, let alone to station inspectors at tenements all night.[25] Similarly, no amount of threat and bluster could induce tenants to remove encumbrances from fire escapes, since city magistrates would not cooperate in punishing offenders. To cope with this problem which had "baffled the ingenuity of every Tenement House Commissioner," Butler borrowed an extra detail of police and wrangled a promise of cooperation from the Board of City Magistrates in 1906. He turned loose his invasion force to round up the worst offenders in a selected thirty-block area. Unfortunately, Butler found that the "City Magistrates failed to live up to their agreement." [26] These magistrates were apparently loath to impose fines on immigrants and workers for violations which they considered relatively trivial.

Administrative confusion within the Department represented a second source of delay in enforcing the law. In some instances the Department held cases for three or four years without sending them to the corporation counsel's office. No time limit was established on how long violations might sit in the Department's files. The Bureau of Municipal Research, which analyzed 2,400 violations filed in Brooklyn and Manhattan in 1907, found that 404 were still pending at the end of a full year in Manhattan, and 244 in Brooklyn.[27] There was no way of knowing how many months or years would elapse before they were forwarded to the corporation counsel. For many years some landlords simply ignored notices of violation, secure in the knowledge that if they complied (even after legal proceedings had begun), the Department would dismiss the case. Commissioner

24. *Ibid.*, 80, 81; Tenement House Department, *Third Report*, 1906, 21.
25. Tenement House Department, *Fourth Report*, 1907-08, 12.
26. Tenement House Department, *Third Report*, 1906, 14.
27. Bureau of Municipal Research, *Tenement House Administration*, 39.

Murphy ended this practice in 1912 by refusing to withdraw summonses despite compliance.

A third and critically important cause of delay had its source in the corporation counsel's office, where enforcement was handled by a special tenement bureau. Just as some cases rested for years in the Tenement House Department's files, others slumbered equally long at the bureau. At the beginning of 1908, the corporation counsel had not filed *lis pendens* (pending suits listed on the court docket) on almost 10,000 cases forwarded by the Tenement House Department. Approximately 9,000 of them had been held anywhere up to eighteen months, another 752 for one and one-half to two years, the remainder between two and four years.[28]

If the Tenement House Department could legitimately complain that delays in the legal machinery of enforcement left no choice but to hold violations for months or years (with the hope that persuasion might effect compliance), the corporation counsel could argue that congested court dockets hampered prompt filing of *lis pendens*. Commissioner Butler, who observed that delays in obtaining compliance with Department orders were becoming detrimental to the prestige and effectiveness of the Department, suggested the creation of a special court to handle municipal cases. Otherwise, the "congested condition of the courts" would continue to hamper the Department's effectiveness.[29]

The fact that the Tenement House Department experienced frustrating delays in enforcing the law does not indicate that it made no progress. If the number of violations issued was any index to its achievements, the Department supervised New York's tenements more zealously than any agency in the city's history. Thus 111,789 violations were pending in the Department's files on January 1, 1915, while another 211,371 were issued during the year. Of this total, 181,381 were dismissed or canceled, leaving 141,779 pending on December 31. The total number of violations issued the following year increased to

28. *Ibid.*, 77.
29. Tenement House Department, *Fourth Report*, 1907-08, 36.

216,429. However, since only 155,440 were cancelled or dismissed, the number pending had again increased to 202,768.[30] Each year the Department issued thousands of violations and succeeded in forcing compliance upon thousands. The problem, in the final analysis, was not in the ability of the Tenement House Department to issue orders and enforce many of them, but in the element of uncertainty involved each time an order was issued. It might be enforced immediately, in weeks, in months, or even years. If, as in the case of encumbered fire escapes, the magistrates proved uncooperative, it would never be enforced.

One cannot expect perfection when a few hundred men are responsible for the supervision of more than 100,000 tenements, and depend, moreover, upon the cooperation of tenants, landlords, courts, and the corporation counsel. Less excusable, however, was any failure of the Department's building bureau to supervise the construction of new tenements, which did not total more than several hundred each year. Ideally, each new tenement should have been inspected four times: first, after the foundation had been laid; second, upon completion of the first tier of beams to ensure that court dimensions met the requirements of the law; third, after interior partitions had taken shape to ensure their proper dimensions; and, finally, after the plaster was laid and the building completed. In the absence of any violations, the builder might then apply for his certificate from the Department. The Butler administration proved lax in vacating new tenements which had been occupied without the proper certificate of compliance. The Bureau of Municipal Research discovered that 493 buildings, for which plans had been filed between 1902 and 1904, were occupied as of March 1908 without having received the Department's final approval. Moreover, 633 violations were pending against the buildings. Over 65 per cent of these violations had been pending between two and four years.[31] Beginning in 1909, however, the Department re-established its authority over the builders. Within three years, over

30. Tenement House Department, *Eighth Report*, 1915-16, 109.
31. Bureau of Municipal Research, *Tenement House Administration*, 87.

2,000 vacancy proceedings were begun, forcing owners to re-move violations and obtain certificates of compliance. The episode suggests that the chronic, day-to-day problems of ad-ministration in a large bureaucracy like the New York Tenement House Department could be intensified by a breakdown at special points. Continual vigilance was necessary to maintain the Department's authority at every link in its complex chain of operations.

The major task of the Butler administration had been to sal-vage the wreckage of the Crain regime and re-establish in some measure the prestige and efficiency of the Veiller-de Forest years. Butler's successor, John J. Murphy, inherited a Depart-ment which, despite numerous weaknesses, functioned fairly smoothly. Murphy's most notable innovation was to introduce a policy of cooperation and education to supplement and (he hoped) to facilitate enforcement of the law. Use the "mailed fist" if necessary, Murphy advised, "but always use education to reach the people whom you desire to affect." [32] Thus Murphy inaugurated a number of experiments designed to win the co-operation of landlords, builders, and tenants. In an effort to re-solve the ever-irksome riddle of the encumbered fire escapes, for example, Murphy decided to enlist the aid of the tenement children. With the cooperation of the Board of Education, the Department sent speakers to public schools hoping to reach parents through their offspring. At the same time, pamphlets were printed in several languages and distributed in the schools. These described the need for unobstructed fire escapes and other fire protection measures. Also for the edification of tenants, the Department cooperated with the COS Tenement House Com-mittee in distributing to tenement families thousands of pamph-lets entitled "For You." In simple words, "For You" described the work of the Department as well as basic principles of sani-tation and personal hygiene.

32. National Housing Association, *Proceedings*, II (1912), 161. Murphy be-lieved that "in the final analysis the most effective work for law enforcement has been through constant urging by the department and the explanation to owners and others of the necessity for the proposed changes rather than through the actual operation of the law." John J. Murphy, "Law Enforce-ment," National Housing Association, *Proceedings*, I (1911), 51.

To placate landlords, Murphy launched a new policy concerning violations. Previously, any violation filed by an inspector became a matter of record. After 1912, the Department agreed not to record the violation should the landlord comply within ten days. Murphy also encouraged "free and open discussion" with landlords, builders, and architects about Department rulings and amendments to the tenement code.

In line with Murphy's policy of enlightenment before force, Model District No. 142 was established in 1916. The district comprised several blocks in the lower East Side, where an attempt was made to induce landlords and tenants to remove violations through personal moral suasion rather than correspondence and threats. In the majority of cases, the Department reported, "the hearty co-operation of owners, lessees, janitors and tenants was cheerfully furnished." [33]

After Murphy left in 1917 (to join the COS Tenement House Committee), the Department again became strictly an enforcing agency. Neither the "mailed fist" nor education had succeeded in overcoming the many obstacles to enforcement. A lack of adequate manpower, heavy turnover of personnel, uncooperative landlords and tenants encouraged by delays in the corporation counsel's office and the courts, continued to hamper the efficiency of the Department. Yet in view of the magnitude of the task confronting the Department, it had more than justified its existence. Between 1902 and 1914, the Department had answered more than 500,000 tenant complaints, filing violations against 193,000 of them. It supervised the construction of more than 24,000 new-law tenements. If the removal of violations was sometimes slow, the Department did gradually progress in the Herculean task of cleaning the tenements. By 1915, two important stipulations of the Tenement House Law of 1901 had been satisfied: windows had been installed in 300,000 interior rooms of old-law tenements and several thousand school sinks had been replaced by water closets.[34] Although thirty-eight lives were lost in fires in old-law tenements in 1915 alone, not a single life

33. Tenement House Department, *Eighth Report*, 1915-16, 11-12.
34. *Ibid.*, 7.

had been lost to fire in a new law tenement since 1902 as a consequence of faulty construction or means of egress.

Edith Elmer Wood, a well-informed student of housing conditions, described New York almost two decades after the Tenement House Law of 1901 was enacted and the Tenement House Department established as "swept and garnished and repaired." She admitted that not all tenements were "immaculate," but there were "no accumulations of filth," "no dilapidation or extreme disrepair," no privy vaults, and few old hall sinks.[35] In 1915, Commissioner Murphy reported that since 1901 New York's death rate had declined from 19.90 to 13.52 per 1,000. With justice, he believed that the Tenement House Department of the City of New York deserved some credit for this achievement.

[3]

Lawrence Veiller realized that his work had only begun after he had incorporated the Tenement House Department into the city's charter. The Department, as well as the tenement law, was subject to political pressures almost any time. A bureaucracy like the Tenement House Department, unless continually prodded, would ossify as routine replaced initiative and imagination. Events confirmed Veiller's wisdom in establishing a permanent tenement house committee to look after the interests of reform. An organized, well-informed body of private citizens was needed to defend (as well as improve) both the tenement laws and the machinery of enforcement. Almost every session of the state legislature brought with it an avalanche of bills attacking this or that provision of the tenement code. As the agent of the COS Tenement House Committee at Albany, Veiller usually possessed sufficient political leverage to prevent damage. In defending and improving the tenement laws after 1901 he displayed in full measure those political and technical skills which had lifted him, by the age of twenty-eight, to the pinnacle of the reform empire.

No sooner had Veiller and de Forest taken office in 1902 than

35. Edith Elmer Wood, *The Housing of the Unskilled Wage Earner: America's Next Problem*, 75-76.

an assault was launched against the Tenement House Law of 1901 by a combination which included, in Veiller's words, "the building interests of the city, the speculative builders, the material men, the institutions which made loans on such property, the architects who had to learn their trade all over again and did not like it, combined with the owners of the existing tenement house who found that they were required to spend in some cases over $1,000 to make their houses comply with the law. . . ." [36] Altogether thirty-one bills adversely affecting the Tenement Law were introduced in 1902 and 1903, all of which Veiller and de Forest successfully defeated.[37]

The most vocal opposition these years and afterward came from builders who resented the additional expenses imposed by Veiller's code, and from owners of old-law tenements reluctant to finance the alterations it required.[38] A chief spokesman for the landlords was the United Real Estate Owners' Association, which decided to test in court the provision of the Law of 1901 compelling the removal of school sinks. After several years of litigation, the United States Supreme Court decided in favor of the constitutionality of the law. Had the courts ruled against the Tenement House Department in the "Katie Moeschen" case, it would have barred the state from "retroactively" raising housing standards. Landlords who had complied with the tenement laws at a particular time would be safe from interference, despite the evolution of higher minimum standards. The United Real Estate Owners' Association was joined by other organized groups of small property owners — the House and Real Estate

36. Veiller, Reminiscences, 44, 45.
37. Tenement House Department, *First Report*, 1902-03, I 59, 68, 259, 260, 261, 262, 266, 267, 268, 269, 279.
38. For information concerning the many assaults upon the Tenement Law, consult the following: Tenement House Committee, Minutes, June 25, Oct. 5, 10, 1901; the annual *Reports* of the COS; Robert W. de Forest, "Introduction, Tenement House Reform in New York since 1901," in de Forest and Veiller, eds., *The Tenement House Problem*, I, xiii-xiv; *Catholic World*, LXXVI (1902-03), 851; *The Nation*, LXXVI (1903), 46; Robert W. de Forest, "Recent Progress in Tenement House Reform," *Annals*, XXIII (1904), 298; New York *Times*, Sept. 13, 1901, 12, Oct. 12, 1901, 16, Oct. 13, 1901, 24, Oct. 20, 1901, 6, Jan. 2, 1902, 3, Jan. 8, 1902, 3, Feb. 21, 1902, 5, Feb. 28, 1902, 5, Mar. 25, 1902, 5; New York *Herald Tribune*, Feb. 28, 1902, 5; *Charities*, VIII (1902), 249-50; *Charities and the Commons*, XV (1905-06), 661-63.

Owners' Association of the 12th and 19th Wards; the West Side
Tax Payers' Association; the Real Estate Owners' Protective
Association of the 12th and 22nd Wards — who labored inces-
santly to amend the tenement code in their favor.[39]

The chief opposition from tenement builders, associated in
various builders' leagues, originated in Brooklyn. At no time was
Veiller unwilling to consult with these landlords and builders,
amending the law to their satisfaction if the change did not seriously affect the welfare of tenants. If experience proved that
certain provisions of the law involved hardships for owners or
builders without compensating advantages to tenants, Veiller
cooperated in changing the law. At one time he even agreed
to persuade Tenement Commissioner Butler to liberalize his interpretation of certain sections of the tenement code for the
benefit of property owners.[40] Veiller never denied the right of
builders and landlords to their profits, if they were not earned
at the expense of the health and welfare of the tenement population.

Veiller traveled to Albany often to defend and promote desirable legislation, and he kept the Committee informed on bills
introduced into the legislature. Conversely, he once sent a letter
to legislators "warning them in regard to introducing bills affecting the tenement house law, and offering the expert advice of
the Committee in regard to such bills."[41] Restless and aggressive,
Veiller frequently prodded the Committee to assume new
responsibilities, to experiment and innovate.[42] He never assumed
that the merits of housing reform were self-evident, and explored
every channel of community education. The prosperous suburban burgher, remote from the stench and troubles of the tenements, had to be informed of the Committee's work, persuaded
of his personal stake in housing reform, converted from indifference to intelligent awareness. Thus Veiller labored to raise
the prestige of the Committee in the public's eye, creating an

39. Adolph Bloch to Lawrence Veiller, Mar. 9, 1905, Veiller MSS.
40. Tenement House Committee, Minutes, Mar. 26, 1909.
41. *Ibid.*, Jan. 13, 1910.
42. See, for example, Lawrence Veiller, "A Housing Programme for New
York, February 1, 1912" (Pamphlet marked confidential for members of the
COS Tenement House Committee), Veiller MSS.

image of competence and disinterested benevolence. In 1913, for example, a battle raged over the advisability of allowing open-stair tenements with water closets situated on each floor landing. Veiller, who opposed this type of construction, drafted a letter for the Committee, advising that it "be sent to news-papers where members of the Committee had personal relations and could send it as a personal communication putting the news-papers on their guard against . . . unfair or untrue statements."[43] Under Veiller's direction the Committee sought to arouse grass-roots support for tenement reform through pamphlets, lectures, newspaper appeals, and similar devices.[44]

As a result of Veiller's efforts the COS Tenement House Committee successfully defended the Tenement Law of 1901 and the Tenement House Department for almost two decades. Only once did Veiller's carefully raised edifice of legislation and enforcement come near disaster; and then only his swift and calculated political counterattack saved it. In February 1912 the New York Court of Appeals ruled that an "apartment house" differed from a tenement for purposes of legal regulation. The Court argued that an apartment house was not a tenement if each family had its own toilet, kitchen, and set bathtub. Since each family in thousands of new-law tenements had its own toilet and usually the other conveniences as well, the Court's decision, if unaltered, threatened to pluck millions of people in existing and future multiple dwellings from the supervision of the Tenement House Department. Veiller, de Forest, and Tene-ment Commissioner Murphy immediately consulted and decided upon a triple strategy. They agreed to persuade the state legis-lature to amend the Tenement Law to prevent a similar catas-trophe, seek similar action from the New York City Board of

43. Tenement House Committee, Minutes, Mar. 24, 1913.

44. COS, *Twenty-fourth Annual Report*, Oct. 1, 1905, to Sept. 30, 1906, 66-67. The following pamphlets printed for public distribution indicate the scope of the Committee's educational work: "The Building Code and Tuberculosis Prevention," (May 15, 1912); "Shall the Law Permit Rooms in Tenement Houses to be Six Feet Wide?" (Mar. 23, 1913); "Shall Water Closets be Per-mitted to get Light and Ventilation from Public Stairs?" (Mar. 28, 1913); "The Tenement House Committee and Its Work," (Dec. 1907). These publi-cations are included in the Edith Elmer Wood papers at Columbia University.

Aldermen, and convince the Court of Appeals to reopen the case.

Veiller hastened to Albany. He contacted Senator Robert F. Wagner, majority leader. After explaining the situation, Veiller implored him to sponsor a bill he had prepared. Veiller urged haste, for any delay would strengthen the opposition from owners and builders who jubilantly accepted the Court's verdict. He suggested that Wagner persuade Governor Dix, also a Democrat, to deliver an emergency message to the legislature. Veiller made similar arrangements with acquaintances in the Republican-controlled assembly. In only a day's time his bill passed both houses.

Governor Dix, however, could not approve the bill. It required the personal signature of the assembly speaker, who was out of town. In the three days that elapsed before the bill was ready for the governor with the speaker's signature, Dix and members of the legislature were flooded by letters and telegrams opposing Veiller's amendment. Wavering under the pressure, Dix granted an extension of several days to hear arguments pro and con. Wagner also weakened to the point of being ready to recall the bill, but was dissuaded by Veiller. Finally, after a delay of ten days, Dix approved the measure.[45]

The episode proved, once again, that political adroitness was essential to success in housing reform. Veiller accepted Albany politics as a game with its own rules, which he learned early and thoroughly. It did not surprise him, three years after he had saved the Tenement House Law of 1901, that storm warnings were raised in Albany again. This time political vigilance was needed to prevent a combination of loft and factory owners, abetted by speculative tenement builders, from sweeping the Tenement House Department out of existence. These interests sought to consolidate building inspection in the hands of the superintendents of building in each borough. They argued that

45. Veiller Reminiscences, 74-81; Report of the Tenement House Committee of the Charity Organization Society of New York, 1911, 1912, 1913, *Housing Reform in New York City* (Jan., 1914), 11-13; COS, *Thirtieth Annual Report for the Year Ending September 30, 1912*, 14-18; *Housing Betterment*, I (Sept., 1912), 1-7. Once the amendment had been secured from the state legislature, Veiller dropped the court and board of aldermen actions.

the division of responsibility among the Fire; Water, Gas and Electricity; State Labor; and Tenement House Departments had resulted in "over-regulation." The Consolidation measure, known as the Lockwood-Ellenbogen Bill, was vigorously opposed by the COS Tenement House Committee, the City Club, the New York press, and the city departments affected. Nonetheless, the state legislature passed the measure, which Mayor Mitchell vetoed. The COS referred to the Consolidation bill as "the most formidable attack upon the integrity" of housing code administration which reformers ever had to face.[46]

Year after year the attacks upon the Tenement House Law or its administration continued. Year after year the COS Tenement House Committee defended them. No attack was more persistent and unyielding than the demand of Brooklyn builders to relieve the three-story, three-family tenement from the stringent provisions of the Law of 1901. This was a popular mode of construction in Brooklyn, and builders pressed for every concession which promised to enhance their profits.

For Veiller, the defense of the law against the assaults of the Brooklyn interests was an issue which he would not compromise. For all his political calculation and flexibility, his willingness to compromise on details, his preoccupation with organization, administration, and technical proficiency, Veiller never lost sight of his ultimate goal — the protection of the moral and physical welfare of the people of New York. Thus he adamantly refused to permit Brooklyn builders to reintroduce the air shaft, despite pressure from a majority of his own Committee. The air shaft was to Veiller what the Mulberry Street Bend had been to Jacob Riis, the hated symbol of those evils which he was pledged to destroy. In the final analysis, Veiller's struggle against the Brooklyn builders represented a defense of his own integrity, as well as that of the Tenement House Law of 1901.

Until 1916 Veiller was able to hold the Tenement House Committee in line. It staunchly opposed amendment of the law regulating the three-family tenement. In 1916, however, the

46. COS, *Thirty-third Annual Report for the Year Ending September 30, 1915*, 59-62; *Housing Betterment*, IV (June 1915), 4-7.

Brooklyn members of the Committee, led by the formidable Alfred T. White and the Committee's chairman, Paul D. Cravath, rebelled. At a meeting on March 25 both White and Cravath expressed their willingness to amend the law at the behest of the Brooklyn men. Veiller objected to any concessions, claiming that under the present law the builders could anticipate a satisfactory 20 per cent profit.[47] A subcommittee headed by White was appointed to examine the question and consult with the builders. In December, White outlined a series of concessions, chiefly pertaining to the size of courts and fire protection. Veiller again opposed retreat, though a majority of the Committee voted for the measures. The following month the Committee, despite Veiller's continued opposition, once more approved amendment of the law to encourage three-family tenements.[48]

In the following months, the issue shifted from the construction of new three-family tenements to the alteration of private one-family homes into three-family tenements. In March 1917, White reported to the Committee that "Mr. Bailey and the other Brooklyn real estate men interested in the three-family house amendment felt that it was essential to the success of any measure introduced into the Legislature on this subject, that it embody changes in the law to facilitate the alteration of old private houses into three-family tenements."[49] The Tenement Committee's discussion focused upon the advisability of allowing an air shaft to replace the court required by the Tenement House Law. This time the Committee voted against such a concession.

Some 20,000 one-family homes in Brooklyn, located in neighborhoods abandoned by the original owners, was the prize so attractive in the eyes of builders. The maximization of their value depended upon their conversion into tenements as cheaply as possible.[50] Accordingly, State Senator Lawson introduced a

47. Tenement House Committee, Minutes, Mar. 25, 1916; Lawson Purdy, Reminiscences, 34.
48. Tenement House Committee, Minutes, Dec. 19, 1916, Jan. 10, 1917.
49. *Ibid.*, Mar. 12, 1917.
50. COS, *Thirty-fifth Annual Report for the Year Ending September 30, 1917*, 19-21; Lawson Purdy, Reminiscences, 34.

bill on March 27, 1917, permitting the use of air shafts in houses converted into three-family tenements. Two days later the Tenement House Committee agreed to oppose the measure.[51]

The sponsors of the Lawson bill then requested a conference with representatives of the Committee. The Brooklyn men, in an effort to win favor with the powerful COS reformers, agreed to a modification of the bill whereby only the second story toilet would be ventilated and lighted by a 3 by 5 foot air shaft extending from the roof to the ceiling of the toilet. On April 13, in Veiller's absence, the Tenement House Committee voted to accept the amended Lawson bill. After Veiller's return, the Committee on April 16 confirmed its decision by a majority vote.[52] Veiller immediately resigned from the Committee; he also announced his intention of opposing the Lawson bill in the legislature. He severed all allegiance to a Committee which, in his opinion, devoted "more attention to the interests of those dealing in real estate and financing houses than to the welfare of the great mass of people of New York City who are unable to protect themselves."[53]

Veiller, however, could not block a measure which had the combined endorsement of his own influential Committee and United States Senator William M. Calder, a builder by profession and leader in the Brooklyn Republican organization. The Lawson bill, enacted by the legislature, was soon on Governor Whitman's desk. Veiller tried to dissuade Whitman, but only succeeded in delaying the inevitable. At a "Sunday School Parade in Brooklyn," Senator Calder won the consent of Whitman and Mayor Mitchell.[54]

The breach between Veiller and the COS Tenement House Committee never healed. Veiller continued to work for the COS as director of the Department for the Improvement of Social Conditions and secretary of the Committee on Criminal Courts.

51. Tenement House Committee, Minutes, Mar. 29, 1917.
52. Ibid., Apr. 11, 13, 16, 1917.
53. New York Times, Apr. 18, 1917, 8. Veiller added that he was "entirely out of sympathy with the judgment of a majority of the committee that it was desirable to increase the fire hazards and return to the unspeakable airshaft."
54. Veiller, Reminiscences, 84.

Feeling, however, that he had been betrayed by the Committee he had sired and led to astounding successes, Veiller remained irreconcilable. He devoted most of his time and bountiful talents in the next two decades to promoting the national housing movement.

[4]

Pioneering welfare associations, such as the AICP and the Council of Hygiene, transmitted to their successors in the Progressive generation an environmental philosophy of housing reform: inferior housing adversely affected health and morals; it resulted in crime, pauperism, intemperance, indolence, and a train of other evils. As the housing problem became increasingly identified with the immigrant in the nation's great urban centers, reformers insisted that improved housing would contribute to Americanization and the reunification of a divided urban community.

In the 1890's, Jacob Riis added a new ingredient to the philosophy: the reconstruction of the tenement neighborhood through a program of parks, playgrounds, schools, educational reform, boys' clubs, and similar projects. In his impressionistic, unsystematic way, Riis realized that improved housing had only limited value in regenerating character, family life, and social structure. But Riis's contemporary housing reformers did not usually think along lines of neighborhood reconstruction, except for settlement workers interested in housing to whom neighborhood regeneration was an article of faith. Although in practice both professional and lay housing reformers supported a wide variety of associated good causes, they tended to view the mere establishment of minimum housing standards as a key to social control. Perhaps it was easier to believe then than now that a private bathroom, more apartment space, a plentitude of light and air, security from fire, good health, and a grass-filled court would make model citizens out of juvenile delinquents and drunkards.

Veiller contributed little to this philosophy. He accepted with no reflection the hypothesis that better housing implied not only healthier but morally superior citizens, that inferior housing surely resulted in physical and moral blight. The assumption that better housing was a basic, indeed, *the* basic need of the immigrant and working-class poor was so self-evident to him that it apparently needed no further analysis.

Veiller's historical contribution to housing reform, apart from the codes he sired, was in method not philosophy. He inherited a three-fold program from his predecessors — restrictive legislation, the model tenement, and the Octavia Hill idea of enlightened management. For all practical purposes, he ignored the last two but put teeth into remedial legislation. Veiller added a fourth new element: the ideal of scientific housing reform based upon expert knowledge and strong, centralized organization. In Veiller's estimation the most lasting results could not be attained by well-meaning, moral-minded amateurs unable to cope with the machinations of experienced politicians and real estate interests.

As we have mentioned, Veiller was skeptical of model tenements as a solution to the housing problem. They were a kind of housing folly which deflected the attention of reformers from the more important goal of effective restrictive legislation. He doubted that enough individuals would become interested in "investment philanthropy" to house more than a handful of people. In support of his argument Veiller pointed out in 1910 that the "efforts of philanthropically inclined persons" had over forty years resulted in twenty-five groups of model tenements in Manhattan, sufficient to house only 3,588 families or 17,940 persons. Meanwhile, speculative builders had erected 27,100 tenements holding 253,510 families, or over a million persons.[55]

The same criticism applied to model tenement and model housing schemes outside of New York. They were superior in quality to the product of the commercial builder, but deficient in number. We have already referred to the Cooperative Building Company of the 1870's and Robert Treat Paine's Workingmen's Building Association, both in Boston. In the nation's

55. Lawrence Veiller, *Housing Reform: A Hand-Book for Practical Use in American Cities* (New York, 1910), 71, 72. Hereafter referred to as Veiller, *Housing Reform*.

capitol, General George M. Sternberg directed a model housing campaign from 1897 until his death in 1915. A prominent sanitarian, former Surgeon General of the Army, and chairman of Roosevelt's Homes Commission in 1908, Sternberg organized a Sanitary Improvement Company which rejected the tenement in favor of two-flat dwellings with separate entrances and backyards for each family. Within twenty years the Company had erected about 310 flats, accommodating 620 families. Each flat, designed for the same type of steadily employed, higher paid wage-earner found in the City and Suburban Homes Company buildings, included two to four rooms, bath, and toilet. The Company limited dividends to 5 per cent. For the benefit of poorer workers, particularly the Negroes of Washington's alley slums, Sternberg organized the Sanitary Housing Company in 1904. He had great difficulty in attracting capital for this venture, however, and the Company built less than a hundred flats. Dr. George M. Kober, Dean of the Georgetown University Medical School, had been associated with Sternberg in this model housing work, and he assumed the presidency of both companies after the general's death.

Another philanthropist who rejected the tenement in favor of the flat was Jacob G. Schmidlapp of Cincinnati. In 1911 he began constructing flats patterned after the Washington variety, but experimented also with detached and semi-detached single-family homes as well as double-detached four-family houses. Landscape gardening brightened the Schmidlapp homes, which contained two to four rooms and bath. Within ten years, he had built about eighty-eight houses for 326 families, a majority of whom were Negroes.

A few other minor model housing schemes appeared outside of New York before World War I. For example an Improved Housing Association in New Haven erected eight two-flat houses in 1914, and in Massachusetts Rev. C. H. Williams organized the Billerica Garden Suburb, which limited dividends to 5 per cent and constructed about thirty detached houses and semi-detached cottages. The relative scarcity of model housing in New York and elsewhere led Veiller to insist that "until adequate restrictive legislation has been passed and the certainty of its enforcement secured, there should be no talk of any other form of effort in housing reform." He preferred that reformers apply their energies to legislation affecting thousands of existing and future dwellings in a community rather than divert their resources to a few model projects.

Veiller did not think that the purpose of restrictive legislation was to create an ideal environment, but rather to insure a minimum of safety and comfort for all. Beyond that minimum which the state was obligated to establish, the laws of supply and demand could legitimately operate. He realized, however, that even minimum standards would be bitterly contested. As he learned from many campaigns, real estate interests were sure to resist any limitations upon their freedom. For this reason, practicality and moderation were necessary. One might aim high, yet the reformer had to accept whatever concessions could be wrested from recalcitrant builders, landlords, and their legislative spokesmen. At best, housing legislation represented a compromise between many conflicting interests, and whoever exerted the most pressure would capture the lion's share in the compromise. In the course of the struggle, someone was "sure to be hurt." Veiller accepted this fact as part of the job: it "is inherent in the situation and cannot be avoided."[56]

Veiller stressed the dangers inherent in poorly drafted restrictive legislation. No law was preferable to a faulty measure pushed through in a burst of enthusiasm. A housing code had to be based upon careful, meticulous examination of local conditions. Slavish imitation of the housing laws of other localities might be disastrous if it resulted in lower standards than those prevailing in the community at the time. The drafters of a housing code also had to insure its constitutionality. Reformers might be loath to begin over again if a housing code, won after arduous struggle, was discredited by the courts. The law had to be practical, as utopian standards were likely to arouse great antagonism, if not disobedience. Excessively high standards, if enforced, might discourage building altogether and thus create

56. Veiller, *A Model Housing Law*, 16.

a serious housing shortage. The framers of a housing code, finally, had to guard against the delegation of discretionary power to regulatory agencies. The practice nearly always "led to abuse and ultimately to nullification of the law."[57]

Lawrence Veiller was a practical-minded man of action who refused to pursue idealistic will-o'-the-wisps, however attractive in theory. He was a conservative who resisted radical innovation in social or economic affairs:

> How delightful it would be to be able to believe that all that is needed to bring about proper housing conditions is a change in the economic status of the working people! That given enough wages, slums would vanish! Flying carpets, wishing caps, and magic philters have from time immemorial had an indescribable charm for humanity. But alas, it is not to be done so easily. City slums cannot by the wave of a neocromancer's wand become gardens of delight.[58]

In housing he spurned what he thought excessive government interference with the laws of supply and demand. Restrictive legislation was both necessary and desirable; but government-built, -owned or -subsidized housing was neither. Well informed on contemporary housing developments in Europe, Veiller knew that the industrial nations of Europe had embarked upon a program of state-built and financed working-class housing. America's rapid urban growth after 1870 was not unique. To cope with their housing problems, both Germany and Belgium had developed an elaborate system of state loans to building and loan societies, or cooperative building associations pledged to provide low-cost working-class housing. Some German cities built and managed low-income housing projects. England's Housing of the Working Class Act of 1890 encouraged municipal slum clearance and the erection of municipal tenements. The urban housing problem was not restricted to the United States; it taxed the resources of western Europe as well.[59]

57. Veiller, *Housing Reform*, 90.
58. Veiller, *A Model Housing Law*, 3.
59. European housing reform after 1890 can be traced in the following: E. R. L. Gould, *The Housing of the Working People;* Wood, *The Housing of the Unskilled Wage Earner;* United States Department of Labor, Bureau of

By the time of the First World War, a few architects and housing economists — Edith Elmer Wood, Carol Aronovici, Charles H. Whitaker, Frederick L. Ackerman, Robert D. Kohn — had rebelled against Veiller's almost exclusive emphasis upon restrictive legislation. Influenced by the European program of state-financing and the abortive but influential federal housing projects of World War I,[60] they argued that America also needed "constructive" housing legislation. "The best restrictive legislation," according to Mrs. Wood, "is only negative. It will prevent the bad. It will not produce the good." She justified a policy of constructive legislation on the grounds that private enterprise had not and could not profitably "supply the demand for good, cheap houses." Unskilled workers, particularly, could not be "supplied with decent homes under existing economic conditions on a business basis."[61]

Mrs. Wood singled out Veiller as the high priest in America's temple of restrictive or "negative" housing legislation. "For this policy," she complained, "the report of the New York Tenement House Commission of 1900, the success of the New York tenement house law, and the activity of Lawrence Veiller and his associates of the National Housing Association are largely responsible."[62] Certainly Veiller threw his influence against any constructive housing legislation, but it was inaccurate to blame him for the failure of any such program to develop. It is difficult to imagine the average middle-class American of the Progressive era tolerating increased taxes in order to subsidize government housing for the poor. To him such housing was both socialistic and the product of special class legislation, neither of which he thought desirable.

In the authoritative and influential report of the Tenement

Labor Statistics, *Government Aid to Home Owning and Housing of Working People in Foreign Countries*, Bulletin, Whole No. 158, Miscellaneous Series No. 5 (Washington, 1915). Also Catherine Bauer, *Modern Housing* (New York, 1934), deals primarily with the 1920's, but contains an account of the preceding period.

60. On the federal housing program of World War I, see my article, "Homes and 'A Few Well Placed Fruit Trees': An Object Lesson in Federal Housing," *Social Research*, XXVII (Winter 1960), 469-86.

61. Wood, *The Housing of the Unskilled Worker*, 20, 19.

62. *Ibid.*, 61.

House Commission of 1900, Veiller justified his opposition to constructive housing reform. Municipal tenements would house only a "favored few" and at the "sacrifice of self-dependence." The municipality was unlikely to prove an efficient landlord "under the necessarily cumbrous and mechanical methods of government system." Municipal tenements promised to enlarge an already ponderous bureaucracy. If they were "tenanted with a view to votes, they might be so located and utilized by the political party in power as to perpetuate its control."[63]

Veiller's most serious objections to municipal housing, however, were economic. From the taxpayer's point of view, why should the state enter housing any more than it should go into the bakery or butcher business, both of which supplied necessities of life which the poor could not always afford in ample quantity? More important, "if the city is to enter the field of building operations and compete with private capital . . . private enterprise will in a short time be driven out of the field. It cannot compete with municipal undertaking."[64] Such a prospect, in Veiller's opinion, was financially appalling. The city would become bankrupt before it could begin to meet the need. On economic grounds Veiller also opposed the proposal to exempt model tenements from municipal taxation as an inducement to philanthropists. Tax exemption would diminish municipal revenues and represented a "distinct departure from our present public policy, which taxes alike all real estate used for housing or private purposes."[65]

Certain of Veiller's assumptions appear dubious. In the case of government housing, he adhered to the established American belief that government enterprise is inherently inefficient, when, in fact, the municipality was potentially more efficient than the average tenement landlord with his limited budget, small-scale operations, and indifferent social policy. Although Veiller admitted that really high standards of restrictive legislation, effec-

63. Robert W. de Forest and Lawrence Veiller, "The Tenement House Problem," 44, 45.

64. Veiller, *Housing Reform*, 81-82.

65. Robert W. de Forest and Lawrence Veiller, "The Tenement House Problem," 45, 46.

tively enforced, could discourage private building enterprise, he did not conclude that some kind of government financial aid was needed to help reduce housing costs or rentals. Housing standards constantly evolve; what proves satisfactory to one generation may not to the next. Minimum standards, for example, were higher in 1900 than in 1867, when New York's first tenement law was enacted. If standards (and costs) spiral upward, the framer of housing legislation is faced with a difficult problem. He must either sacrifice the standards or cause rents to be raised higher than the supposed beneficiaries of the legislation can pay. New York's poorest workers did not, in fact, occupy the new-law tenements built after 1901. Indeed, in that year Jacob Riis had feared that "our tenement house reform was taking a shape that tended to make it impossible for anyone not able to pay [up to] $75 to live on Manhattan Island." He expressed his doubts to Veiller and de Forest, but "was overruled." Later on, Edith Elmer Wood complained that new-law tenements, with the exception of a few jerry-built ones in Brooklyn which had evaded the scrutiny of the Tenement House Department, were financially inaccessible to unskilled workers.[66] Veiller never really examined or resolved this difficult question of how one applied the benefits of rising minimum standards in housing to those unable to afford them.

Finally, it was not necessarily true that government-built or -financed housing must accommodate either everyone or no one because of its threat to private building. The supporters of federal housing in the 1930's argued that private enterprise was not building at all for the lowest income groups. Such housing was not profitable enough because immigration and the rate of urban expansion had declined, thus reducing the low income market. In this case, municipal housing was not competing with the private builder. It was supplementary rather than competitive.

In the 1920's Veiller advocated a program of municipal slum-clearance involving sale of the land to limited dividend

66. Jacob A. Riis to [probably] Dr. Jane Robbins, Oct. 10, 1901, Jacob A. Riis, MSS; Wood, *The House of the Unskilled Worker*, 24.

companies, but he consistently opposed government-built or
-financed housing. He criticized not only the housing but the
entire spending program of the New Deal. Nevertheless the
impressive European public housing program of the 1920's, the
persisting blight and slums in our cities, new ideals of large-
scale community development, and the catastrophic depression
focused the attention of the new generation of housing reformers upon the inadequacy of restrictive legislation. The new goal
was not simply the prevention of poor housing through restrictive legislation, but the creation of physically integrated, aesthet-
ically satisfying residential environments for all classes.

Although Veiller's exclusive emphasis upon restrictive legislation had been challenged by 1917 and had fallen into disrepute
by the 1930's, it is understandable why the reformers of the
Progressive era found the idea attractive. In the first place,
depression unemployment in the thirties combined with the
decline of immigration and relatively stable rates of urban
growth to encourage government subsidized housing. The early
twentieth century, in contrast, was a period of rapid urban
expansion and heavy immigration, when it seemed to reformers
like Veiller that government subsidy in any form would involve
colossal expenditures with no end or limits in sight. On the
other hand, a modest local, state, or federal housing program
would benefit only a few, like the model tenement, and thus
fail to meet the city's housing needs.

Second, the commercial builder, for better or worse, did cater
to low-income groups in the early twentieth century. Tenements and flats were profitable speculative ventures in a period
of rising land values and population growth. Opponents of a
"constructive" housing program argued, therefore, that private
enterprise could supply enough housing for basic shelter needs
if not discouraged by government competition. Restrictive legislation insured that the commercial builder's product attained
minimum safety and health standards. This argument became
less convincing when builders after World War I concentrated
increasingly upon homes and apartment houses beyond the
reach of the lower economic third of the population, and even

the middle third. The economics of housing in the 1920's was discussed at length by Edith Elmer Wood in her *Recent Trends in American Housing* (1931), and the heart of her message was that "two thirds of the population cannot pay a rental or purchase price high enough to produce a commercial profit on a new dwelling, satisfactory to the commercial builder. . . . Therefore, he does not build for them."[67]

Restrictive legislation, finally, attracted housing reformers in the early twentieth century because it promised to eliminate urban blight and slums more swiftly and with less expenditure than any alternative method. In contrast to earlier building codes and sanitary ordinances, Veiller's program of effective restrictive legislation came as a revelation with vast potentialities for urban sanitary and social control. It took many years of experience to prove that restrictive legislation alone did not and never could entirely eliminate slums and create a desirable urban residential environment. Yet Veiller's uncompromising drive for such legislation, viewed in historical perspective, performed a valuable service. Even if the poorest workers in New York could not afford the new-law tenement, they could not afford the dumb-bell either, in terms of the accommodations offered for the price. At least the Tenement House Law of 1901 did guarantee to those able to afford the new-law houses a satisfactory minimum (for the time) of light and ventilation, fire protection, and sanitary facilities. Equally important, his zealous campaign for restrictive legislation helped arouse other cities to their housing problem. Veiller's work insured that high standards of restrictive housing legislation would be accepted, in principle, as basic to the safety and welfare of an urban society.

Lawrence Veiller was the technician of housing reform, and it sometimes happens with the technician that the means become the ends; but if he erred in opposing all forms of "constructive" housing legislation, he compensated for this rigidity by introducing the concept of expert professional service and efficient

67. Edith Elmer Wood, *Recent Trends in American Housing* (New York, 1931), 46.

organization in housing reform. Long after Veiller had retired in the mid-1930's, he remarked that the generation of social reformers who succeeded him viewed him as conservative, if not reactionary. Remembering back to the turn of the century when Seth Low considered him too "radical" for the post of tenement house commissioner, Veiller observed simply that "such is life."[68]

68. Veiller, Reminiscences, 39.

7.

The Professional Good Neighbor

Well, I tell you, it's a wonderful movement, this Hudson Guild. And in those years when I was a boy, you have no idea what it meant.

EDWARD LAFFERTY,
New York cop, 1916

[1]

By any standards the decade and a half following 1900 was a golden age of American reform. From the settlements, charities, and social reform organizations like the Consumers' League came the dedication to salve the nation's misery. Housing reformers could always depend upon these groups for moral and political support; and in turn, although the settlements or charities were not primarily identified with housing reform, their efforts to improve living and working conditions were inseparably linked to the housing crusade.

The housing reformer represented, almost exclusively, what Mary E. Richmond termed the "wholesale" method of reform which endeavored to stamp out exploitation and injustice on a grand scale. By sweeping legislative and environmental change the wholesaler hoped to eradicate poverty, disease, crime and ignorance. The settlements and charities, however, also stressed the importance of individual, face-to-face relations with the poor — the "retail" method. Material aid, housing codes, or wages and hours laws had their share in the rehabilitation of the individual and the reconstruction of the slum, but they could not substitute for personal sympathy, understanding, and friendship.

Yet the settlement and charity worker, the embodiment of the retail method, invariably employed wholesale methods when necessary. The Progressive social reformer was, above all else, a pragmatist. If a social evil — the tenement and tenement home work, unsanitary and dangerous working conditions, prostitution — could be repressed most quickly and effectively by the wholesale method, it was adopted without hesitation. The tenement inhabitant benefited from the environmental as well as the personal approach of organized social work.

Broadly speaking, housing reform was merely one manisfestation of this organized social welfare crusade of the Progressive era. The dominant themes of the housing movement — leadership by professionals like Veiller and Gould as well as the reliance upon restrictive legislation to impose minimum standards — were reflections in a mirror rather than unique phenomena. An age which numbered its poor, its immigrants, its underpaid women and child workers, and its slum housing in the millions could no longer depend upon socially conscious ministers, laymen, and philanthropic matrons to guide the destinies of its charities and reform organizations. As social problems increased in scope and complexity welfare agencies were forced to rely increasingly upon a new breed of philanthropist — the full-time salaried professional. Thus Lawrence Veiller had his counterparts at every strategic point of the welfare empire of the early twentieth century. Charity organization, for example, could point to such resourceful professionals as Mary E. Richmond, casework theorist, and Edward T. Devine, social work administrator, educator and general secretary of the New York COS after 1896. Homer Folks left his mark as an authority on public charities and child welfare. Florence Kelley, Mary Van Kleeck, Josephine and Pauline Goldmark, Grace and Edith Abbott, and Sophonisba Breckinridge were a few of the distinguished experts on labor legislation of the period. Dr. Alice Hamilton, from her base at Hull House in Chicago, achieved renown as an authority on industrial disease. Even urban vice had its professional investigator in George J. Kneeland.

The professional philanthropist, the social engineer of the Progressive era, commonly assumed that poverty was an unnatural, abnormal condition. It was the outgrowth of social maladjustments subject to investigation, analysis, and, ultimately, eradication. If the commitment of organized social work to what Devine called "conscious social action" can be summarized in a single concept, it would be the universal attainment of a normal standard of living. The state was to "fix the levels below which the exploitation of workers and consumers would not be tolerated, above which the principles of free competition might safely and advantageously be left free to operate."[1] Here was the social worker's equivalent of the housing reformer's goal of minimum health and safety standards enforced by legislative fiat. Both the wholesalers and retailers of reform shared in common the belief that society could establish the criteria for a normal standard of living and then gradually assist every individual to attain the standard by eliminating the evils which dragged him below the line. The right of every individual to the normal life, to those material and cultural necessities without which he could not function as a healthy, productive member of society, was a goal which linked together the disparate reform crusades of the Progressive era.

[2]

Mary K. Simkhovitch expressed the settlement worker's point of view when she wrote that an income standard was a "social necessity in just the sense and for precisely the same reason as is a cubic air space standard." The mission of this generation and the next, she insisted, was to "recognize and establish standards of health, education, leisure and income." Democracy could not coexist with any lesser ideal.[2]

When Dr. Stanton Coit returned from England to establish the Neighborhood Guild (later University Settlement) in New York's lower East Side in 1886, he created one of the most dramatic and successful vehicles for neighborhood improvement ever known in America. The settlement idea spread rapidly for

1. Edward T. Devine, *When Social Work Was Young* (New York, 1939), 4.
2. Mary K. Simkhovitch, *The City Worker's World in America* (New York, 1917), 169, 176.

it fulfilled the spiritual and moral needs of middle-class humanitarians as much as those of the working-class, immigrant poor. Whether in New York, Chicago, Boston, Philadelphia, or Pittsburgh, the settlement formula was simple. Members of the "privileged classes" would live with the poor as friends and neighbors, interpreting their needs and aspirations to the community while introducing into the life of the poor the spiritual and cultural advantages which poverty had denied them.

The neighborhood ideal, the desire to create an organic unity among the people and institutions of the neighborhood, inspired the work of the settlement. Felix Adler, a lay housing reformer who, like Riis, looked beyond the immediate problems of sanitary improvement to achieve social control, explained that the unique function of the settlement was to "rescue for us and to develop a department of ethics which has almost been lost to us, namely, the ethics of neighborhood." The educated, the well-to-do, could not "truly in any real sense live" unless they participated in neighborhood building. They had to refresh their own lives by "dipping into the current of life of the multitude of their fellow-beings."[3] The settlement worker, neighbor and friend of the immigrant, served as "interpreter of American customs and ideals." In the midst of the slum, where the "advantages are least and the evil influences greatest," the settlement planted the seeds of American culture, education, and social ideals.[4]

The settlement worker's struggle for civic betterment and Americanization developed out of her personal contact with the poor and a firsthand understanding of their problems. In this sense she was a leading exponent of the retail method of reform. The settlement, observed Mary Simkhovitch, was "really another home for the neighbors who met there, a place where the needs and desires of each were sympathetically considered."[5] The settlement invariably organized play groups, clubs, and

3. Felix Adler, "The Ethics of Neighborhood," *University Settlement Studies*, II (July 1906), 30, 28.

4. College Settlements Association, *Report*, 1911-12, 8, 9.

5. Mary K. Simkhovitch, *Neighborhood: My Story of Greenwich House* (New York, 1938), 70.

classes where the children of the neighborhood received, under a resident's personal guidance and attention, their training for future citizenship. Indeed, the child's loyalty and affection were fundamental goals of the settlement. It endeavored to influence and mould his total personality, thus aiding the "public schools in the transformation of the crude immigration material into the real citizens and citizenesses."[6]

Out of her personal understanding and sympathy for the people of the neighborhood, her devotion to a higher standard of life for them and their children, the settlement worker plunged into a crusade to eradicate every influence for moral evil and physical degeneration. An ethical pragmatism was her only guide and doctrine. Nothing which deteriorated the quality of neighborhood life was immune from attack; nothing which promised relief and improvement was rejected.

Although housing and sanitary reform were hardly exclusive interests in view of the settlement's sweeping vision of an organic community of neighbors, they always ranked high in the struggle for neighborhood regeneration. Thus it was the poignant spectacle of a sick woman in a squalid rear tenement that convinced Lillian Wald to devote her life to the poor. A graduate of a nurses' training school, Miss Wald had been giving courses in home nursing on the East Side in the early 1890's. One morning a child led her to a tenement where "open and unscreened closets were promiscuously used by men and women." In her brief journey to an ill mother, of a family neither criminal nor depraved, Miss Wald saw epitomized "all the maladjustments of our social and economic relations."[7]

The Henry Street Settlement established by Lillian Wald included a visiting nursing service which succored the ill and disseminated principles of personal hygiene. From the small beginnings in 1893 when Miss Wald and Mary Brewster comprised the entire staff, the service expanded to fifteen in 1900 and forty-seven by 1909. Like public baths, sandlots and playgrounds, kindergartens and manual training, child welfare clinics

6. College Settlements Association, *Report*, 1905-06, 36.
7. Lillian D. Wald, *The House on Henry Street* (New York, 1915), 5, 6.

and pure milk stations, visiting nursing was a settlement activity eventually assumed by the municipality. Henry Street had lent a nurse to the New York Board of Health in 1902 to follow up cases of children sent home because of illness. In a month's time the Board adopted the school nursing service as its own, and soon expanded this activity to include home nursing of contagious disease.

Henry Street became involved in numerous other health and hygiene programs. The Settlement established a milk station in 1903 to insure that East Side mothers could obtain pure milk for their children. The success of this experiment eventually resulted in fifteen municipal milk stations in 1911. A nurse was attached to each of them to train tenement mothers in the principles of hygiene, infant care, and nutrition. Henry Street also pioneered in tuberculosis control. In 1893, shortly before the Board of Health inaugurated its campaign of preventive work and education, the Settlement nurses obtained the names of tuberculosis patients in the neighborhood, visited them, supplied sputum cups and disinfectant, and taught them how to protect others from infection.

No other settlement contributed so much to public health, but all actively promoted good housing and hygiene. Residents nagged the city to clean local streets, testified before tenement house commissions, reported violations of housing and sanitary codes to the proper authorities. The West Side's Greenwich House, for example, which included Jacob Riis and Felix Adler among its founders, prepared a tenant's manual and worked closely with the poor on housekeeping and hygiene matters. The same settlement pestered the sanitation department to collect refuse more efficiently and successfully fought to have the city asphalt local streets. In the Veiller-de Forest years of the Tenement House Department, Greenwich House cooperated closely with the inspectors—"many of whom were our friends," Mrs. Simkhovitch recalled.[8] The Settlement took particular pride in the work of Dr. Hans Zinsser, a resident who started

8. Simkhovitch, *Neighborhood*, 130.

an infant welfare clinic, anticipating the establishment of the Bureau of Child Hygiene in the New York Board of Health.

It is difficult today, when we take municipal parks, playgrounds, and other recreation services for granted, to appreciate the profound commitment of the social settlement to recreation facilities for tenement neighborhoods. Even health and housing reform did not rank higher in importance to the settlement resident than the provision of wholesome play facilities, which she viewed as a form of discipline, education, and exercise. Elizabeth S. Williams, headworker at New York's College Settlement, was one of many "deeply impressed with the horror of the overcrowding in this part of the city and with the necessity for renewed effort to obtain more parks and playgrounds near at hand, besides access to nature's playground on the ocean beaches."[9] The tenement resident needed fresh air to breath, and a refreshing contrast to the monotonous miles of tenements, fire escapes, and clotheslines. Equally important, the "streets, the moving picture show, the cheap vaudeville, the penny arcade, the dance halls and academies" had become dangerously alluring to tenement youth.[10] If the settlement wished to retain its influence over the tenement boy and girl, it would have to supply alternative attractions.

Under Elizabeth William's direction the College Settlement became a seedbed for the recreation movement of the late 1890's. It was the headquarters of the East Side Recreation Society as well as the Outdoor Recreation League. The University Settlement, in the persons of Charles Stover and James Paulding, had played a prominent role in organizing the League. One of the most distinguished champions of recreation in the Progressive era, Stover was appointed New York's Park Commissioner in 1910. In cooperation with Stover's University Settlement and others, the College Settlement on Rivington Street labored incessantly for neighborhood recreation facilities.

Most settlements improvised some play area for tenement chil-

9. College Settlements Association, *Report*, 1903-04, 15.
10. College Settlements Association, *Report*, 1908-09, 39.

dren. No sooner, for example, did Lillian Wald establish her nursing service before she transformed three yards into a small playground for the neighborhood children. In her opinion, the "young offender's presence in the courts may be traced to a play-impulse for which there was no safe outlet."[11] Similarly, the Friendly Aid House on East 34th Street, to which Mary Simkhovitch had moved in 1898 after a year's exposure to the College Settlement's lively recreation campaign, converted two adjoining lots into its "Kip's Bay Playground." After Mrs. Simkhovitch became head resident at Greenwich House, she was instrumental in creating a neighborhood center out of Hudson Park. According to one contemporary, "if a tablet were to be erected to commemorate the service of Mary Simkhovitch and the settlement to the neighborhood, it might appropriately be placed in Hudson Park." Thanks to Greenwich House, there were "grouped about the park . . . in addition to the public school, public baths and a branch public library."[12]

As far as Mary Simkhovitch was concerned, the efforts of her settlement to reduce neighborhood congestion, establish school social centers, and create a "community spirit" were equally important.[13] Like most settlements, Greenwich House engaged in a bewildering array of activities. Every settlement fought for more and better schools, and it was common to find a settlement resident serving on local school boards. Settlements were active also in labor affairs. University Settlement, for example, encouraged the use of its rooms and other facilities by labor unions. Lillian Wald favored union organization among women and helped found Clinton Hall, a large assembly house in the East Side which served as headquarters for over twenty unions. The knowledge gained by College Settlement residents of violations of the factory laws resulted in an important investi-

11. Wald, *House on Henry Street*, 95.

12. Anne O'Hagan Shinn, "Where Barrow Street and Bleecker Meet," *Survey*, XXXIX, 247.

13. One of Greenwich House's contributions to "community spirit" was the establishment of the Greenwich Village Improvement Society, "the first neighborhood association in New York, to bring together citizens of all walks of life in the vicinity for the common object of securing improvements. . . ." Simkhovitch, *Neighborhood*, 98.

gation by Mary Van Kleeck.[14] Settlements usually participated in the work of civic reform organizations — the Consumers' League, Child Labor Committee, Women's Trade Union League, and others. The child labor cause was always a favorite; according to Lillian Wald, no single activity met with more enthusiastic and unanimous approval from residents. Appropriately, Florence Kelley, a veteran in the struggle for child labor reform, resided at Henry Street.

In contrast to many philanthropists and reformers, the settlement worker's passion for improvement did not spring out of superficial contact with the immigrant and working-class poor, out of some abstract conception of justice or some arbitrary definition of a normal standard of living. The reforms she promoted were grounded in a concrete knowledge of the people and institutions of her neighborhood, a knowledge unrivalled by any other category of middle-class reformers. Like the housing reformer, the settlement worker was anxious to Americanize the immigrant and disseminate middle-class norms of social behavior. She did not, however, overestimate the potentialities of housing codes, assuming that they could substitute for time, patience, personal influence and a wide variety of environmental changes.

[3]

The settlement was not a charitable institution, but residents often participated in the work of neighborhood charitable societies. The ties, for example, between the College Settlement and the Corlear's Hook District Committee of the COS were close. Once a week settlement workers traveled to the offices of the Committee to ponder relief cases and determine the most suitable form of. aid. Josephine Shaw Lowell, founder of the COS in 1882, was chairman of this Committee in the 1890's, and Mary Simkhovitch, one of the College Settlement group active in its affairs remembered that although Mrs. Lowell was sympathetic to the housing and recreation movements of the time, she "never forsook the humble work of help for people

14. Mary Van Kleeck, "Working Hours of Women in Factories," *Charities and the Commons*, XVII (1906-07), 13-21.

in need. Personal help was to her at the heart of all social problems."[15]

By 1900 Mrs. Lowell's Society had become one of the largest and most influential charity organization associations in the United States. It supplemented its basic casework activities with various work-relief and thrift programs, such as a woodyard, laundry, and penny provident bank. After Devine became general secretary in 1896, the Society became closely identified with a program of preventive social reform encompassing housing, court reform, and tuberculosis control. The employment of trained, paid agents was a conspicuous feature of the Society's operations. It pioneered in the development of professional social work education when it inaugurated a summer school of philanthropy in 1898.

The agents of the COS and other charity societies were probably more conscious than any other group of social reformers of the need to define the concept of a normal standard of living with some measure of precision. How could relief be "adequate," sufficient to cover at least the minimum needs of a family unless an agency knew the income required by the average working-class family for food, clothing, or shelter over a period of time in a particular community?

Equally important, the long range goal of the Charity Organization Society depended upon a sophisticated understanding of the factors which entered into a normal standard of living. The purpose of a society's casework as well as its preventive reform activities was to eliminate dependency and social maladjustment. Casework rehabilitated the individual while housing reform, better working conditions, minimum wage levels, workmen's compensation, or tuberculosis control prevented the physical and moral degeneration which led to dependence. Thus to rehabilitate and to reform efficiently, the social worker had to know the norm for which she was striving.

The interest of social workers in a normal standard of life resulted in a number of studies of working-class family budgets and costs of living in the first decade of the twentieth century.

15. Simkhovitch, *Neighborhood*, 72-73.

One of the earliest was Caroline Goodyear's analysis of the food purchasing and management of 100 tenement families. Miss Goodyear, a district agent of the New York COS, discovered that the average income of these families was only $9.00 a week. She estimated that insufficient or improper nourishment was the cause of poor health in thirty-seven families; in thirty-three of the families inadequate diet resulted in the "delicate" physique of two or more members.[16]

On a broader scale, Lee K. Frankel analyzed 100 families who had applied for relief to the United Hebrew Charities. According to his calculations, sickness was the immediate cause of distress in sixty-two cases, widowhood in fourteen and insufficient earnings in eighteen. Social conditions rather than personal moral inadequacy were responsible for the bulk of this dependency. Here were typical instances of "living, suffering human beings . . . submerged not because they are dissolute, submerged not by reason of any evil acts of their own, but because they live in an industrial environment, where it is a physical impossibility to eke out a decent living and to maintain a decent standard of existence." Frankel concluded that all philanthropic effort had to be expressed "in terms of exact justice." Every individual had a right to the opportunity to earn a livelihood "under conditions which permit of decent living, proper housing, wholesome nourishment and providing for the proverbial rainy day."[17] The intrinsically social roots of poverty and the right of every individual to a normal or minimum standard of living as the fruits of his labors were staple articles of faith among social workers.

They were the faith, certainly, of John A. Ryan, the Catholic social theorist who published his influential book on *A Living Wage* in 1906. Ryan summarized his view of the normal

16. Caroline Goodyear, "Special Report of an Investigation in Regard to the Purchase and Management of Food by One Hundred Tenement House Families, New York," COS, *Twenty-Third Annual Report*, 1904-05, 89, 90. For another discussion of the problem of food in relation to relief see Frederic Almy, "Standards of Living as Standards of Relief," *Charities and the Commons*, XXI (1908-09), 1227-29.

17. Lee K. Frankel, "The Relation Between Standards of Living and Standards of Compensation," New York State Conference of Charities and Correction, *Proceedings*, 1906, 30, 31.

standard of life before the National Conference of Charities and Correction. It had to include, first, a supply of food "sufficient and of such quality as to maintain health and industrial efficiency." Clothing had to be adequate "not only to the requirements of health and rudimentary comfort, but to those of decent social intercourse and recreation." No family had attained a normal standard if the mother or child had to work, or if provision could not be made for old age or emergencies. A normal standard implied also some surplus for the amenities of life, including a "regular supply of reading matter, membership in a church and in some other organizations, and as much recreation and amusement as are adequate to health and moderate contentment."[18]

No analysis of the cost of living or the normal standard of life was complete without some consideration of the housing problem. Housing reform and the charities intersected at this point of a common interest in minimum living standards. In Ryan's formulation "health and decency" required that "each family should have five, or at the very least four rooms." The dwelling had to provide not only elementary comfort, but had to "satisfy in some little degree the desire for beauty and refinement."[19] Social workers, a group in close personal contact with the poor, frequently stressed the importance of amenities which the sanitary minded housing reformer sometimes overlooked. Thus Mary Simkhovitch insisted that "tenement houses erected purely on sanitary lines without regard to the aesthetic demands of the tenants are a failure." Status and respectability demanded a parlor or front room.[20] Similarly, Florence Nesbitt of the United Charities of Chicago and author of a text on household management thought that a "pleasant sitting-room" was a "potent factor in preventing adolescent boys and girls from seeking all their pleasure on the street, or in the dance hall and pool room."[21]

18. John A. Ryan, "The Standard of Living and the Problem of Dependency," National Conference of Charities and Correction, *Proceedings*, 1907, 343, 344.
19. *Ibid.*, 343.
20. Simkhovitch, *The City Worker's World*, 33, 31.
21. Florence Nesbitt, *Household Management* (New York, 1918), 135.

The investigations into living costs by social workers resulted in various estimates of the minimum income required to maintain a normal standard in New York. After an intensive study of 391 workingmen's families Robert C. Chapin concluded that an absolute minimum of $900 a year was necessary in 1909 to "get food enough to keep soul and body together, and clothing and shelter enough to meet the most urgent demands of decency."[22] A committee of the New York State Conference of Charities and Correction, after a survey of 244 families, concluded that $825 would suffice for the average family of five.[23] Particularly significant was the discovery that families below the minimum estimate frequently relied upon lodgers to supplement their incomes while even families above the minimum who lived in better, higher-priced tenements often accommodated lodgers as well.

Chapin found that in Manhattan 61 of the 173 families who earned less than $900 took in lodgers, as well as 22 of the 70 families whose incomes ranged between $900 and $1,099. The surprisingly large number of families with higher incomes who accommodated lodgers were apparently forced to this expedient because of the higher rents they paid. Eighteen of the 22 families were in the highest rent brackets, $14 a month and up. The investigation by the New York State Conference of Charities and Correction confirmed the importance of the lodger in the working-class budget. Of the 72 families earning $600 to $700 a year, 17 kept lodgers. Twenty-six of the 79 families earning between $700 and $800 accommodated lodgers, as did

22. Robert C. Chapin, *The Standard of Living Among Workingmen's Families in New York City* (New York, 1909), 246.

23. "Report of the Special Committee on Standard of Living," New York State Conference of Charities and Correction, *Proceedings*, 1907 (reprinted in Chapin, *The Standard of Living Among Workingmen's Families in New York City*, 281). For other standard of living studies consult: Caroline Goodyear, "A Study of the Minimum Practicable Cost of an Adequate Standard of Living in New York City," New York State Conference of Charities and Correction, *Proceedings*, 1906, 40-53; Sue A. Clark and Edith Wyatt, *Making Both Ends Meet: Income and Outlay of New York Working Girls* (New York, 1911); Frank H. Streightoff, *The Standard of Living Among the Industrial People of America* (Boston, 1911); Louise B. More, *Wage-Earners' Budgets: A Study of Standards and Cost of Living in New York City* (New York, 1907).

25 of the 73 families in the $800 to $900 category. Thus lodgers were accepted not only by families with substandard income, but by those whose income reached and exceeded the minimum. When many families tried to raise their standard of living by moving into better housing, the increased rentals frequently forced them to sacrifice the privacy and extra living accommodations they had gained. The Charities' study concluded that the lodger problem, in most instances, was ultimately a question of wages. In all the groups, lodgers were "necessarily kept to meet additional expenditures." The social worker was conscious not only of the low-income family's need for sanitary, spacious and structurally sound housing, but of its need for an income sufficient to meet the inevitably higher rents.

[4]

Better housing and higher wages were just two concerns of the charity agent. Like the settlement worker, she was pledged to abolish all those social evils responsible for slums and poverty. If the tenement poor were to achieve a normal standard of living, then the case worker (the retailer) and the preventive social reformer (the wholesaler) would have to eliminate every obstacle which a callous industrial society placed in the worker's path.

The chief spokesman for the retail, casework approach to social improvement was Mary E. Richmond. Perhaps it would be more accurate to say that Miss Richmond approved of all wholesale methods but warned social workers not to ignore the beneficent potentialities of the retail method. She began her social work career in the adolescent years of the charity organization movement as assistant treasurer of the Baltimore COS in 1889, advancing to the post of general secretary in 1891. Her work attracted the attention of the Philadelphia Society for Organizing Charity, which acquired her as its secretary in 1900. Miss Richmond's administrative achievements in Baltimore and Philadelphia, along with her writings on charity organization and friendly visiting, eventually commanded the attention of the powerful and influential New Yorkers associated with the COS and the Russell Sage Foundation. When the COS publication *Charities* merged with the *Commons* of Chicago in 1905, Miss Richmond became field editor of the newly established Field Department (for organizing charity) of *Charities and the Commons*. After the Russell Sage Foundation was created in 1907, the directors decided to assume the work of promoting charity organization. Mary Richmond became director of the Foundation's Charity Organization Department in 1909.

Her interests traversed the entire range of charity and relief work. Although no one worked harder and more effectively to create professional standards in social work, she always returned to the volunteer and friendly visitor as a vital force in the social agency. The friendly visitor was the "good neighbor" whose personal work with dependent families was bridging the gap between classes which had emerged in an urban-industrial society. Tapping all the progressive influences in our culture, she worked "with the democratic spirit of the age to forward the advance of the plain and common people into a better and larger life."[24] To Miss Richmond's often-expressed regret, however, officialdom and professionalism were creating social work bureaucracies in which the volunteer was ignored entirely or severed from direct contact with clients. As early as 1905 she complained that "our national habit of thought has exalted the expert and the professional at the expense of the volunteer." Had we arrived at the point, she wondered, where "it is assumed that only officials should be permitted to be charitable?"[25] A few years later she warned against a "certain opinionated and self-righteous attitude in some of the trained social workers." The world was not yet a stage "upon which

24. Mary E. Richmond, *Friendly Visiting Among the Poor: A Handbook for Charity Workers* (New York, 1899), 195.

25. Mary E. Richmond, "The Retail Method of Reform," in Joanna C. Colcord and Ruth Z. S. Mann, eds., Mary E. Richmond, *The Long View: Papers and Addresses* (New York, 1930), 220.

we professional workers are to exercise our talents, while the volunteers do nothing but furnish the gate receipts and an open-mouthed admiration of our performances."[26]

The trend toward professional social work was inexorable, despite Mary Richmond's firm belief in the real or potential value of volunteer service. The complex social problems of the twentieth century and the ideal of "scientific philanthropy" promulgated by the charity organization societies imposed demands upon social workers, in terms of time, skill, and training, which the volunteer could not always satisfy. Edward T. Devine and the New York COS offered tribute to the importance of the volunteer but Devine also pointed out that "preference" was given in private agencies to "those who besides ordinary physical and moral qualifications can give some evidence of having studied the specific problems involved, of having had training for the work to be done."[27]

The lofty ideals of individual and family casework treatment adopted by charity organization societies encouraged the use of trained, paid workers. Basic to the casework process was the assumption that relief, at best, was merely a means to the end of permanent rehabilitation. The caseworker was obliged to uncover the fundamental reasons for destitution and dependency, and by removing them restore the client to social or financial independence. Her function, therefore, was not to separate the "worthy" from the "unworthy," or relentlessly expose frauds and professional paupers; nor was it the dispensation of money with a few kind words of sympathy and advice. Casework, as Mary Richmond defined it, was dedicated to bringing about *"better adjustments in the social relationships of individual men, women, or children."* This involved, "first, skill in discovering the social relationships by which a given personality had been shaped; second, ability to get at the central core of difficulty in these relationships; and third, power to

26. Mary E. Richmond, "The Case for the Volunteer," in Colcord and Mann, eds., *The Long View*, 345.

27. Edward T. Devine, "Social Ideals Implied in Present American Programs of Voluntary Philanthropy," American Sociological Society, *Publications*, VII (1912), 185-86.

utilize the direct action of mind upon mind in their adjustment."[28]

At this point, however, the caseworker's responsibilities had only begun. Her job, in Mary Richmond's view, implied not only subtle psychological insight allied with patient, painstaking work with individuals or families over a period of time, but participation in the entire fabric of social reconstruction. In order to help individuals most effectively, she had to consider the implications of changes for which her colleagues in preventive social reform were responsible. For example, the casework division of a charity organization society could anticipate increased burdens following the passage and enforcement of a child labor or tenement home-work law. If the society failed to help the poor adapt to the new situation, tiding many families over until they could tap new sources of income, the law might be discredited. At the same time the society had to ensure that relief did not accustom the families to a condition of permanent dependency.

Besides contributing to the success of preventive social work, the caseworker had to engage directly in preventive reform. She had to take a long range view of the tuberculosis problem, among others, and not remain content with relief to families whose wage-earner was incapacitated. The caseworker was expected to "meet the tuberculosis nurses more than half way in planning aid that will really cure the disease," incidentally acquiring experience that "reacts favorably upon [an agency's] relief program in all other cases of physical handicap."[29] Similarly, Mary Richmond viewed the caseworker as a "sort of deputy housing and sanitary inspector." She had to assume this obligation because housing affected "health, morals, economic efficiency, child-nurture, and the foundations of the family."[30] The caseworker, therefore, had to report unsanitary and dangerous housing conditions to the proper authorities and

28. Mary E. Richmond, "The Social Case Worker's Task," in Colcord and Mann, eds., *The Long View*, 398, 399.

29. Mary E. Richmond, "The Interrelation of Social Movements," in Colcord and Mann, eds., *The Long View*, 288.

30. Mary E. Richmond, "How Social Workers Can Aid Housing Reform," in Colcord and Mann, eds., *The Long View*, 325.

simultaneously assume an Octavia Hill role by helping tenants to "make necessary changes and adjustments."

However the caseworker contributed to social reform, her ultimate loyalty was to the retail method, to work with individuals and families. "Whatever the legislative and governmental changes of the next fifty years," Miss Richmond observed, "whatever the industrial changes, whatever the improvements in conditions and in folks, it will still be necessary to do different things for and with different people, if the results of our doing are to be more good than bad."[31] If the high standards of social casework adopted (as an ideal if not always in practice) by charity organization societies in the early twentieth century diminished the status of the volunteer philanthropist, there is no doubt that such standards represented a response to the knotty social problems of an urban society as well as the new understanding of personality afforded by psychiatry and psychology. The caseworker was responsible now for a realistic assessment of her clients' needs based upon thorough investigation of their social environment and social relationships. Assistance, at least in theory, was supposed to be adequate and appropriate — adequate in relation to the normal standard of living for a community, and appropriate in terms of the material or counseling services which could best insure permanent rehabilitation or social adjustment. Here again was the kind of social control for which housing codes or any form of restrictive legislation could not substitute.

The concept of the normal standard of living was fundamental to Mary Richmond's theory of casework. "Social rehabilitation, like rehabilitation in health," she believed, "must proceed from the normal as its starting point toward the normal as its goal."[32] Edward T. Devine, a most distinguished exponent of preventive social work in the early twentieth century, shared this assumption. Two years after Devine had assumed his post as general secretary of the New York COS, the agency

31. Mary E. Richmond, "The Case Worker in a Changing World," in Colcord and Mann, eds., *The Long View*, 376.
32. Mary E. Richmond, "On the Art of Beginning in Social Work," in Colcord and Mann, eds., *The Long View*, 317.

launched its famous adventure in housing reform. No issue of interest to social reformers escaped his attention. Like Riis and Robert W. de Forest, president of the COS, he was among the most versatile handymen in the world of philanthropy. Devine's principle of preventive philanthropy, of the charity to abolish charity, was a second leading theme of early twentieth century social work (never wholly at rest with the casework, retail method advanced by Mary Richmond). According to Devine, the key to history was exploitation and the struggle against it. Behind every form of degeneracy and dependency he saw lurking some entrenched pecuniary interest — the tenement landlord who obstructed the establishment of minimum standards, the manufacturer too miserly to install safety devices for his employees, the corporation which refused to ease the tempo of work for its women and child employees, the department store owners whose prosperity was sucked from the sweat and wages of shopgirls. The social worker's task was to diminish the power of all those interests which obstructed the "conservation and development" of the human personality, while advancing a "recognition of normal standards of comfort, normal standards of activity, normal standards of life."[33]

The only safe generalization about the poor, Devine argued, was their poverty. The Darwinian categories, the divisions of society into the fit and unfit, superior and inferior, were untenable in view of the social handicaps which confronted them. More to the point, the poor like every other social group included the weak and strong, cowardly and heroic, vicious and gentle, lazy and ambitious, miserly and generous. The "differentiating factors" between them and the rest of society were "economic rather than moral or religious, social rather than personal, accidental and remediable rather than characteristic and fundamental."[34] Mostly, the poor were a product of their environment and opportunities — an environment subject to the beneficent touch of the social engineer and opportunities capable of infinite expansion.

33. Edward T. Devine, *Social Forces* (New York, 1910), 62.
34. *Ibid.*, 47.

Devine specified ten prerequisites to the just and prosperous community of the future. Taken together they constituted almost the complete social reform program of the Progressive era, the index of the social worker's achievement and the measure of the normal standard of life. In Devine's normal community a sound physical heredity would be the birthright of every child.[35] The privilege of the feeble-minded, alcoholic, or syphilitic to breed would be carefully controlled. A protected, nurtured childhood was next, and implied first and foremost, the abolition of child labor. Let the mills, factories, shops, and mines rise or fall, prosper or perish, without sacrificing the nation's youth. At the opposite extreme, the nation had to benefit more than in the past from the experience and work capacity of middle-aged and older citizens. If employers could be persuaded to hire older men and women, then family income and savings could be increased and the family strengthened "to the third and fourth generation."

The normal community would be safe from preventable disease. Progressive social workers were acutely conscious of health and sanitary problems in relation to the social environment. The real race suicide, Devine argued, was not the failure to propagate, but the failure to protect the people's health through appropriate social measures: popular education in the prevention and care of disease, particularly tuberculosis; the abolition of slums or at least universal minimum standards in matters of light, ventilation, sanitation and waste facilities; the reduction of industrial accidents and disease through legislative action. Ill health, observed Devine, was not only the "most constant of the attendants of poverty," but a fundamental cause.

In the fifth place, Devine predicted "freedom from professional crime" in the normal community. Just as he viewed prevention as the basic weapon against poverty and the "dominant note" of modern philanthropy, he anticipated the time when our prisons and reformatories would become true correctional institutions. They would seek to reform rather than merely

35. For Devine's ten points see his book *Misery and Its Causes* (New York, 1909), 241-51.

segregate the offender. Devine's interest in criminal problems was reflected in the establishment in 1910 of a Criminal Courts Committee within the COS. The Committee, as we have mentioned, was particularly concerned with the Police or Magistrates' courts, which were "indissolubly bound up with the improvement of social conditions." These courts represented American justice to the "ignorant and foreign born."[36]

When old age, sickness, accident, or unemployment struck a family in the normal community, it would be protected by an elaborate system of social insurance. Children would not be forced to work and deprived of their education by the death or incapacity of the breadwinner, nor mothers deprived of the right to produce and rear healthy children because they left home to suffer the stain of sterile, time-consuming work.

Seventh, "elementary education shall be adopted to present-day needs and resources" in the normal community. The strict enforcement of child labor laws would be coupled with schools adequate in number and attractive enough in curriculum to hold the child's interest. A vocational training program would become a significant feature of the curriculum, and by teaching the child a trade would save him from the dead ends of messenger, newsboy, factory automaton, or warehouse clerk.

In the normal community, a "liberal relief system" would prevail for the protection of the individual. But fortunately, in the ninth place, a "standard of living high enough to insure full nourishment, reasonable recreation, shelter," would minimize the necessity for relief. Finally, a socialized religious ethos would inspire the philanthropic work of the community. A "militant, aggressive religious faith" would protect agencies from the senility of mechanized efficiency, unimaginative routine, and the ruthlessness of the charity lacking sympathy and compassion.

[5]

After Alice Woodbridge, secretary of the Working Women's Society, prepared a report on the working conditions of New

36. COS, *Twenty-Ninth Annual Report for the Year Ending September 30, 1911*, 71.

York shop girls in 1890, she turned to Josephine Shaw Lowell for assistance; and Mrs. Lowell, with her infinite capacity for moral indignation, immediately adopted the struggle of the shop girls as her own. Enlisting the cooperation of Dr. Mary Putnam Jacobi, she called a meeting of leisure-class women to consider the predicament of their less fortunate sisters. They were startled by Alice Woodbridge's account of the harsh life of department store employees. None of them "had ever dreamed that women and children working in retail stores were often obliged to work under conditions injurious to health and morals."[37] The aroused humanitarians sponsored a mass meeting at Chickering Hall in May 1890. The New York Consumers' League was born when a committee was appointed to cooperate with the Working Women's Society in preparing a list of stores which treated their employees fairly.

The Consumers' League, formally organized in January 1891, ranked high in power and prestige among the reform associations of the Progressive era. It became one of the most effective participants in the combat waged by the settlements, charities, and housing reformers to improve the living conditions of the tenement poor. The general object of the League was to "ameliorate the condition of the women and children employed in New York City, by helping to form a public opinion which will lead consumers to recognize their responsibilities." The problem of the working woman was the League's pet concern, for there was "no limit beyond which the wages of women may not be depressed down, unless artificially maintained at a living rate by combinations, either of the workers themselves, or of consumers." The League relied, in part, upon economic pressure to accomplish its ends. It prepared a "white list" of department stores which met the League's minimum standards as to working conditions and hours, and recommended these establishments to the general public.

The League's ultimate sanction, however, was ethical. It relied, in the final analysis, upon the conscience of the public:

37. Maud Nathan, *The Story of an Epoch-Making Movement* (Garden City, N. Y., 1926), 20.

"We beg of all dreamers to wake, to study conditions for themselves. And then, perhaps, when they provide for their wants, they will remember that everything they purchase is the product of human toil; and in buying the article, they will see to it that they are not buying tortured flesh and blood as well."[38] The League maintained that modern commerce and industry had severed all moral bonds and mutual responsibilities among producer, consumer, and employee. Their relationship was impersonal. The merchant or manufacturer had become less interested in the quality of his product or the welfare of his employees than in underselling his competitors. The consumer, regrettably, was only interested in satisfying her wants as economically as possible, not in the conditions under which articles were produced or sold. The consumer's selfishness often left the producer no choice but to employ and exploit women and child workers; he had to satisfy a fickle, bargain hunting public as best he could. If the consumer could be aroused from her ignorance and indifference, she could become a powerful instrument of reform. The manufacturer and merchant would have to heed her demands for an end to tenement home work and child labor, for shorter hours and higher wages, for safe and comfortable working conditions.

The ethical idealism personified by the Consumers' League idea spread from New York to other cities and states. In 1899 the National League was formed. Florence Kelley, a resident of Hull House and former chief factory inspector for Illinois, moved to New York to serve as its executive secretary. Establishing her home at Lillian Wald's Henry Street Settlement, she worked at the United Charities Building, which also accommodated the COS, Association for Improving the Condition of the Poor, and Child Labor Committee. Through Florence Kelley the powerful reform impulse generated by New York's settlements and charities passed from the National Consumers' League into the sixty leagues in twenty different states which had organized by 1909. New York's pioneer league, headed by Maud Nathan, could always depend upon Florence Kelley and

38. The Consumers' League of the City of New York, Report, 1909, 21.

the National League to underwrite its efforts to raise the general standard of living. Among its many activities, three were particularly relevant to the welfare of the tenement population: the improvement of women's working conditions, the regulation of sweatshop or tenement home work, and the crusade for pure food.

Five years of agitation by the New York League on the subject of department store working conditions resulted in the passage of a Mercantile Inspection Law by the state legislature in 1896. It limited the work week of shop girls to sixty hours and required employers to provide seats for female employees. The law vested enforcement power in the Board of Health, already overburdened with a multitude of housing and sanitary inspection duties. Even though the Board appointed Maud Nathan, president of the League, as an inspector, the League fought to have enforcement responsibilities transferred to the State Department of Labor. Much to the Consumers' League's satisfaction, this was accomplished in 1908. Supplementing official inspectors, representatives of the League visited department stores to ferret out violations of mercantile and child labor laws, and obtain the facts upon which further reform legislation could be based. The League combined these activities with a persistent campaign of consumer education. It constantly reminded consumers to shop early for Christmas and Easter in order to reduce the last minute rush, to avoid shopping on Saturdays or after 6 P.M., and to refuse to receive deliveries made at night.

The Consumers' League was interested in wages as well as general working conditions and hours. In 1908, three years before the "white slave" hysteria ushered in an era of vice commissions and investigations whose recommendations frequently included minimum wage levels, Maud Nathan implied a casual connection between low wages and prostitution.[39] In 1909 the League's Committee on Investigations complained that many of the saleswomen in seventeen department stores earned only $6.00 a week, a "wage which affords the absolutely

39. The Consumers' League of the City of New York, *Report*, 1908, 11.

self-supporting girl a mere economic *existence*, and exposes her to very great temptation and peril."[40] The League thus plunged into a campaign to raise the working girl's wage, arguing that too many of them earned only $6.00 a week when $8.00 or $9.00 was the least they required for support. Although several states secured minimum wage boards before World War I, the efforts of the Consumers' League and allied organizations such as the Child Labor Committee and Women's Trade Union League to secure similar legislation for New York State failed.[41] The League had to remain content with improvements in working conditions and hours.

The efforts of the Consumers' League to brighten the life of the working girl included migrations to Albany to oppose undesirable legislation. Thus in 1902 the League successfully thwarted an attempt to exempt all women over twenty-one from hour restrictions. Another time the League took the initiative in defeating a proposal permitting a sixty-six hour work week for women engaged in the manufacture of perishable, seasonal goods.[42] Labor legislation, like housing codes, had to be carefully guarded against undesirable amendment.

The struggle of the Consumers' League to raise the living standard of the tenement mother and daughter through restrictive labor laws was paralleled by a crusade against tenement-home work. In the tenements virtually no controls existed over the working conditions and hours of women. The League crossed paths with the New York and National Child Labor Committees in this fight against the sweatshop, for of all the evils of tenement home work none was more conspicuous than

40. The Consumers' League of the City of New York, *Report*, 1909, 23.

41. More than a dozen states enacted women's minimum wage laws in the decade following 1913. In most states, payment of the minimum by employers was compulsory. The Supreme Court affirmed the constitutionality of the laws in 1917. Many of the minimum wage commissions were established in 1913, when California, Colorado, Minnesota, Nebraska, Oregon, Washington, and Wisconsin acted and when Illinois, Indiana, Ohio, and Connecticut appointed committees to investigate the subject. See Florence Kelley, "Status of Legislation in the United States," *Survey*, XXXIII (1914-15), 487-89; and Robert W. Bruère, "The Meaning of the Minimum Wage," *Harper's New Monthly Magazine*, CXXXII (Jan., 1916), 276-82.

42. The Consumers' League of the City of New York, *Report*, 1902, 16, *Report*, 1907, 15.

the exploitation of the child. The abolition of child labor was posed as the consumer's greatest challenge and most profound moral responsibility.

Dr. Annie S. Daniel, a foe of the sweating system since the 1890's whose experience as visiting tenement physician for the New York Dispensary for Women and Children had convinced her that nothing short of total prohibition would suffice, summarized the evils of tenement home work as they appeared to reformers around 1905. First, there were the long hours of toil. In the busy season, Dr. Daniel reported, a "woman will frequently not have more than five hours rest in the twenty-four." The long hours, however, were not relieved by payment of a living wage. The amount varied with the kind of work, "from 1½ cents an hour to 10 cents — very rarely more." Dr. Daniel complained that "in order to make the income reach the outgo, boarders, lodgers, two and three families huddle together, until not even the ghost of decency remains." Finally, children were drawn into the tenement home work economy from the moment they could perform the simplest tasks. Even the three year old could straighten tobacco leaves while the four year old could put the cover on boxes.[43] In one instance an investigator for the Consumers' League encountered a seven year old girl, already a four year veteran of garment manufacture, who had sat "day after day with little legs crossed, pulling out bastings from garments." Her legs, contorted from lack of use, had become paralyzed.[44]

The Consumers' League initially endeavored to improve tenement home work conditions through regulation. Since 1899 New York State law had required the licensing of individual tenement apartments to insure that the working environment did not menace the health of consumer or worker. The Consumers' League realized that such regulation was unsatisfactory, for it was difficult to enforce and did not prevent home work in an apartment even though unsanitary conditions prevailed elsewhere in a tenement. Thus in 1903 the League prepared

43. Annie S. Daniel, "The Wreck of the Home: How Wearing Apparel is Fashioned in the Tenements," *Charities*, XIV (1905), 624-29.
44. The Consumers' League of the City of New York, *Report*, 1906, 17-18.

legislation aimed at licensing the entire tenement rather than individual apartments. Lawrence Veiller perfected the bill which was pushed through the legislature with the assistance of League representatives. It was not long, however, before the Consumers' League decided that licensing was futile and moved towards a position of total prohibition.

Beginning in the fall of 1906, Mary Van Kleeck's investigation into tenement home work confirmed the failure of regulation. The Van Kleeck study, which was sponsored by the College Settlements Association, the New York and National Child Labor Committees, and the New York and National Consumers' Leagues, showed that "work in unlicensed houses is not prevented, nor is the list of articles named in the law inclusive enough to regulate all existing forms of home work." The Department of Labor's inspection staff was totally inadequate to "comply even with that provision of the law requiring that every licensed tenement be inspected twice a year." Nor did the licensing laws strike at the roots of the tenement home work evil: the long hours, low pay, and, above all, exploitation of young children. The exploitation of these children, most of them between five and ten years of age, was the supreme evil. It "ought to be a spur to unremitting effort against a system of industry which makes child labor possible in New York state, where public opinion years ago demanded its prohibition."[45] In light of the facts uncovered by the Van Kleeck study, it was apparent that the "licensing of a tenement for home work would seem to be scarcely more than a form."[46] The Consumers' League decided to press for abolition of a system which permitted manufacturers of garments, food and tobacco products, artificial flowers, toys, and other commodities to exploit the labor of women and children as well as men. In alliance with the Child Labor Committees, the League

45. Mary Van Kleeck, "Child Labor in New York City Tenements" (Pamphlet, 1908, reprinted from *Charities and the Commons,* Jan. 18, 1908). A few years later the author examined one branch of the home work industry in her book *Artificial Flower Makers* (New York, 1913). She found that more than half the flower making trade was carried on at home. Only 24 of 114 firms investigated did all their work at the plant.
46. The Consumers' League of the City of New York, *Report,* 1907, 41.

achieved a major, if not a total, victory in 1913. The manufacture of babies' and children's clothing was prohibited in tenements, and the employment of children under fourteen was forbidden.

The 1913 legislation also prohibited the manufacture of food products in tenements. Indeed, the efforts of the Consumers' League to insure a pure and wholesome food supply for the tenement population was of fundamental importance in its general crusade to raise living standards. The New York League had launched its pure food campaign in 1905 with the appointment of a Committee on Food Investigation. The establishment of this Committee grew out of an investigation of tenement food preparation by Mary Sherman of the National League. Her exposure of the filthy conditions under which macaroni, nuts, candy, and ice cream were prepared in tenements startled New Yorkers. In one case a macaroni manufacturer went straight from his child stricken with diphtheria to his macaroni machine. Similarly, an Italian on Oliver Street suffering from tuberculous joints picked nuts from shells.[47] Too often, the New York League observed, the workers "live in small, overcrowded rooms that are far from clean." The situation menaced the health of tenement consumers (as well as others who did not realize that their neatly packaged food had been fondled by diseased hands in filthy surroundings). "Nothing," concluded the Consumers' League, "more vitally affects the wage-earning class than this question of food. One of the beneficent purposes of the League will have been finally achieved when the poor consumer can be as certain of securing a supply of clean, pure food, as is his more fortunate brother."[48]

The Consumers' League did not restrict its interest to the problem of·tenement food manufacture, but watched over all phases of the preparation and distribution of the city's food supply. It requested the Health Department to enforce more rigorously the provisions of the sanitary code regulating foods exposed in streets, pushcarts, and stores. The Committee on

47. Mary Sherman, "Manufacturing of Foods in the Tenements," *Charities and the Commons*, XV (1905-06), 670.
48. The Consumers' League of the City of New York, *Report*, 1906, 34.

Food Investigation dispatched its own investigators to survey conditions in markets and streets. The fruit vendor received special attention. In many instances he was "filthy in person as well as in practices." The tenement districts, where he "holds sway," would be better off if the sale of food from pushcarts was prohibited entirely, the Committee believed.[49]

The food inspection work was supplemented by a broad educational campaign. In the summer cards were distributed to markets and stores throughout the city reminding proprietors to keep their food clean and protected from insects. The League sponsored a series of lectures on food problems in cooperation with the settlements, public schools, New York Federation of Women's Clubs, and other civic organizations. In 1910 the League's Food Committee began an investigation of cellar bake-shops, a major source of supply for the tenement population's bread. It publicized the fact that virtually no such bakeries were "clean and wholesome enough to be desirable places for the making of bread for this great city."[50] The conditions exposed by the League contributed to a stricter enforcement of the city's sanitary code, for towards the end of 1912 the Board of Health issued 287 public nuisance and vacation orders against offending bakeries.

[6]

Like the settlements, charities, and housing movements, the Consumers' League embodied the struggle of middle-class reformers to heal the wounds of an industrial society whose class divisions were exascerbated by ethnic cleavages. In the cities, where the wounds cut deepest, these middle-class reformers organized into philanthropic pressure groups which endeavored to convert American society to the morality of social cooperation in place of the older agrarian individualism. Because society had become highly specialized, it had become interdependent; and men had to assume a moral responsibility, a social stewardship, over the activities of their fellows. The obligation of social stewardship applied especially to the consumer. Because her

49. The Consumers' League of the City of New York, *Report*, 1909, 29, 30.
50. The Consumers' League of the City of New York, *Report*, 1910, 33.

purchasing decisions determined what would be produced, she was as responsible as the manufacturer or merchant for the conditions under which goods were manufactured and distributed. The thoughtless, self-centered consumer who condoned the exploitation of child labor or the tenement system of manufacture bathed deep in ignominy.

The middle-class reformers of the Progressive era struggled to envelop the entire fabric of social relationships with the morality of social cooperation and stewardship, to substitute the ideal of service for that of personal profit and power. As Felix Adler, chairman of the National Child Labor Committee, explained: "It is because the chief end of life is held to be money-making that the young child cannot too soon be induced or forced to dedicate himself to the chief end of life."[51] Once we realized that life's purpose was not personal aggrandizement but service, not only child labor but every form of social and economic injustice would disappear.

The Progressive era spawned an army of dedicated, professional reformers imbued with the ideal of service — service to the ill-housed and ill-fed and to the community whose vision of a classless, democratic society was belied by the stratifications of race and class. Reform had to be full-time, organized, and proficient because of the alleged exploiters: the corrupt politicians, the monster corporations against whom the individual was powerless, the tenement builders and landlords unwilling or unable to maintain minimum standards, the garment, food or flower manufacturers who prospered from the desperation of tenement women and children whose breadwinner could not earn a living wage. In a sense the professional reformers, men and women like Edward T. Devine, Mary Richmond, Lawrence Veiller, Florence Kelley, or Josephine Goldmark, were humanitarian efficiency experts anxious to organize the social environment in such a way that every individual could attain his maximum physical, mental and cultural development.

It is not surprising that the crusade of Progressive reformers

51. Felix Adler, "Annual Address of the Chairman," *The Child Labor Bulletin*, IV (Aug., 1915), 95.

for an efficient utilization of the nation's physical and human resources led to an interest in social planning. As Devine interpreted the social worker's faith, progress was possible, but not inevitable. It was "dependent upon our efforts. We [were] the architects and builders of our own well-being and that of our posterity."[52] The Progressive commitment to planning was reflected in the conservation movement of the era. Samuel P. Hays has explained that the conservation movement was, in large measure, an effort of scientists, engineers, and other technicians to substitute planned, centrally controlled resource development for the individual, inefficient, and wasteful exploitation of the past.[53] The social ideal of the disinterested technician, the impartial servant of society, greatly influenced the thinking of conservation leaders, who viewed the expert as the key figure in a new age of planned economic growth, the saviour of a society which would no longer afford the physical and human waste of days gone by.

The concept of a planned urban society also arose during the Progressive era. Housing reformers grasped the planning movement as a young but powerful ally. They joined with the engineers, architects, and landscape architects who provided its leadership in a common effort to rebuild our cities and direct their future growth. City planning became a new ingredient in the philosophy and methods of housing reformers, who now realized that the maximum effectiveness of their own work depended upon its coordination with other elements of urban life. Along with conservation, the city planning movement symbolized the Progressive infatuation with efficient social organization. In both cases the morality of social responsibility and cooperation had superseded that of agrarian individualism.

52. Edward T. Devine, *The Normal Life* (New York, 1915), 5.
53. Samuel P. Hays, *Conservation and the Gospel of Efficiency: The Progressive Conservation Movement, 1890-1920* (Cambridge, Mass., 1959).

Progressivism, Planning and Housing

*And when the heavens rolled away and St.
John beheld the new Jerusalem, so a new
vision of a new London, a new Washington, Chicago, or New York breaks with
the morning's sunshine upon the degradation, discomfort, and baseness of modern
city life. There are born a new dream and
a new hope.*

CHARLES M. ROBINSON,
Modern Civic Art, 1918

[1]

The initial spur to city planning in the United States came from
the spectacular Chicago Fair of 1893. Chicago's "White City"
has been aptly described as "a laboratory — a testing ground —
not only for the problems of civic design but also for determining the best hygienic and protective methods for urban
application."[1] Thanks to the skill of its chief architect, Daniel
H. Burnham, and landscape architect, Frederick Law Olmsted,
the planned unity and classic dignity of the Fair became for
Americans "a revelation" and "a benediction." Here, for the
first time, they glimpsed "what an ideal city might be."[2]

The Fair did not represent simply an experiment in civic
art and architecture. Its organizers faced many practical problems: police and fire protection, the creation of water, sewerage,
and transportation systems, the provision of cultural and recreational facilities. The Columbian Exposition suggested that the

1. Maurice F. Neufeld, The Contribution of the World's Columbian Exposition of 1893 to the Idea of a Planned Society in the United States, Ph.D. Thesis
(University of Wisconsin, 1935), 133.
2. John Coleman Adams, "What a Great City Might Be — a Lesson from the
White City," *New England Magazine*, XX (1896), 10, 3.

217

aesthetic and utilitarian could be coordinated to produce a higher form of urban civilization. That "glorious fairy city which sprung up almost overnight in Jackson Park, in Chicago"[3] was America's hope and promise of what the twentieth-century city might be.

The classic facade of the White City has been criticized by some, notably Lewis Mumford, as a dubious contribution to America's architectural and civic development. The architects had "chanted a Roman litany above the Babel of individual styles." The World's Fair triumph had "suggested to the civic enthusiast that every city might become a fair: it introduced the notion of·the City Beautiful as a sort of municipal cosmetic."[4] Mumford's savage critique has validity. It is true that the classic vogue in architecture and the City Beautiful concept in civic design which sprang from the Fair had certain baneful consequences. The Fair, however, performed one valuable service which could excuse many faults; it planted the seed basic to the art and science of city planning. From the Exposition came the realization that a city is an organism of inter-related, interdependent parts whose efficiency depends upon planned and orderly growth.

The dominating quality of the Exposition, that which made the most lasting impression upon spectators, was its unity. "It remained for Chicago," the president of the American Civic Association observed, "to awaken our dormant sense of form and appropriateness in architecture and environment, and to show what planning could accomplish."[5] Never before, affirmed a contemporary, "was the unity of a single design so triumphant." The lesson of the Fair was the dependence of the city upon "proportion, balance, and ordered suitability of parts."[6] However one might disparage the somewhat sterile classicism

3. George B. Ford, "Digging Deeper in City Planning," *American City*, VI (1912), 557.

4. Lewis Mumford, *Sticks and Stones: A Study of American Architecture and Civilization* (Dover Publications: New York, 1955), 127, 130-31.

5. J. Horace McFarland, "The Growth of City Planning in America," *Charities and the Commons*, XVIX (1907-08), 1525.

6. Alice Freeman Palmer, "Some Lasting Results of the World's Fair," *Forum*, XVI (1893-94), 520.

of the Fair, its ultimate influence was salutary. In contrast to the typically ugly, sprawling, squalid American industrial city of the nineteenth century, the White City was a beatific vision of blue lagoons, luxurious green lawns, and monumental splendor. Americans saw in its planned beauty, order and picturesque design an irresistible alternative to the dirt, monotony and pervading dinginess of their existing municipalities. This was the real meaning of the Chicago Fair; it created new ideals and standards by which to measure the quality of urban life.

Until about 1909 the City Beautiful was the principal expression of the newly discovered passion for planned civic growth.[7] Cities hired architects to produce elaborate schemes for civic centers, tree-lined boulevards in the European manner, parks, and a variety of other forms of ornamentation: public art, plant decoration, sculpture, street signs, even lamp posts. The City Beautiful also included several negative ideals, such as noise abatement and the control of street advertising.

Besides Daniel H. Burnham, the chief exponent of the City Beautiful for many years was Charles Mulford Robinson, a Rochester, New York, architect. A prolific author, Robinson labored to convert "the spirit of aesthetic renaissance," "civic art's transforming touch," into a secular municipal religion. For Robinson the City Beautiful was not merely an aesthete's delight, a genteel pastime, but an inspired social vision: "The moral and spiritual standards of the people will be advanced by this art, and their political ideals will rise with a civic pride and a community spirit born of the appreciation that they are citizens of 'no mean city.' "[8] The tenement population, particularly, would benefit from the sensual delights of the City Beautiful: ". . . to make the homes not only livable but attractive, to awaken ambition, to encourage the life of the beautiful — would not this, this glorious aggregate, be the first task that civic art would undertake?"[9] Robinson and other exponents of

7. Consult the issues of *Municipal Affairs* (1897-1902) for many articles relevant to the City Beautiful.

8. Charles M. Robinson, *The Improvement of Towns and Cities or the Practical Basis of Civic Aesthetics*, 4th ed., (New York, 1913), 211, 200, 292.

9. Charles M. Robinson, *Modern Civic Art or the City Made Beautiful*, 4th ed. (New York, 1918), 247.

the City Beautiful interpreted civic art much as Jacob Riis interpreted nature; it was a moral force able to elevate the character and ideals of those touched by its magic wand.

In time the almost exclusive dominion of the City Beautiful was challenged. After 1909 the "City Useful" overtook, then surpassed the City Beautiful in the theoretical formulations of city planners, if not always in their actual plans.[10] The desire for urban unity and harmony aroused by the Chicago Fair achieved a more mature expression in the new utilitarian-oriented planning movement.

There were several reasons for the new point of view. The City Beautiful was a narrow and pathetically fragile ideal, remote from business, commerce, industry, transportation, poverty, and similar mundane but integral features of urban life. Once the glow of the White City had dimmed, the need to incorporate these features into a planning scheme became apparent. In addition, new men who achieved prominence in planning insisted that the City Beautiful must be subordinate to the City Useful if the goal of "a better, more orderly, more livable city"[11] was to be attained. Conspicuous among the champions of utilitarian planning was John Nolen, a Massachusetts landscape architect and founding father of modern planning in America. Very different from Robinson's ideal was the social and practical emphasis of Nolen. The absence of beauty troubled him less than the faulty street arrangement, the condition of the waterfronts, the uncoordinated transportation system, the "unsanitary and demoralizing influences of slums."[12] If housing reform in the broadest sense signified the

10. In the plans made for cities after 1909, there are still many traces of the City Beautiful concept. However, the overwhelmingly utilitarian emphasis in theory can readily be ascertained by reference to National Conference on City Planning, *Proceedings*, 1910-17. Most of the articles and papers dealt with practical problems of city planning. Also, *American City*, 1909-17; *The City Plan*, and *Housing Betterment*, the organs respectively of the National Conference on City Planning and the National Housing Association; the papers of planners at the National Housing Association published in the annual *Proceedings; Charities and the Commons* and its successor, *Survey*.

11. Arnold W. Brunner, "The Meaning of City Planning," National Conference on City Planning, *Proceedings*, 1912, 22.

12. John Nolen, *New Ideals in the Planning of Cities, Towns, and Villages* (New York, 1919), 17.

belief that the health and welfare of the people in an urban-industrial society were too important to remain in the hands of the entrepreneur exclusively, the utilitarian-minded city planning movement after 1909 evolved from the conviction that urban growth in general was too important to continue unplanned and uncoordinated, the product of countless short-sighted and selfish private decisions.

[2]

Most significant in explaining the character of the planning movement after 1909, particularly in relation to housing, were two European developments. The City Beautiful remained dominant until planners and housing reformers had digested the implications of the garden city in England and the zoning program in Germany. The garden city was the product of a book by an obscure court stenographer named Ebenezer Howard; and Germany's zoning legislation unfolded from the experiments of Franz Adickes, Bürgermeister of Altona, a Hamburg suburb, and then of Frankfurt-am-Main. The concept of the garden city and zoning equipped American planners, for the first time, with a concrete formula for urban reconstruction based upon dispersion of population and industry.

In his book *Tomorrow* (1898), Howard proposed an alternative to city or country life possessing the advantages of both, but none of their inconveniences. The alternative would be a magnet, producing the "spontaneous movement" of people from crowded cities to the country. "Town and country *must be married*," Howard affirmed, for out of the union would "spring a new hope, a new life, a new civilisation."[13]

Howard outlined a plan for a garden city limited in population to about 32,000. Neither the first nor future garden cities would expand beyond that size, for any excess population would simply serve as the nucleus for an entirely new community. Each garden city would be surrounded forever by an agricultural belt producing food for the community and pre-

13. Ebenezer Howard, *Garden Cities of To-morrow* (London, 1902), 15, 18 (3rd ed. of *To-morrow: A Peaceful Path to Reform*).

venting suburban sprawl. Howard located factories, warehouses, and other business establishments in the outer ring of his circular city, separated from the people's homes in the inner circle. Besides homes, the inner circle would include attractive radial boulevards, parks, and civic, cultural, and shopping facilities.

Garden city was to be governed by a central council composed of the officers of various departments elected by the inhabitants. Its revenues depended entirely upon rents. Since the community as a whole owned the land, any increase in its value would revert back to the people. Thus no "unearned increment" would flow into the pockets of landlords and speculators as a consequence of the community's growth and prosperity.

A year after Howard's book appeared, a Garden City Association in England was formed to promote the plan. Its efforts resulted in 1903 in the formation of the First Garden City, Ltd., which purchased and developed on garden city principles a 4,000-acre estate at Letchworth. Letchworth suggested to planners and housing reformers in America and Europe that garden city was no idle, impractical dream fit only for a small cult of enthusiasts. It was a financial and social success.[14]

Garden city's appeal to reformers in England and America is not difficult to explain. On paper, at least, it was a simple scheme. One had only to grasp a few elementary principles, locate a site, and gather sufficient funds to purchase and develop it. The cooperative benefits of garden city impressed a generation of municipal reformers who attributed many of the evils of urban life to unsocialized individualism and private greed. Here at last was a way to insure that landed wealth created by the community would return to its source to benefit all the people instead of a few monopolists. At the same time, however, there was plenty of scope for private initiative in the agricultural, industrial, and retail trades integral to garden city's

14. For accounts of the evolution of the Garden City movement in England consult: C. B. Purdom, *The Garden City: A Study in the Development of a Modern Town* (London, 1913); E. G. Culpin, *The Garden City Movement Up-to-Date* (London, 1912); *Town Planning in Theory and Practice* (a report of a conference arranged by the Garden City Association, October 25, 1907).

economy. The balance between industry and agriculture in Howard's machine-age utopia particularly interested a generation which feared that man was losing touch with nature, stifling himself in the smoke and soot of the great industrial city.[15] Finally, garden city was influential as a thoroughly planned community. In contrast to Chicago's White City, an ephemeral fairyland meant to vanish when the Fair had ended, people actually lived and worked there. It was the most concrete example of the potentialities inherent in city planning for creating a new civilization.

Certain features of the garden city plan particularly impressed housing reformers. The limitations on population and the number of houses per acre seemed an ideal system for preventing the congestion out of which the slum had evolved. Equally important, the garden city program, revolutionary in principle but conservative in method, could be used against existing slums. It did not involve expensive and confiscatory slum clearance schemes in the core of the city where congestion had inflated land and property values. If enough of the urban population could be removed to garden cities, the inflated structure of values would collapse of its own weight. Land would become cheap enough to house people comfortably again, even in the heart of the city.

Although the garden city was the ideal goal, two modifications of its principles received even greater attention from planners and housing reformers in America. The garden suburb and garden village involved the identical end of urban decentralization, but were less ambitious in scope and thus were better suited for immediate application. The garden suburb was a planned residential community on the outskirts of a city. Although it was only an appendage which lacked the self-sufficiency of garden city, it seemed a practical way to house a sizeable percentage of the urban working population in attrac-

15. In Howard's words: "It is well-nigh universally agreed by men of all parties, not only in England, but all over Europe and America and our colonies, that it is deeply to be deplored that the people should continue to stream into the already over-crowded cities, and should thus further deplete the country districts." Howard, *Garden Cities of To-Morrow*, 10-11.

tive surroundings. The inspiration for the garden suburb also derived from England, where it formed a part of the great cooperative movement. In 1901 the Ealing Tenants, Ltd. had been formed by a group of cooperators to develop a suburban residential estate. Their success resulted in the organization of similar associations in English cities. The Co-Partnership Tenant's Council provided central leadership as an organizing and propagandizing agency; the associations themselves were affiliated in the Co-Partnership Tenants, Ltd. of London. By 1909 workers' cooperative associations owned almost $40,000,000 worth of property.[16]

There was also a middle road between the self-sufficiency of the garden city and the strictly residential character of the garden suburb. The garden village was a residential community organized around one or a few industries. The influence of two of the English garden villages upon planners and housing reformers in the Progressive era cannot be overestimated. In Port Sunlight and Bournville they saw a brilliant alternative to the evils of crowded city life. Port Sunlight, a garden village located outside Liverpool, was founded by Sir William Lever, the soap manufacturer. Here was a planned community of winding, tree-lined roads, spacious parks, and handsome cottages with gardens. Lever operated the village for his employees at a loss, but found recompense in their contentment and good health. Observers were usually charmed by what they saw at Port Sunlight. One of them, prior to a visit, "had not known that there was anywhere in the world a village in which there was nowhere to be found one ugly, inartistic, unsanitary, or other demoralizing feature."[17]

Bournville was also an industrial village founded by a benevolent employer. It was developed as a model community after 1895 by George Cadbury, the cocoa manufacturer. In 1900 Cadbury turned over the property, located outside Birmingham,

16. James Ford, *The Housing Problem* (Cambridge, Mass. 1911), 15, 16 (A Summary of Conditions and Remedies Prepared to Accompany the Housing Exhibit in May, 1911 of the Harvard Social Museum).

17. Annie L. Diggs, "The Garden City Movement," *Arena*, XXVIII (1902), 627.

in trust to the nation. Besides its spacious, well-designed cottages, Bournville displayed such amenities as a meeting house; an institute containing a library, lecture hall, classrooms and similar facilities; children's playgrounds; wooded areas and village greens. According to Bournville's architect, it was the village of the future, "a village of healthy homes and pleasant. surroundings, where fresh air is abundant and beauty present."[18]

After the inspiring examples of Port Sunlight and Bournville had permeated the thinking of American planners and housing reformers, they discovered that America actually had a tradition of industrial villages. Unfortunately, many of them were mining and cotton-mill towns, merely squalid caricatures of the English prototypes in physical layout and management. Not even the best specimens of the American industrial village, such as Pullman, Illinois, could compare with Port Sunlight or Bournville in the quality of planning or the benefits conferred upon their inhabitants.

Nonetheless, housing reformers were optimistic about the future of the industrial village. In model garden villages detached or row cottages, limited in number per acre, would provide excellent housing in contrast to the dreary flats or tenements to which so many workers were accustomed. The garden village was practical, for industrialists would surely find a contented and healthy working force to their advantage, not to mention the low taxes and land prices of suburban locations. It was not necessary or even desirable for a company to build and manage an industrial village. The work could be delegated to a subsidiary company or to private developers subject to strict standards of planning and design. In any case, the company must avoid both the paternalism which created resentment

18. W. Alexander Harvey, *The Model Village and Its Cottages: Bournville* (London, 1906), 15. For the significance of the Garden Village as interpreted by Americans consult: Edward E. Pratt, "Garden Cities in Europe," *American City*, VII (1912), 503-10; Lyra D. Trueblood, "The Bournville Village Experiment: a Twentieth-Century Attempt at Housing the Workers," *Arena*, XXXIV (1905), 449-58; Robert Brown, "Progress of the Garden City Movement in England," *Arena*, XL (1908), 459-60; Carol Aronovici, *Housing and the Housing Problem* (Chicago, 1920); Edith Elmer Wood, *The Housing of the Unskilled Wage Earner: America's Next Problem* (New York, 1919).

at Pullman and the despotism of most mining and cotton-mill towns.

A number of planned or semi-planned industrial suburbs had appeared before World War I. Gary, Indiana, one of the largest, showed little evidence of planning or the social responsibility reformers hoped to stimulate among companies engaged in real estate operations. Within three years (1906-9), the United States Steel Corporation transformed marshland and sand dunes into a city of 12,000 equipped with paved streets, sidewalks, utilities, public schools, shops and residences; but since the Corporation had been more interested in expanding its steel production than in city-building it did not employ planners and it acquiesced in the speculative development of homes by private realtors on land south of the Wabash Railroad tracks. Hundreds of box-shaped, frame houses sprang up for unskilled workers, and no housing codes interfered with the builders.

More satisfactory specimens of industrial suburbs encouraged reformers to retain faith in the garden village. The Goodyear Tire and Rubber Company organized a subsidiary in 1912, which hired the landscape architect Warren H. Manning to develop a 100-acre tract adjoining Akron, Ohio. About 250 brick and stucco homes of five to eight rooms had been erected by 1916 and sold to employees. Similarly, the Norton Grinding Company of Worcester, Massachusetts, commissioned Grosvenor Atterbury to develop a ninety-acre site. Under Atterbury's supervision, the Company built some sixty detached and semi-detached frame and stucco houses. John Nolen, a fervid champion of industrial housing, planned a garden village at Kistler, Pennsylvania, for the Mount Union Refractories Company. Nolen's plans for the fifty-acre tract included parks, playgrounds, and a school.

Emile Perrot, a Philadelphia architect familiar with the English garden village, helped plan Marcus Hook near Chester, Pennsylvania, for the Viscose Company. The Marcus Hook development included 215 brick row houses, a store, and a recreation building. Two additional experiments which aroused the interest of housing reformers were Morgan Park outside of

Duluth, where the Minnesota Steel Company erected single-family detached and row houses for more than 400 families, and Eclipse Park, near Beloit, Wisconsin, where the Fairbank Morse Company built 350 detached houses for employees, ranging in price from $2,400 for four rooms to $3,100 for eight rooms.[19]

No garden cities appeared in America, and reformers could claim an extremely limited success in promoting the garden village. With a few exceptions like the Homewood project of the City and Suburban Homes Company, reformers could refer only to Forest Hills Gardens in Long Island to illustrate the planned garden suburb in America. Designed by Frederick Law Olmsted, Jr., and Grosvenor Atterbury, Forest Hills Gardens was sponsored by the Russell Sage Foundation in 1909. Its Tudor-style homes with spacious lawns, network of winding roads, shopping center, small parks and public schools illustrated the virtues of large-scale comprehensive planning. Yet Forest Hills proved nothing except the obvious — that attractive suburban communities could be created for those able to afford them.

In a report which appeared in the United States Bureau of Labor Statistics *Monthly Review* for November 1917, Leifur Magnusson examined 236 company housing projects. Few of the companies hired architects and planners of the caliber of Nolen, Atterbury, or Perrot. No American industrial communities matched Bournville or Port Sunlight, and many of them like Gary, or the mining towns of the Colorado Fuel and Iron Company, exhibited no housing or planning features worthy of emulation. For the reformer, however, the industrial

19. The American industrial village is discussed in Graham R. Taylor, *Satellite Cities: A Study of Industrial Suburbs* (New York, 1915); Leifur Magnusson, "Housing by Employers in the United States," National Housing Association, *Proceedings*, 1917, 106-29; Grosvenor Atterbury, *Model Towns in America* (National Housing Association, Publications, No. 17, Jan., 1913); E. R. L. Gould, *The Housing of the Working People*, Eighth Special Report of the Commissioner of Labor (Washington, D.C., 1895); Leonora B. Ellis, "A Model Factory Town," *Forum*, XXXII (1901-02), 60-65, a favorable discussion of Pelzer, S. C. A detailed description of conditions in one of the most famous of American industrial towns is Margaret F. Byington, *Homestead, The Households of a Mill Town* (New York, 1910).

village and garden suburb seemed in theory a promising alternative to the city tenement or flat. If only enough industrialists and philanthropists could be convinced of the economic and social advantages of the garden village and suburb, the reformer could strike at the heart of the housing problem by relieving the congestion of the industrial city. Here was a key point at which the housing and planning movements of the Progressive era intersected — relief of the congestion responsible for the tenement and slum through dispersion of work and population from the central city.

All Progressive housing reformers endorsed the garden city program or its modifications. Even Lawrence Veiller, the leading exponent of restrictive legislation, could not resist the allure of planned garden communities. Although Veiller observed that workers in most American industrial towns "live in squalid and sordid surroundings," in time, perhaps, "far-sighted employers of labor" might "develop their community in such a way that it will not only furnish a delightful dwelling place for their workers, but will be a real asset to the industry."[20] Referring to the garden city, Veiller noted that by 1920 Letchworth contained eighty-two factories and workshops, 2,282 houses, and many shops and public buildings. It was a thriving community. England had demonstrated to his satisfaction that "the Garden City is a practical scheme; of benefit to the workers, of benefit to industry, of benefit to the community, of benefit to the nation."[21]

The COS Tenement House Committee promoted the garden city ideal and its variations whenever possible. It learned, for example, that Proctor and Gamble was planning to establish a plant in Staten Island, and offered some free advice to William C. Proctor. The Committee explained the merits of the industrial village, referring specifically to Port Sunlight, Bournville,

20. Lawrence Veiller, *Industrial Housing* (National Housing Association Publications, No. 36, June 1917), 1, 25. A discussion of the practical problems of establishing an industrial village in terms of finance and design can be found in John Nolen, *The Industrial Village* (National Housing Association, Publications, No. 50, Sept. 1918).

21. Lawrence Veiller, *Are Great Cities a Menace? The Garden City a Way Out* (National Housing Association, Publications, No. 57, Feb., 1922), 9, 10.

and some American towns. It stressed its point by outlining the alternative to the planned, industrial village — the New York speculative tenement with its "increase in excessive drinking and gambling; overindulgence in all the dissipations which gain influence as the home ceases to be attractive; increase in crime, and decrease in reliability, intelligence, contentment and efficiency."[22] Though nothing came of the Committee's proposal, it reflects the interest of the Progressive housing reformer in directing the flow of population and industry away from the congested core of the city and into the country.[23]

[3]

The garden city program provided only for the planned development of new communities. It did not affect the expansion of existing municipalities or protect their better neighborhoods from future congestion. In zoning, housing reformers and planners thought they had found a device which would insure the orderly growth of existing cities. A planning weapon which had achieved maturity in Germany after 1900, zoning combined with the garden city movement after 1909 to enhance the utilitarian impulse superseding the City Beautiful. Although businessmen would promote zoning mainly to protect their financial interests, reformers viewed it in the broader perspective of the general social welfare; zoning would improve urban housing and living conditions by controlling population distribution.

German municipalities in rapid succession adopted zoning or districting regulations after 1900 in order to regulate expansion outward from the old (often medieval) central city.[24] The German zoning program consisted essentially of three series of restrictions over building development. First, the city was dis-

22. COS Tenement House Committee, Minutes, June 21, 1906.
23. See Carol Aronovici's plea for decentralization in "Suburban Development," *Annals*, LI(1914), 234-38.
24. Frank Backus Williams, "The German Zone Building Regulations," Heights of Buildings Commission to the Committee on the Height, Size and Arrangement of Buildings of the Board of Estimate and Apportionment of the City of New York, *Report*, Dec. 23, 1913, 94-119.

tricted into specific use areas: residential, industrial, commercial, and mixed. In residential neighborhoods, protected against industrial or commercial invasion, property values would presumably remain stable because home owners were safeguarded against indiscriminate land use; property values would not fluctuate wildly, for speculators could not exploit the uncertainty and fears of home owners.

German zoning also involved the establishment of height districts. Building heights in designated areas were limited to a certain multiple of the street width. Height regulation had a dual purpose: it prevented congestion by limiting the number of people who could live or work in a particular area and simultaneously insured a minimum of light and air for all the structures. Height districting, in addition, protected property owners. A developer, for example, was prohibited from erecting a tall tenement in a neighborhood of one-family homes.

German zoning, finally, involved the creation of bulk or area restrictions. These regulated such items as court and yard sizes and the percentage of a lot which could be covered. Like height regulations, these area restrictions also insured a minimum of light and air for commercial as well as residential structures, and reduced overcrowding by limiting the amount of land which developers could improve.

American housing reformers and planners believed they had found in zoning a tool with which to control land speculation, the fluctuation of property values and, above all, congestion. Indeed, American municipal reformers commonly assumed that if we imposed zoning regulations to prevent overcrowding, we would plug the fountain from which many of the physical and social evils of urban life flowed. No program of social betterment could achieve results unless "accompanied by a reasonably successful attempt to lessen the congestion of population which now exists."[25]

25. Frank J. Goodnow, "Report of the Committee on Congestion of Population," First New York City Conference of Charities and Correction, *Proceedings*, 1910, 13.

[4]

The crusade to reduce urban congestion in the Progressive era was part of, but distinct from, the housing reform and planning movements. It enlisted the support of social reformers of all varieties, including those interested in land, taxation, and child welfare. In New York City it developed its own program and organization, and no discussion of housing or city planning is complete without some mention of the anti-congestion campaign.

Early in the winter of 1907 a group of New York social workers decided to form an association dedicated to the relief of congestion and to the stimulation of public interest in its causes, consequences, and remedies. This group, which included such distinguished settlement leaders as Mary K. Simkhovitch, Lillian D. Wald, and Gaylord S. White, as well as Florence Kelley of the National Consumers' League, organized the Committee on Congestion of Population in New York (CCP).[26] The Committee appointed Benjamin C. Marsh as its secretary.[27] Like Veiller, Marsh was a talented organizer and administrator, outspoken in his convictions and gifted with a quick, original mind. He differed from Veiller and de Forest, however, in his receptivity to economic reforms unacceptable to the more conservative New Yorkers. Marsh remembered that when he first came to New York, Veiller introduced him to de Forest, pointing out that Marsh was particularly interested in the land problem. According to Marsh, "Mr. de Forrest [sic] looked at me with the maddening tolerance of a wise old man for a well-intentioned young fool and said, 'If you touch the land problem in New York, you probably won't last here two years.' "[28]

After graduating from Iowa's Grinnell College in 1898, Marsh served a short term as assistant state secretary for the YMCA, followed by courses in political economy at the Uni-

26. Benjamin C. Marsh, *Lobbyist for the People, a Record of Fifty Years* (Washington, D.C., 1953), 17.
27. Marsh also served as secretary of a second land and tax reform group—the Society to Lower Rents and Reduce Taxes on Homes in New York.
28. Marsh, *Lobbyist for the People*, 35.

versity of Chicago. He spent two years raising funds for the Congregationalist Board of Commissioners for Foreign Missions, exploring America's industrial cities and observing first-hand the living conditions of the nation's workers. Distressed by the widespread misery he encountered, he decided to learn more. Marsh accepted a fellowship in 1902 at the University of Pennsylvania in order to study the "homeless man" under the direction of Professor Simon Patten, and left for Europe the following summer to examine the old world's system of control over the beggar and tramp. His background in social work soon qualified him for appointment as secretary of the Pennsylvania Society to Protect Children from Cruelty, and in 1907 he received the call from the newly organized CCP.

Under Marsh's direction the CCP quickly spread its influence in the fields of congestion relief, housing reform, and planning. He scored an early triumph with the organization of New York's first congestion exhibit. Held in the Museum of Natural History in March 1908, the exhibit was patterned after those which Lawrence Veiller had arranged for the COS on housing and tuberculosis. Exhibitors included the Tenement House Department, COS and AICP, City and Suburban Homes Company, National Consumers' League, New York Child Labor Committee, and other welfare and reform agencies.[29] Marsh toured the premises with Governor Hughes, pointing out to him "the most striking features." The exhibit aroused considerable public interest, which the CCP exploited to induce the New York City legislature to authorize the creation of an official congestion commission.[30]

The New York Congestion Commission, appointed by Mayor Gaynor in 1910 and including Benjamin Marsh as its secretary, published a lengthy report in 1911. This unique social document

29. *Exhibit of Congestion of Population in New York* (brochure, 1908, distributed by the CCP).

30. Marsh, *Lobbyist for the People*, 18. The CCP was also responsible for the appointment of a State Commission on Congestion of Population. See Robert W. Hebberd, "The Work of the State Commission on Distribution of Population," Eleventh New York State Conference of Charities and Correction, *Proceedings*, 1910, 907-15 (published in New York State Board of Charities, *Forty-fourth Annual Report*, I, 1910).

involved a comprehensive examination of the causes, consequences, and possible remedies for New York's oppressive overcrowding of land and people. It discovered that the population
and density for all New York's boroughs had increased between
1900-10. In Manhattan, for example, the population had leaped
from 1,850,000 to 2,321,000; the density per acre rose from
131.8 to 166.1. The Commission argued that "for a good standard of housing for unskilled wage earners the maximum value
of land should not exceed 50 cents per square foot." Land in
districts of Manhattan, however, ranged in value between $2.74
and $16 per square foot.[31] In general, the Commission attributed
to congestion a variety of physical and social evils similar to
those emphasized by housing reformers for many years.[32]

The Commission presented a series of fourteen recommendations designed to reduce existing congestion and discourage
future overcrowding. The most important of these included
restrictions upon the height and lot coverage of buildings;
measures to encourage a more efficient distribution of industry;
a reduction of taxation upon buildings in order to discourage
the holding of land for speculative purposes; extension of the
rapid transit system to facilitate suburban migration; promotion
of farm schools and garden training to help people adopt agriculture as a profession; a campaign by the Bureau of Industries
and Immigration of the State Department of Labor to "encourage the immigrants to become farm laborers and to discourage
the segregating of immigrants in congested sections of the city."
These recommendations illustrate the intense interest of the
Progressive municipal reformer in urban decentralization and,
particularly, his desire to deflect immigrants from the congested
industrial cities. For all practical purposes, however, nothing
resulted from the Commission's labors. Its report was significant
mainly as a symptom of the fact that municipal reformers and

31. New York City Commission on Congestion of Population, *Report*
(transmitted to the Mayor and the Board of Aldermen, Feb. 28, 1911), 12.
32. For example: ". . . there seems to be very little doubt among those who
have worked in the congested districts that a very large part of the juvenile
delinquencies, which are becoming so serious, are directly traceable to the
congested conditions of population among a large portion of the families from
which the juvenile delinquents come," *ibid.*, 15.

officials viewed congestion as a problem so unique and urgent that it merited the appointment of a special government commission of inquiry.

Perhaps the outstanding accomplishment of the New York CCP was in the field of city planning. In connection with a city planning exhibit held in Washington, D. C., in 1909, the CCP sponsored a conference with the intention of establishing a national planning association. Held in the spring of 1909 this meeting resulted in the creation of a National Conference on City Planning.[33] On the national level the conference became a significant link between the housing and planning movements. Lawrence Veiller, for example, served on its executive committee and contributed numerous papers at the annual meetings. Planners, likewise, often participated in the sessions of the National Housing Association. Thus, after 1910, both the housing and planning movements had achieved national organization and shared a common interest in problems relating to housing, congestion, and urban decentralization.[34]

The New York CCP, with similar interests, urged both planners and housing reformers to adopt its own special formula for the improvement of housing conditions and the relief of congestion. It stressed a program of land and taxation reform identified particularly with Benjamin C. Marsh. Though Marsh was not a doctrinaire single-taxer, he borrowed heavily from the theories of Henry George and his disciples.

The high cost of land, the CCP argued, was "an essential, eternal and irremediable cause of congestion of population so

33. Mrs. V. G. Simkhovitch, "Report of Committee on Congestion of Population," Eleventh New York State Conference of Charities and Correction, Proceedings, 1910, 900-07 (published in New York State Board of Charities, Forty-fourth Annual Report, I, 1910). Also National Conference on City Planning, Proceedings, 1910, 3.

34. Veiller's papers at the National Conference on City Planning include "The Safe Load of Population on Land," 1910; "Buildings in Relation to Street and Site," 1911; "Protecting Residential Districts," 1914; "Districting by Municipal Regulation," 1916. Attending the National Housing Association Conferences were such men as Frederick Law Olmsted, Jr., landscape architect; John Nolen; Arthur Coleman Comey, an architect and member of the Massachusetts Homestead Commission; E. H. Bennett, a Chicago city planner; Robert H. Whitten, Secretary of the Committee on the City Plan of the New York Board of Estimate.

far as housing conditions are concerned. With expensive land no remedy for congestion among unskilled workers can permanently be found."[35] Well-versed in European land and tax programs, Marsh saw in them clues to the radical improvement of housing conditions and congestion relief. Speaking of Frankfurt, Marsh noted that it had "pursued a consistent policy of land purchase and owned in 1907 about 48.9 [per cent] of the land within the city limits, and a large percentage outside the city limits."[36] Other German cities owned large parcels of land. In the opinion of the CCP the American city might wisely emulate their example, acquiring land "for its purposes early — before speculation increases its cost."[37] Municipal land ownership, the Committee argued, had numerous advantages. The city possessed a greater measure of control over the character and pace of its expansion, while it was assured a cheap supply of land for public improvements. Municipal land, if rented out or sold to limited-dividend companies, would encourage the production of better housing at lower costs. Tenements or homes erected upon land acquired at agricultural prices would be much cheaper than dwellings erected upon private land which had undergone the process of speculative transfer and subdivision.

As important as municipal land ownership, in the view of Marsh and the CCP, was the differential or graded tax. This involved a progressive tax upon increases in land values, of which the community received one-tenth to one-quarter, as well as the proceeds from the regular land tax. The differential tax, which taxed land at a much higher rate than buildings (thus transferring at least part of the "unearned increment" to the community) was clearly designed to discourage land speculation or monopoly and, conversely, to encourage improvements. Landowners, presumably, would find it too costly to keep land

35. *The True Story of the Worst Congestion in any Civilized City* (A Summary of a Report by the Committee on Congestion of Population in New York) (New York, 1910), 14. Hereafter referred to as *The True Story of Congestion*.

36. Benjamin C. Marsh, *An Introduction to City Planning: Democracy's Challenge to the American City* (Privately printed, 1909), 52.

37. *The True Story of Congestion*, 15.

idle, waiting for it to increase in value. Large amounts of unimproved land would be thrown onto the market, depreciating the value of all land and promoting construction of homes and public improvements. Land, not improvements, bore the brunt of taxation.

Marsh envisioned vast benefits to the working class and city as a whole from the differential tax, at the expense only of the landholder and speculator. Cheaper land, in the first place, promised to reduce building costs and thus rents. Rents would drop also because landowners would have to pay the taxes currently assessed upon owners of improved property. Marsh thought the differential tax would take a "heavy burden" off industry, permitting the payment of higher wages and encouraging the "appropriate" use of land. Finally, it would provide sufficient revenue to meet the "social needs" of the city.

The differential taxer like Marsh and the uncompromising single-taxer like Frederic C. Howe of Cleveland clearly regarded a program of restrictive legislation as a superficial response to the urban housing problem. From the point of view of tax reformers, any plan for "constructive" housing legislation was equally futile if it failed to control land values. "While poverty is explained by immigration," Howe argued, "by improvident marriages, by the Malthusian law of population, by the drink evil . . . the real cause is nearer at hand. It is to be found in the burden of rent, which is slowly, but none the less finally, appropriating the surplus wealth of the people." The speculator, Howe continued, throttled and strangled the development of the city. He withdrew a large percentage of every city's total land area from circulation to create scarcity, and thus appreciate values. As rents increased on remaining improved land, private dwellings gave way to apartment houses, and homes to slums.[38]

The tax reformer hoped to accomplish directly what the exponent of the garden city anticipated indirectly — the reduction of congestion, the depreciation of land values, the lessening

38. Benjamin C. Marsh, *Taxation of Land Values in American Cities: The Next Step in Exterminating Poverty* (New York, 1911), 77; Frederic C. Howe, *Privilege and Democracy in America* (New York, 1910), 157, 168.

of rents, more and better housing. However, few American cities adopted a differential tax, and only two large ones — Seattle and Pittsburgh. The Pittsburgh law of 1913 reduced the tax on land compared to buildings by 10 per cent for 1914 and 1915, and continued the 10 per cent reductions every third year until the tax on buildings equalled half that on land. Despite the fond hopes of Marsh and Howe, radical tax reform had limited success. As we have seen, no garden city such as Letchworth appeared, no garden villages of the charm and beauty of Port Sunlight and Bournville; though some progress in good industrial housing had been made, there were few garden suburbs. The garden city ideal, especially where it involved cooperative landholding, presumed a degree of planning, of economic and social cooperation, and a predilection for wholesale community planning for which the average middle-class American was unprepared. The job- and wages-oriented labor movement represented by the AF of L had little inclination to indulge in cooperative housing experiments, let alone schemes of urban reconstruction. The reformer thus lacked a wide base of support for his community planning ideals. He had to depend upon a few benevolent businessmen or philanthropic agencies to promote his model communities. Similarly, few Americans would endorse experiments in municipal land ownership on a scale sufficient to affect radically the cost of land and character of urban expansion.

Yet the intensive concern of housing reformers, city planners, and the CCP in controlled urban growth finally paid a handsome dividend. Both the Boston tenement house law of 1899 and Veiller's Tenement House Law of 1901 restricted building heights to a certain multiple of street widths, and Los Angeles in 1909 had established use districts, prohibiting industry in a certain section of the city. In 1916 New York City adopted America's first comprehensive zoning code, enacted through the combined pressure of housing, taxation, and other social reformers in alliance with conservative business interests. Indeed, one small but powerful segment of New York's business community triggered the events which resulted in New York's pioneering zoning measure. The reformer was not isolated in his zoning campaign, for businessmen possessed a direct, tangible economic stake in zoning which they lacked in the more visionary garden city ideal.

[5]

Prior to 1900 New York's garment industry had been concentrated in the East Side and lower Broadway. Then garment factories and warehouses began spilling over onto Fifth Avenue; the exclusive department stores and shops responded to the invasion by a migration farther up the avenue, between 27th and 50th Streets. Besides the congestion and other inconveniences caused by the presence of thousands of garment industry employees in shopping districts, the Fifth Avenue merchants discovered that land values were plummeting downwards. To their chagrin the garment manufacturers continued to encroach upon their territory. Instead of retreating once again, the merchants inaugurated a campaign to preserve Fifth Avenue from further desecration, climaxed shortly before the zoning resolution of 1916 by the desperate expedient of a boycott. The merchants agreed to boycott any garment manufacturers who did not remove their plants outside of certain stipulated districts. Full page ads appeared in New York papers signed by such distinguished names as B. Altman, Bonwit Teller, Gimbel Brothers, Lord and Taylor, R. H. Macy, Saks, Stern Brothers, and Franklin Simon. The signers threatened that as of February 1, 1917, they would give preference in purchasing clothes to producers whose plants were located outside of the area bounded by 33rd to 59th Streets, Third to Seventh Avenues.[39]

George McAneny, borough president of Manhattan (1910-1913), shared the merchants' distress. Possessing a legal and journalistic background, McAneny was a progressive New York politician especially committed to civil service reform and efficient government. Between 1892 and 1902 he had served on

39. *Housing Betterment*, V (May 1916), 9-10; "Building Zones in New York," *World's Work*, XXXII 488; Lawson Purdy, Reminiscences, Columbia Oral History Project, 26; George B. Ford, "City Planning by Coercion or Legislation," *American City*, XIV (1916), 328-33.

the New York Civil Service Reform Commission and the National Civil Service Reform League. In 1906, the year Veiller left the City Club, McAneny became its president. His interests expanded beyond the Mugwumpish infatuation with honest government to a broader concern for social welfare. He stressed a positive program of municipal government "for the betterment of the health, and comfort, and the social well-being of the individual." Like many others in the Progressive era, McAneny was "bent on reducing the volume of misery or dependency in the city through the correction, so far as possible, of the conditions that breed misery."[40] In city planning and zoning McAneny found an instrument of municipal control which promised to benefit the tenement population as well as Fifth Avenue merchants. Between 1911 and 1916 he was a leading combatant in New York's struggle for zoning legislation.

McAneny's first contribution was his appointment in the winter of 1911-12 of a Fifth Avenue Commission to examine the question of preserving the Avenue as an exclusive shopping district. The recommendation of this Commission — that the height of buildings on Fifth Avenue be restricted to 125 feet within a distance 300 feet east and west of the thoroughfare — McAneny introduced with some modification into the Board of Estimate.[41] Though no action was taken, McAneny introduced a second more important resolution the following year. This authorized the appointment of a committee to study the general question of the height, size, and use of buildings throughout New York. The Board of Estimate cooperated this time; it appointed a "Committee on the Height, Size and Arrangement of Buildings," including McAneny and the borough presidents of Brooklyn and the Bronx. The Committee, in turn, appointed an advisory "Heights of Buildings Commission."

Between the appointment of this Advisory Commission in 1913 and the final zoning resolution in 1916 came a succession of other commissions, committees, and reports, revealing the

40. Draft of a lecture dated May 1, 1914, one of six delivered by McAneny at Yale, McAneny MSS.
41. Heights of Buildings Commission, *Report*, Dec. 23, 1913, 51.

careful, almost tortuous preparation out of which the zoning legislation evolved. The experts in planning, housing, and real estate who staffed the commissions were determined to ensure the support of the business community, to allay any lingering fears that zoning would jeopardize rather than stabilize property values. They stressed the fact that zoning was designed to promote business interests, not injure them for the benefit of the working class poor; that zoning was not a conspiracy of idealistic reformers whose only concern was for the under-privileged.

Edward M. Bassett, a lawyer destined to become one of America's outstanding authorities on zoning legislation, was named chairman of the Advisory Commission. Its secretary was George B. Ford, an architect and lecturer on city planning at Columbia, who along with Bassett and McAneny was among the pioneers of early planning and zoning activity in America. The Commission also included Lawson Purdy and Lawrence Veiller, who refused to sign the final report because it was too moderate in its recommendations.

Purdy, a lawyer, deserves particular mention as one of New York's most versatile and influential reformers in the Progressive era. He had been converted to Henry George's single-tax program, and between 1896 and 1906 served as secretary of the New York Tax Reform Association.[42] He worked success-fully for legislation requiring the publication of assessment rolls and the separation of land from total value in real estate assess-ments. Mayor McClellan appointed Purdy to the presidency of the New York Department of Taxes and Assessments, a post he held until 1917. Unlike Veiller, Purdy was a strategically-placed municipal official for many years. The two were good friends who saw eye to eye on matters of housing reform and city planning. After 1917 Purdy held high posts in the COS and its Tenement House Committee, and in the 1920's he became secretary of the state commission which revised Veiller's tenement code. It is evidence of the interlocking hierarchy in the New York reform empire in the Progressive era that Purdy

42. Purdy, Reminiscences, 3.

was also a friend of Marsh. The latter was indebted to him for "great help in studying the land-values and land problem of Greater New York, pointing out the effect of taxing buildings at the same rate as land values in creating speculative land values, encouraging slums, and discouraging the construction of healthy buildings."[43]

The Heights of Buildings Commission, staffed by some of New York's most distinguished authorities on housing, planning and real estate problems, proceeded in 1913 to make a comprehensive study of zoning precedents in Europe and America. It justified the control of building development on the grounds of public health and safety, relief from street congestion, the protection of property values, and the advancement of the general welfare. In the eyes of the Commission, Fifth Avenue's experience was a case in point of how indiscriminate building development adversely affected the well-being of a city.[44] The Commission recommended that the state legislature authorize the Board of Estimate to establish use, height, and area restrictions in New York, and that the Board appoint a second commission to consider the precise boundaries of the districts.

In 1914 the state legislature amended New York's charter, permitting the Board of Estimate to zone the city. Earlier in the same year the Board had appointed a standing "Committee on the City Plan," responsible for coordinating all public improvements. This Committee, whose establishment indicated the high priority which a zoning and planning program had achieved in New York's official quarters, endorsed the report of the Heights of Building Commission, recommending to the Board of Estimate that it appoint a "Commission on Building Districts and Restrictions."[45]

The new Commission, appointed in June 1914, included many members of the 1913 Heights of Buildings Commission.

43. Marsh, *Lobbyist for the People*, 19.
44. Heights of Buildings Commission, *Report*, 10, 51.
45. Committee on the City Plan of the Board of Estimate and Apportionment of the City of New York, *Development and Present Status of City Planning in New York* (Being the Report of the Committee on the City Plan, Dec. 31, 1914, together with papers presented at a meeting of the Advisory Commission on City Plan, Dec. 17, 1914), 10.

Bassett was chairman again; Purdy, vice-chairman. George B. Ford, now a consultant, was replaced as secretary by the equally competent Robert H. Whitten. In its prolonged, intensive two-year investigation, the Commission covered much the same ground as its predecessor. It justified its work in similar terms:

> The bigger a city grows the more essential a plan be-comes. Traffic problems, the congestion of population, the intensive use of land, the magnitude of the property values involved, make the control of building development more and more essential to the health, comfort and welfare of the city and its inhabitants. New York City has reached a point beyond which continued unplanned growth can-not take.place without inviting social and economic disas-ter. It is too big a city, the social and economic interests involved are too great to permit the continuance of the *laissez faire* methods of earlier days.[46]

Here was a mature statement of the significance of planning for the modern industrial city. What the AICP and Council of Hygiene had glimpsed long before — that the interdepend-ence, complexity, and heterogeneity of city life necessitated municipal supervision over such fundamental determinants of social welfare as sanitary conditions and housing — the Bassett Commission made explicit. In the Progressive era, many munic-ipal reformers likened the city to an organism whose health and prosperity depended upon enlightened social legislation and the sacrifice of individual interests for the benefit of the whole.[47]

Both the Bassett Commission and the Board of Estimate held lengthy public hearings on the impending zoning legislation. Finally, in July 1916 the Board adopted the nation's first com-prehensive zoning resolution based upon the recommendations and meticulous groundwork of the Commission on Building Districts and Restrictions. The city was divided into three categories of use districts: residential, commercial and unre-

46. Commission on Building Districts and Restrictions, *Final Report*, June 2, 1916, 6.

47. For an analysis of the "organic" concept in Progressive municipal thought consult my article, "The Twentieth Century City: The Progressive as Municipal Reformer," *Mid-America*, XLI (1959), 195-209.

stricted. The zoning law also divided New York into five kinds
of height districts, in which building heights were regulated
by multiples of the adjoining street width. These height districts
were supplemented by area districts, regulating the size of yards
and courts.

The skillful work of the zoning commissions was apparent
in the almost unanimous support accorded to the zoning resolution. The Board of Estimate reported that "the real estate,
lending and building interests are united in their support of
the plan; as are also the commercial and civic associations. Not
a single organization of any kind has opposed the general
plan."[48] Similarly, the Bassett Commission observed that the
districting plan had not only received widespread endorsement,
but that many organizations had requested "more stringent
restrictions than those proposed."[49] The Commission also pointed
out that the life insurance, title and trust companies, and savings
banks which financed real estate operations in New York had
united in support of the zoning ordinance. Many of them,
including such giants as the Metropolitan, Mutual, and New
York Life Insurance Companies, the Astor Trust Company and
Bowery Savings Bank, complained in a petition that haphazard
development had already impaired the "capital values of large
areas," thus "affecting the market value of real estate for investment purposes."[50] With the support of New York's most powerful business and civic organizations, the zoning resolution
crushed the opposition of property owners and speculators who
preferred the opportunity to capitalize their property on the
basis of prezoning values.

New York's zoning legislation was the product of many
years of intensive agitation and education by housing reformers,
planners, and social workers, reinforced by the costly experience
of businessmen who discovered that indiscriminate land use
affected their pocketbooks. It is understandable why real estate
investors supported the zoning program of municipal reformers
in contrast to the garden city ideal. The latter had for its

48. Commission on Building Districts and Restrictions, *Final Report*, 213.
49. *Ibid.*, 73.
50. *Ibid.*, 75.

objective urban decentralization, the radical deflation of those identical land and property values which investors finally realized they could best protect through zoning. In contrast to zoning, the garden city program represented a kind of economic suicide both for real estate interests and the businessmen who profited from the concentrated urban population.

The New York zoning law of 1916, in which the interest of the social reformer like Veiller or Purdy in promoting the general welfare coincided with that of the businessman in protecting his investment, ranks with the New York Tenement House Law of 1901 as among the most significant municipal reforms of the Progressive era. By today's standards, certainly, the zoning resolution was inadequate. In striving to win unanimous support and to insure that the restrictions would not discourage real estate investment, the zoning commissions proved overgenerous to developers. The 1916 measure with subsequent amendments permitted New York City a potential resident population of more than 55 million.[51] Just as Veiller had discouraged literal adoption of New York's housing laws, George B. Ford in 1916 warned other cities against slavish imitation of New York's zoning measure: "It would be most unfortunate if the law were applied as it stands to other cities for it is full of unduly liberal provisions in the way of height and size that tend strongly to defeat the object of the law but were necessitated by the exceptional economic conditions of New York."[52]

The zoning legislation possessed a flaw, besides its liberality, which was not apparent to the housing reformers and planners of the early twentieth century. The zoning resolution of 1916 was a pioneering effort which aroused national interest and resulted in acceptance of zoning by hundreds of American communities in the following decade, but, like restrictive housing legislation, it was primarily negative in effect. Restrictive legislation and zoning provided municipalities with indispensable tools of control over physical development, and in this sense Progressive housing reform and planning marks an important

51. New York *Times*, Dec. 21, 1959, 22.
52. George B. Ford, "How New York City Now Controls the Development of Private Property," *City Plan*, II (Oct., 1916), 3.

transitional era; the problem, however, was that such negative legislation in itself represented a dead end. It could not clear slums, nor provide adequate housing for those elements of the population whom the commercial builder could not profitably accommodate, nor establish criteria for satisfactory residential environments. The planner of the period was at heart a social reformer anxious to improve housing conditions, but he thwarted his own purpose by embracing a negative zoning program and a wistful garden city rhetoric, thus surrendering any hopes of dealing with housing directly. The response of the first generation of American planners to the urban housing problem was deconcentration attained through zoning and the garden city and its variations, a strikingly indirect approach which proved ultimately ineffectual. It left the slums standing, and although it pointed to the need for relating housing and planning, it provided no concrete, workable basis for the coordination of housing and planning policy.

[6]

RETROSPECT AND CONCLUSION

We have seen that a serious housing problem arose in New York City as early as the 1840's. It originated in the lower wards of Manhattan where immigrants concentrated in order to be near their sources of employment and their countrymen. Builders and property owners responded to the demand for cheap housing by partitioning the original one-family homes of native Americans into multi-family tenements, and by erecting barrack-like structures several stories in height which sprawled over all or most of the lot. The prevalent *laissez-faire* doctrine and the failure of New Yorkers to grasp the peculiar nature of housing in a large, heterogeneous industrial city resulted for a long while in little or no regulation of housing standards. New Yorkers, for the most part, did not realize that the community had no choice but to control housing conditions; that its health and welfare were dependent upon providing an adequate supply of safe and sanitary dwellings.

The AICP became New York's first source of organized protest against the city's deteriorating housing conditions. The Association believed that although moral faults caused poverty in the first place, squalid housing intensified these faults, making it exceedingly difficult to inculcate the middle-class virtues. From the start, housing reformers were concerned with the moral and social as well as the physical consequences of inferior housing. In the opinion of the AICP, substandard housing encouraged crime, delinquency, pauperism, intemperance, and other evils.

Neither the AICP nor the state assembly investigating committee of 1857 could persuade the state legislature to enact restrictive legislation. The AICP, however, did inaugurate the model tenement program in the United States when it sponsored the Workmen's Home in the 1850's. At a very early date restrictive legislation and model tenements had become the cornerstones of the housing reformer's strategy.

The Council of Hygiene in 1866 was responsible for the first major advance in housing and sanitary reform. The Council endorsed the model tenement idea but concentrated its attention upon the establishment of a non-political, professional Board of Health which could efficiently remedy New York's sanitary defects. The Council's work represented one of America's first attempts to apply standards of efficiency and *expertise* to the control of urban housing and sanitary conditions.

Composed of physicians and sanitary experts, the Council of Hygiene inherited the environmentalism of the AICP, assuming that improved housing would affect not only the health but the moral fiber of the poor. Stephen Smith and his associates were certain that better housing would elevate the character of the poor, contributing to a more unified, homogeneous community. In the broadest terms, the Council of Hygiene enunciated that basic principle of housing reform which tied together the AICP and Lawrence Veiller, Stephen Smith and Jacob Riis — that the index of municipal and social progress was the health and happiness of the individual, that this could not be

assured in the absence of enlightened social legislation *i*
and enforced by the community.

Between 1867 and 1890 both the urgency of the housing
problem and the concern of middle-class New Yorkers increased. The tenement spread further uptown as hundreds of
thousands of immigrants, many of whom found their way into
Manhattan's slums, responded to America's call for cheap labor.
The structure of the tenement problem for two decades was
set in 1879 with the birth of the infamous dumb-bell tenement.

Housing reformers of the period mostly urged the restrictive
legislation and model tenement program devised before the Civil
War. New York's first tenement law was enacted in 1867,
amended in 1879 and 1887. Neither the laws and amendments
nor their enforcement by an overworked and understaffed
Board of Health proved adequate. The most prominent single
reformer of the time was Alfred T. White, who proved to
the satisfaction of his contemporaries that the model tenement
was a practical solution to the housing problem. White was
perhaps too successful, for the model tenement may have
deflected the attention of reformers from the inadequacy of
the existing housing codes. Around the 1880's, a third method
of housing reform began to attract attention in the form of the
rather limited Octavia Hill principle of enlightened, paternalistic
management.

The social implications of the tenement slum received increasing attention after 1880. The city, it seemed, had become
a world characterized by physical proximity and social distance,
divided by class, race and nationality. Immigrant working-class
ghettos had formed in which foreign speech, customs, and culture prevailed, where crime and vice abounded. Such a development, in the eyes of reformers, threatened the social and
political stability of the entire community. The tenement slum
was a potential volcano, its inhabitants the willing recruits of
the demagogue and revolutionist. Recalling the fearsome Draft
Riots of 1863, Jacob Riis warned that "the sea of a mighty
population, held in galling fetters, heaves uneasily in the tene-

ments." Housing reformers argued that the unenlightened foreigner, a potential anarchist or criminal, was more likely to become a respectable middle-class American citizen if housed decently.

The year 1890 witnessed the publication of *How the Other Half Lives* and the emergence of Jacob Riis. With great skill and imagination Riis awakened New York as never before to a consciousness of its housing problem; and people were prepared to hear his message in the 1890's, a decade of unremitting social and economic strife in which numerical supremacy passed from northern Europe to the "new immigration" from southern and eastern Europe. Riis's nationalism, combined with his glorification of nature, appealed to a generation of Americans who feared for the survival of the Republic under the twin assaults of the new immigration and an increasingly industrial-urban way of life.

As a housing reformer Riis promoted the three traditional methods of amelioration: restrictive legislation, model tenements, and the Octavia Hill plan. Riis was both a prophet and the child of his time. He adhered very often to the simple environmental faith of his contemporaries, assuming that a change in material condition such as housing would result in immeasurable social and moral improvement. Yet he had the insight to transcend his own environmental determinism. For one thing, Riis paid great attention to the tenement child, admitting that the adult was often beyond redemption, despite the quality of his housing. Thus he sensed that a modification of the environment did not automatically insure a change in individual character or social structure. More important, Riis stressed the necessity of reconstructing the total environment of the poor, not simply their housing. He viewed the tenement neighborhood in all its complexity as the basic unit of social control, in which environmental changes must be accompanied by every form of moral influence which the reformer could exert. Riis recognized that the tenement was a way of life, whose social and moral tone was determined by the process of immigrant adaptation to a

PROGRESSIVISM, PLANNING AND HOUSING 249

total environment. The problem of social control, Riis intuitively grasped, was more difficult than earlier generations of housing reformers had assumed.

Riis's distinctive contributions to the theory and practice of housing reform were not developed by his contemporaries, who veered more sharply than ever in the direction of restrictive legislation. Following the Gilder Tenement Committee of 1894, whose work resulted in more ineffectual legislation and in the formation of the City and Suburban Homes Company — the "model" model tenement company of the Progressive era — tenement conditions were substantially influenced by the work of Lawrence Veiller. His impressive achievements between 1898 and 1902 included the establishment of the COS Tenement House Committee, the Tenement House Commission of 1900 and its sweeping reforms, and the organization of the New York Tenement House Department.

Veiller contributed much to the methods, if not the theory, of housing reform. The apostle of restrictive legislation, he stressed the fundamental importance of comprehensive housing codes and taught his generation how to enact them. Before Veiller had stormed onto the scene, New York had neither an adequate housing law nor the machinery to enforce it. If the essential purpose of the housing reformer was to promote restrictive legislation, his success depended upon the quality of his organization and upon his professional skill. The housing reformer, Veiller emphasized, would always have to contend with well-organized opposition from landlords, builders, the lending institutions who financed them, and similar vested real estate interests. Thus he would have to organize in order to maximize his own power and influence over the public. A full-time professional reformer himself, Veiller preferred *expertise* and technical proficiency to high-minded moral fervor. For this reason, and because he assumed that better housing was sufficient for purposes of social control, Veiller minimized the responsibilities of housing reformers in relation to neighborhood reconstruction. He admired Jacob Riis as a humanitarian and human being, but not as a housing reformer adept in legislative and structural technicalities. He appreciated Riis's moral enthusiasm, his dedicated efforts to bring parks and schools to tenement neighborhoods, but did not think that Riis's moral indignation and ideals of neighborhood reconstruction contributed much to the fundamental goal of improving housing conditions.[53]

Like most housing reformers, Veiller viewed the city planning movement as a useful ally. A new ingredient in the philosophy and methods of housing reform, city planning promised to relieve congestion, a problem uppermost in the minds of many Progressive municipal reformers. Overcrowding, they charged, deteriorated the health and morals of the tenement population. It made the tenement problem hopeless, because inflated land and property values, arising from congestion, forced real estate investors to the most intensive development of their land. To relieve overcrowding by dispersing industry and population, housing reformers turned hopefully to the English garden city ideal and to Germany's zoning program. Some reformers like Benjamin Marsh and Lawson Purdy stressed land and tax reforms. Thus housing reformers, more conscious than before of the relationship between their own work and urban physical development as a whole, contributed to the early planning movement.

The significance of Progressive housing reform, in perspective, is threefold. First, the ideal of neighborhood reconstruction identified with Jacob Riis and the social settlement retains significant contemporary implications. Relocation difficulties and the disruption of established neighborhood social patterns connected with wholesale demolition in public housing and urban renewal projects have emphasized the fact that housing, good or bad, is inseparable from a broader neighborhood and community environment. It is likely that in terms of social control Riis overestimated the potency of parks, playgrounds, supervised club activity, and the public school. He did, however, realize

53. Lawrence Veiller to author, Interview, July 13, 1959.

that for purposes of public social policy, housing could not be isolated from other influences which affected personal behavior and family and neighborhood life.

Lawrence Veiller's emphasis upon effective restrictive legislation and a technically proficient, well-organized housing reform movement is a second useful legacy of the Progressive era. No one interested in housing problems today can fail to profit from a perusal of Veiller's model housing laws or his handbook on housing reform, in which he outlined his philosophy of reform and the characteristics of good housing legislation. If Veiller was too narrowly concerned with minimum standards legislation, this does not make such legislation less indispensable to any rounded housing, planning or urban renewal program.

Finally, Progressive housing reform is significant for its affiliation with the early planning movement. Both housing reformers and planners undoubtedly exaggerated the possibilities of creating a satisfactory urban residential environment through zoning and garden city schemes. Hoping to lower housing costs and rents by stabilizing or reducing land values, they favored measures designed to relieve and prevent congestion and encourage migration from high density areas. If a program organized around the prospect of urban decentralization or dispersion is subject to criticism as the product of men who disliked or feared the city of their time, it is equally true that these reformers of the Progressive era launched a continuing search for principles of efficient urban development and control, relating housing to industrial and commercial location, land and tax policy, transportation, population density, zoning, and similar fundamentals.

Any balanced appraisal of Progressive housing reform must consider two important limitations. The first of these, already mentioned, is that restrictive legislation may prevent the worst housing from being erected, but cannot guarantee a sufficient supply of good housing at rents (or costs) suited to low-income or even middle-income groups. Without necessarily endorsing an elaborate and expensive public housing program, it seems essential for reformers to devise some means of providing housing for those whom private enterprise cannot profitably accommodate. Glancing at Europe the rebels against Veiller's exclusive emphasis upon restrictive legislation stressed the need for state loans, municipal land purchase, and other devices to reduce housing costs. New Deal housing reformers, of course, developed a program of federal mortgage insurance and subsidized public housing. Whatever the method, the problem of insuring good housing for those whom private builders cannot profitably accommodate must be faced.

Progressive housing reformers, in the second place, including those who participated in labor, recreation, and other reform movements, did not devote much thought to the elusive relationship between housing, on the one hand, and personality, family life, and social structure, on the other. The relationship seemed so obvious that they did not even consider it an issue. They were sure that better housing would operate to transmit the values and cultural norms of middle-class America to immigrants and workers. Good housing would help in re-establishing the primary group controls of the peasant village or small town which had disintegrated in the modern industrial city.

This question of the social value of housing reform is not mere academic whimsy, but is crucial in relation to the formulation of public policy. Let us admit that certain minimum standards in housing are essential to the health, and probably to the social well-being of any community. For most people it is a serious handicap to grow up and live amidst filth and dilapidation. It is possible, however, that beyond a certain point the social benefits anticipated from improved housing can be achieved more quickly, cheaply, or effectively by alternative methods. Can an apartment in a mammoth public housing project, for example, assist the multiproblem family as much as a supply of trained social workers? Perhaps both are necessary, but to what degree? The crucial point is that the resources of a society are limited; they should be allocated in order to accomplish the most good at the least cost.

Similarly, does better housing solve the basic problem of discrimination? The Negro, for example, would not need public housing if discrimination did not so drastically limit his employment and residence mobility. Indeed, given the high percentage of Negro tenants in public housing projects in New York, Chicago, and other cities, it would seem that public housing has sometimes operated to cement patterns of residential segregation. Housing authorities, of course, have usually had no choice but to follow a policy of involuntary segregation owing to the reluctance of whites to move into public housing, and opposition to the erection of such projects in predominantly white neighborhoods.[54] In any case, it can be argued that Negroes and other low-income minority groups need equal opportunity in employment, private housing, and education as much as the public housing which is a symbol of their depressed status.

Any efficient housing policy depends upon a more exact understanding of the relationship between housing design and family life. Does it make a difference whether a low-income (or any) family lives in a high-rise elevator apartment in contrast to a single-family house or low-rise garden apartment? Exactly how do different forms of housing affect the rearing of children or the parental role? Does the father, for example, in a single-family house gain status in the eyes of his family when they see him assuming the responsibility for its efficient operation, in contrast to his passive reliance upon management in the huge public housing project? What kind of housing design is most conducive to the development of a sense of neighborhood or community? This issue is obviously relevant in the case of the New York City Puerto Ricans whose family cohesiveness and communal roots tend to disintegrate in Manhattan's slums. In short, it is necessary to define social aims more clearly

54. Martin Meyerson and Edward C. Banfield, *Politics, Planning and the Public Interest: The Case of Public Housing in Chicago* (Glencoe, Ill., 1955), is an illuminating account of the struggle of the Chicago Housing Authority to gain public and political approval for the location of projects on vacant sites in middle-class neighborhoods. The Authority, which developed its plans soon after passage of the Housing Act of 1949, had to revise its policy and locate most projects on former slum sites because of the strong opposition.

and then discover the design most appropriate to their attainment.[55]

As a consequence of our growing awareness of the complexities surrounding housing policy, the environmental optimism of the Progressive era, which was transmitted to the New Deal public housing enthusiasts, has greatly diminished. Experience has proved that public housing has often failed to attain its social ends. A recent discussion of the urban housing problem quotes a bitter admission by "a close student of New York's slums": "Once upon a time we thought that if we could only get our problem families out of those dreadful slums, then papa would stop taking dope, mama would stop chasing around, and Junior would stop carrying a knife. Well, we've got them in a nice new apartment with modern kitchens and a recreation center. And they're still the same bunch of bastards they always were."[56]

The disillusionment would have been less had not the hopes been so high. Harrison E. Salisbury, in connection with a series of articles for the New York *Times* on the "Shook-up Generation," has observed that "most visitors to the Fort Greene Houses in Brooklyn prefer to walk up three or four flights instead of taking the elevator. They choose the steep, cold staircases rather than face the stench of stale urine that pervades the elevators." Salisbury bluntly concludes that "nowhere this side of Moscow are you likely to find public housing so closely duplicating the squalor it was designed to supplant."[57] Fort Greene is only one housing project. It does not discredit the public housing program with its many fine accomplishments, but suggests that the social significance of the program must be re-evaluated in the light of twenty years' experience.

55. On the problem of housing and design see Frederick A. Gutheim, *Housing as Environment* (New York, 1953). This is a report on the Research Conference, "The Role of Social Research in Housing Design," sponsored by the Committee on Housing Research, Social Science Research Council (May 24-26, 1951, Ann Arbor, Michigan). Mimeographed copies distributed by the Institute for Urban Land and Housing Studies, Columbia University.

56. Daniel Seligman, "The Enduring Slums," in the Editors of *Fortune*, eds., *The Exploding Metropolis* (Garden City, N. Y., 1958), 106.

57. New York *Times*, Mar. 26, 1958, 1.

In a study made for the Philadelphia Housing Author
competent social scientist has stated the issue succinctly:

> The policy maker . . . often assumes that it is the bad
> *housing* in slums which breeds these social disadvantages
> which he wishes to remove; delinquency, poverty, mental
> disorder, physical disease, broken homes, poor citizenship,
> crime, and so forth. Many studies have shown the high
> degree of spatial association which obtains between poor
> housing and poor social conditions. The temptation is to
> cry, "Remove the slum (i.e., the inferior houses) and the
> social ills will disappear!" But actually there is not much
> evidence to show that these poor social conditions were
> caused by the poor housing *in and of itself.*

The author concludes that bad housing is only one factor in
a total series of functional cultural relationships in any slum
area, that better housing alone will not produce any revolution
in the pattern of "interpersonal relations."[58] And a sociologist,
in attempting to discredit the "myths" of housing reform, has
complained that housing reformers habitually overstressed the
"inadequate *physical* environment of the slums," while mini-
mizing the "connection between the *social* environment of the
slums and the disorders they wanted to cure." The public
housing program was "sold" on the assumption that "slum
clearance would remove the social ills."[59]

One is not justified in criticizing the Progressives too harshly,
if at all, for accepting the relationship between housing and
social control as a matter of faith. We are little more advanced
or enlightened today. Nothing is certain except that minimum
housing standards are necessary for health, and that we need
a more scientific understanding of the exact relationship between

58. Anthony F. C. Wallace, *Housing and Social Structure: A Preliminary
Survey, with Particular Reference to Multi-Story, Low-Rent, Public Housing
Projects* (Philadelphia Housing Authority, 1952), 29-30. Wallace was particularly concerned with the influence upon three aim-variables (mental and
physical health, family, and community structure) of a high-rise project in
contrast to a low-rise project. He examined the Jacob Riis Houses in New
York (high-rise) and the Tasker Homes in Philadelphia (low-rise). Wallace
found the low-rise form preferable in terms of all three aim-variables.

59. John P. Dean, "The Myths of Housing Reform," *American Sociological
Review,* XIV (1949), 283.

housing and social structure before housing reform can achieve maximum effectiveness as an instrument of public policy.[60]

60. Areas of needed research are discussed in Robert K. Merton, "The Social Psychology of Housing," in Wayne Dennis, ed., *Current Trends in Social Psychology* (Pittsburgh, 1948), 163-217. Two articles which illustrate such research are Irving Rosow, "The Social Effects of the Physical Environment," American Institute of Planners, *Journal*, XXVII (May 1961), 127-33; and Herbert J. Gans, "Planning and Social Life: Friendship and Neighbor Relations in Suburban Communities," *ibid.*, 134-40. Rosow, however, makes the unfounded assumption that "housers have effectively won their point that slum clearance pays dividends in terms of social welfare" (p. 127). He cites only three sources in support of this statement, does not consider contrary evidence, and ignores the issues which Dean's article raises, though he cites the same article in a different connection.

APPENDIXES

TENEMENT HOUSES AND POPULATION: MANHATTAN, 1864

Source: Council of Hygiene

Ward	Total No. of Tenements	Total No. of Families	Average No. of Families in Each House	Total Population
1	250	2,181	8.50	8,564
3	54	310	5.75	1,248
4	486	3,636	7.50	17,611
5	462	2,597	5.50	10,370
6	605	4,406	7.25	22,401
7	627	4,586	7.25	19,293
8	625	3,977	6.50	15,630
9	596	3,836	6.50	14,955
10	534	4,487	9.00	18,140
11	2,049	13,433	6.50	64,254
13	540	3,729	6.75	14,997
14	546	4,509	8.50	20,008
15	197	1,358	7.00	4,970
16	1,257	7,088	5.67	31,500
17	1,890	15,974	8.33	63,766
18	836	7,267	8.75	35,869
19	571	3,632	6.50	16,067
20	1,162	8,344	7.33	32,205
21	1,026	7,299	7.00	36,675
22	996	7,714	7.50	31,845

Total Number of Tenements (three or more families): 15,511

Total Population of Tenements: 486,000

Total Cellar Population: 15,224

Total Tenement and Cellar Population: 501,224

APPENDIX II

POPULATION, ACREAGE, AND DENSITY IN MANHATTAN, 1880, 1894

NUMBER OF TENEMENTS IN MANHATTAN, 1893

Source: Tenement House Committee of 1894

Ward	Year	Tenements	Population	Acreage	Density
1	1880		17,939	154	116.5
	1893	210			
	1894		14,369*	264**	54.4
2	1880		1,608	81	19.8
	1893	8			
	1894		1,202	76	15.8
3	1880		3,582	95	37.7
	1893	48			
	1894		4,864	102	47.6
4	1880		20,996	83	252.9
	1893	473			
	1894		23,006	82	280.5
5	1880		15,845	168	94.3
	1893	238			
	1894		16,000	162	98.7
6	1880		20,196	86	233.6
	1893	522			
	1894		29,868	100	298.7
7	1880		50,066	198	252.9
	1893	1,510			
	1894		74,110	202	366.8
8	1880		35,879	183	196.0
	1893	826			
	1894		40,333	170	237.2

* The population figures for 1894 were estimates (as of July 1, 1894) acquired by the Committee from the New York Board of Health.

** The acreage figures differ somewhat between 1880 and 1894. The Committee drew upon Health Department records for the 1880 figures, from U. S. Census Reports for the 1894 figures. There is a particularly wide discrepancy in acreage figures for the 1st and 12th wards. The 1st ward figures for 1894, however, include Governor's, Bedloe's and Ellis Islands; the 12th ward figures for 1894 include several islands in the East River opposite the ward. The 23rd and 24th wards were part of what is now the Bronx.

Ward	Year	Tenements	Population	Acreage	Density
9	1880		54,596	322	169.5
	1893	1,519			
	1894		70,308	316	222.5
10	1880		47,554	110	432.3
	1893	1,196			
	1894		74,401	106	701.9
11	1880		68,778	196	350.9
	1893	2,201			
	1894		97,435	218	446.9
12	1880		81,800	5,504	14.8
	1893	7,702			
	1894		316,529	5,394	58.7
13	1880		37,797	107	353.2
	1893	1,042			
	1894		59,267	109	543.7
14	1880		30,171	96	314.3
	1893	636			
	1894		36,292	102	355.8
15	1880		31,882	198	161
	1893	359			
	1894		32,811	229	143.3
16	1880		52,188	349	149.5
	1893	1,118			
	1894		63,468	332	191.2
17	1880		104,837	331	316.7
	1893	2,770			
	1894		133,257	290	449.5
18	1880		66,611	450	148
	1893	1,321			
	1894		81,734	431	189.6
19	1880		158,191	1,481	106.8
	1893	5,450			
	1894		303,388	1,455	208.5
20	1880		86,015	444	193.7
	1893	2,830			
	1894		108,936	443	245.9

Ward	Year	Tenements	Population	Acreage	Density
21	1880		66,536	411	161.8
	1893	1,458			
	1894		81,400	410	198.5
22	1880		111,606	1,529	72.9
	1893	4,146			
	1894		198,761	1,169	170
23	1880		28,338	4,267	6.6
	1893	1,458			
	1894		69,696	4,241	16.4
24	1880		13,288	8,050	1.6
	1893	97			
	1894		26,014	8,474	3

APPENDIX III

TENEMENTS, TENEMENT POPULATION, ETHNIC DISTRIBUTION, AND WARD BOUNDARIES IN MANHATTAN, 1900

Statistical Source: De Forest and Veiller, *The Tenement House Problem*

Manhattan's 1st ward, extending from the Battery north to Liberty Street and Maiden Lane, was mostly given over to business and thus housed a small tenement population of 7,153 distributed among 216 dwellings. Persons of Irish extraction predominated, with a scattering of Germans and native Americans. The 2nd (Liberty Street, Maiden Lane, Broadway, Park Row, Peck Slip, East River) and 3rd (Liberty Street, Broadway, Reade Street, Hudson River) wards were also commercial areas with negligible tenement populations. Their ethnic composition was similar to that of the 1st ward. An unusual feature of these downtown wards as one proceeded north from the Battery along Greenwich and Washington Streets were the restaurants and shops of the Turks, Arabs, and Syrians who had joined in the great trek to America.

The 4th ward (Peck Slip, Park Row, Catherine Street, East River), a bucolic retreat of the well-to-do in the eighteenth and early nineteenth centuries, had since become a forbidding region of shabby dives, lodging houses and tenements. The 471 tenements of this riverfront ward housed 19,335 people in 1900, mostly of

Irish, German, and Italian extraction. A large colony of Greeks also resided here, in the vicinity of Roosevelt and Marion Streets.

Bounded by Reade and Canal Streets, Broadway and the Hudson River, the 5th was another riverside ward in which business and commerce nudged out population. Its 234 tenements housed 7,777 persons, mostly of Irish and German descent.

In the notorious 6th ward of Five Points, Chinatown, and Mulberry Bend fame, 20,936 persons crowded into 423 tenements. Bounded by Canal Street, the Bowery, Park Row, and Broadway, the house density of the 6th ward was the third highest in the city — 49.49 persons to each tenement. Here the Italians represented the heaviest ethnic concentration and the Irish were second heaviest. Several thousand Jews had spilled over from the Ghetto wards to the east, especially into the district between Centre and Baxter Streets. The 6th ward was characterized by one unsympathetic critic as the mecca for "vermin-laden beggars and banditti of southern Italy, incrusted with dirt, crawling with vermin, given to hard drinking, idling, gambling, gaming and fighting, and presenting the most stubborn front to all efforts to civilize and Americanize them."

The Italians, who had begun emigrating to this country in large numbers after 1880, concentrated most heavily in the lower central wards — the 6th, 8th, 14th, and 15th — expanding from these into surrounding wards. Jews from Russia, Poland, and the Austro-Hungarian empire settled closer to the East River, in the 7th, 10th, and 13th wards. As early as 1890 the Italians had become the largest ethnic group in the 14th ward while the Jews held undisputed numerical supremacy of the 10th. As these southern and eastern European immigrants crowded native Americans and older Irish or German settlers out of these lower wards, they moved uptown and into the surrounding boroughs.

The 7th ward, bounded by Catherine, Division, and Grand Streets and the East River, was a densely populated tenement district. It harbored 72,466 persons in 1,500 dwellings. Long dominated by the Irish, it capitulated after 1880 to a heavy Jewish invasion.

The 8th ward, situated between Broadway and the Hudson River, Canal and Houston Streets, contained a large Negro population in the vicinity east of Varick Street and south of Spring Street. A French colony north of Spring Street added a Gallic flavor. The ward's most notable ethnic feature, however, was the large Italian influx pushing out the older Irish and German residents. The 8th ward's 871 tenements contained a population of 27,093.

The 9th, another West Side ward, was bounded by Houston and 14th Streets, Sixth Avenue and the Hudson River. This Greenwich

Village ward was largely the preserve of native Americans, Irish, and Germans, with a noticeable concentration of Negroes. Its 2,283 tenements housed 51,577 people.

The 10th ward, "New Israel," was the great lower East Side bailiwick of Russian and other eastern European Jews. By 1890, they already numbered 30,467 in this region which was bounded by Division and Rivington Streets, Norfolk Street, and the Bowery. Their closest competitors were the Germans, who numbered about 14,000. These nationalities swamped a scattering of native Americans, Irish, Italians, and Bohemians. The ward's 109 acres contained a population of 76,073, crowded into 1,179 tenements. The average population per tenement, 64.52, was the highest for any ward in Manhattan.

In the sweatshops of New Israel the steam irons hissed and the needles swooped to their targets as the stream of Jewish immigrants scurried into the cheap, ready-made clothing industry. The 10th ward was the setting for the colorful Hester Street "pig-market," where pork was actually scarcer than a native American. On Friday afternoons Hester Street bulged with peddlers, pushcarts, and shoppers anxious to stock up for the Sabbath. Intersecting Hester two blocks west of Essex was Orchard Street. Walhalla Hall, the great civic and fraternal center of the 10th ward, was located here. At Walhalla marriages were celebrated, dances organized, union activities discussed, and revolution plotted by tailor anarchists and peddler socialists.

The 11th ward (Rivington Street, East River, 14th Street, Avenue B, Clinton Street), to the northeast of New Israel, was another sprawling tenement empire. Its 2,031 tenements housed 89,361 persons. The adjoining ward to the west, the 17th (Rivington Street, Avenue B, Clinton Street, 14th Street, the Bowery, 4th Avenue), was the home of 114,559 people divided among 2,877 tenements. Both these wards, especially the 17th, harbored large German populations.

The 12th ward was the largest in Manhattan. Its nearly 6,000 acres extended north from 86th Street to the tip of the Island. The population of 397,571 and the 11,005 tenements included mostly native Americans, Germans, and Irish. Many Italians, however, had penetrated to the gashouse district between 110th and 120th Streets, east of 4th Avenue. Much of the ward, especially above 120th Street, was undeveloped suburban country.

In the 13th ward (Division and Grand Streets, East River, Rivington Street, Norfolk Street) — like the 7th and 10th — the Irish and German population was overwhelmed by Jewish newcomers. Hemmed in between the 10th ward and the East River, the 13th ward in 1900 claimed a tenement population of 55,564 in 1,123 dwellings.

The 14th ward (Canal Street, the Bowery, Houston Street, Broadway) was one of the largest reservoirs of Italian settlement. Immediately north of the "Bloody Sixth," the ward contained a population of 35,250 in 642 tenements. The density per house of 54.9 was the second largest of any ward in the city, exceeded only by New Israel. The overcrowding resulted in part from the fact that much of the land was used for business purposes. Italians after 1890 also moved in large numbers to the adjoining ward to the northwest, the 15th (Houston Street, the Bowery, Fourth Avenue, 14th Street, 6th Avenue), mingling with the established native American, Irish, German, Negro, and French population. The 15,989 tenement inhabitants shared 533 dwellings.

The 16th and 20th wards extended in a straight line north from 14th to 40th Streets. They were bounded by Sixth Avenue and the Hudson River. These wards included artistocratic Chelsea as well as brawling Hell's Kitchen and the vice-ridden Tenderloin. Apart from Chelsea and the gaudy carnival atmosphere of the Tenderloin, the native American, Irish, and German stock inhabited a gloomy region of slaughterhouses, gas works, railroad yards, docks, and seedy tenements. Violence, especially street fighting, was common in these wards, whose gangs included one of the most notorious ever to stomp the pavements of Manhattan — the Gophers. In the summer of 1900 a serious riot occurred which resulted in death and injury to scores of Whites and Negroes. It was sparked by the killing of a policeman by a Negro, though the traditional enmity between the Irish and the colored is a better explanation for the violence than the compassion of Hell's Kitchen for the police. Irish were especially conspicuous in the 16th ward, Germans in the 20th. The former contained 1,533 tenements and a population of 43,467; the latter, 2,791 tenements and 79,732 tenants.

The 19th ward, which extended from 6th Avenue to the East River, and the 22nd ward, which reached from 6th Avenue to the Hudson River, were bounded by 40th Street to the south, 86th Street to the north. Except for a particularly heavy concentration of Germans in the 19th ward, whose territory included the beginnings of Yorkville, and a sizeable Bohemian colony, the ethnic composition was similar to that of most other uptown wards. Both had grown rapidly in the previous few decades as Americans and older immigrant stock moved northward to escape the southern and eastern European immigrants. In 1900, the 19th ward housed 203,815 in 5,720 tenements. The 4,454 tenements of the 22nd ward contained a population of 182,508.

The boundaries for the 18th and 21st wards were exactly those of the 16th and 20th, except for the fact that they fronted on the East River. Americans, Germans, and Irish predominated, and both wards contained a substantial number of private residences as well as tenements. The 18th ward harbored 1,323 tenements with a population of 40,724; the 21st ward, 1,449 tenements and 42,818 population.

APPENDIX IV

TENEMENTS AND TENEMENT POPULATION IN BROOKLYN, BRONX, QUEENS, AND RICHMOND, 1900

TOTAL TENEMENTS AND TENEMENT POPULATION IN GREATER NEW YORK, 1900

Source: DeForest and Veiller, *The Tenement House Problem*

Brooklyn

Tenements:	33,771
Population:	653,431

Bronx

Tenements:	4,365
Population:	106,027

Queens

Tenements:	1,398
Population:	22,334

Richmond

Tenements:	418
Population:	5,287

Totals

Tenements, Manhattan:	42,700
Population, Manhattan:	1,585,000
Average Persons per Tenement, Manhattan:	33.58
Tenements, Other Boroughs:	39,952
Population, Other Boroughs:	787,079
Average Persons per Tenement:	
Brooklyn:	19.34
Bronx:	24.29
Queens:	15.97
Richmond:	12.64

APPENDIX V

ESTIMATED POPULATION OF MANHATTAN
TENEMENTS, DECEMBER 31, 1916

Source: Tenement House Department of the City of New York, *Eighth Report*, 1915-1916

District	New Law	Old Law	Total	Est. Tenement Population
1. Below 14th St., east of Broadway	729	7,662	8,391	508,400
2. Below 14th St., west of Broadway	196	2,245	2,441	92,600
3. 14th St. to 40th St., east of 6th Avenue	165	2,343	2,508	100,900
4. 14th St. to 40th St., west of 6th Avenue	40	2,851	2,891	102,100
5. 40th St. to 86th St., east of 6th Avenue	410	5,245	5,655	235,900
6. 40th St. to 86th St., west of 6th Avenue	172	3,989	4,161	185,100
7. 86th St. to 130th St., east of Lenox Avenue	917	6,123	7,040	372,400
8. 86th St. to 130th St., west of Lenox Avenue	695	3,156	3,851	204,000
9. 130th St. to 155th St.	1,081	1,708	2,789	171,900
10. North of 155th St.	1,019	167	1,186	109,000
Total:	5,424	35,489	40,913	2,082,300

APPENDIX VI

TENEMENTS IN BRONX, BROOKLYN, QUEENS AND RICHMOND, JANUARY 1, 1917

Source: Tenement House Department of the City of New York, *Eighth Report*, 1915-1916

Bronx

Old Law:	4,862
New Law:	5,554

Brooklyn

Old Law:	34,997
New Law:	12,411

Queens

Old Law:	1,877
New Law:	3,735

Richmond

Old Law:	379
New Law:	25

Total Old Law: 42,115 (plus 35,489 in Manhattan)

Total New Law: 21,725 (plus 5,424 in Manhattan)

Total Old and New Law: 63,840 (plus 40,913 in Manhattan)

APPENDIX VII

TENEMENT COURT DIMENSIONS RECOMMENDED BY THE TENEMENT HOUSE COMMISSION OF 1900

Outer courts (courts which extended to the street or yard) of buildings 60 feet in height (5 stories), if the court was situated on the lot line, had to measure at least 6 feet in width. If the outer court was not situated on the lot line but between different wings of the building or between different buildings on the same lot, it had to measure at least 12 feet.

Outer courts of buildings over 60 feet in height, if the court was situated on the lot line, had to increase 6 inches for every additional story (12 feet or a fraction). The outer court had to increase one foot for each additional story if it was situated between the wings of the same building or between different buildings on the same lot. Buildings less than 60 feet in height decreased the size of their courts proportionately. No outer court, however, could be smaller than 4 feet 6 inches in width if situated on the lot line, or 9 feet if situated between wings of the same building or between different buildings on the same lot.

Inner courts (courts which did not extend to the street or yard) situated on the lot line in buildings 60 feet in height had to measure at least 12 feet in width from the lot line to the opposite wall. Its other dimension had to measure at least 24 feet. For each additional story over the fifth, the width of the court had to increase 6 inches; its other dimension, one foot. Buildings less than 60 feet in height could decrease the size of their courts proportionately. No inner court situated on the lot line, however, could measure less than 10 feet 6 inches by 21 feet.

Inner courts not touching the lot line but enclosed on all four sides had to measure at least 24 feet on all sides if the building was 60 feet or 5 stories high. For each additional story, the court had to increase one foot in every direction. The size of inner courts could decrease proportionately for buildings less than 60 feet in height. No inner court situated on the lot line, however, could measure less than 21 feet in any direction. Enclosed courts had to be provided with at least one duct at the bottom, 5 square feet or more in area, in order to insure adequate circulation of air.

APPENDIX VIII

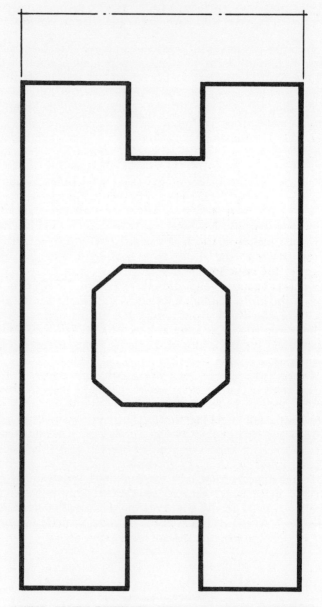

OUTER COURT BETWEEN WINGS OF SAME BUILDING

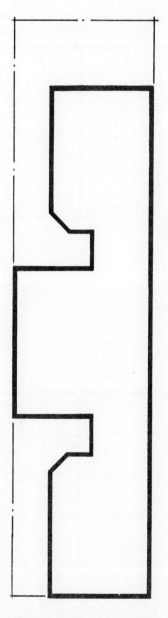

OUTER COURT SITUATED ON LOT LINE

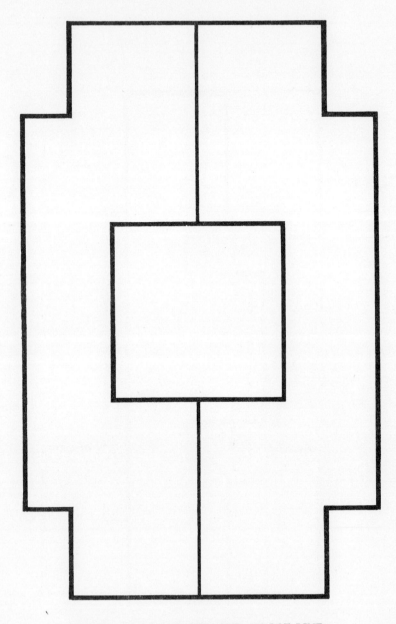

INNER COURT NOT SITUATED ON LOT LINE

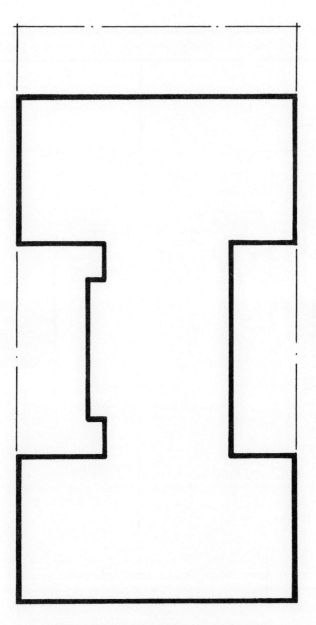

INNER COURT SITUATED ON LOT LINE

272 THE PROGRESSIVES AND THE SLUMS

APPENDIX IX

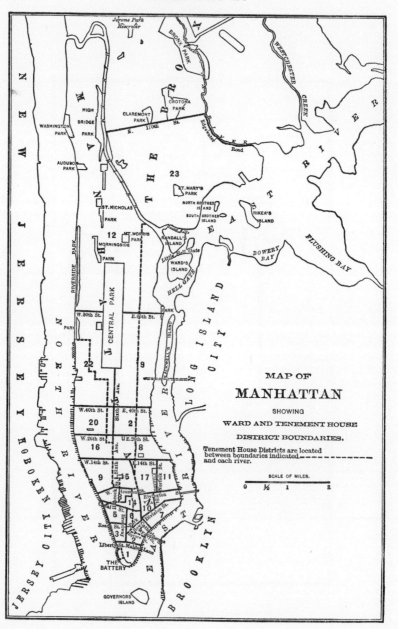

MAP OF

MANHATTAN

SHOWING

WARD AND TENEMENT HOUSE

DISTRICT BOUNDARIES.

Tenement House Districts are located
between boundaries indicated - - - - - - - -
and each river.

SCALE OF MILES.

BIBLIOGRAPHICAL NOTE

Manuscript materials referred to in the footnotes are located in the following libraries:

The Century Collection: New York Public Library.
Richard Watson Gilder Papers: New York Public Library.
Seth Low Papers: Columbia University.
George McAneny Papers: Columbia University.
Jacob A. Riis Papers: Library of Congress.
Lawrence Veiller Papers: Columbia University.
Lillian Wald Papers: New York Public Library.
Edith Elmer Wood Papers: Columbia University.

Tenement House Committee of the Charity Organization Society, Minutes, 1898-1917: Archives, Community Service Society of New York.

Reminiscences, Columbia University Oral History Project:
William H. Allen
William S. Bennet
Robert S. Binkerd
Homer Folks
George McAneny
Lawson Purdy
Jackson E. Reynolds
William Jay Schieffelin
Norman Thomas
Lawrence Veiller

INDEX

Abbott, Edith, 186
Abbott, Grace, 186
Ackerman, Frederick L., 179
Adams, John Quincy, 3
Addams, Jane, 67
Adickes, Franz, 221
Adler, Felix: criticizes tenements in 1884, 33; favors municipal land purchase, 105; expounds neighborhood ethic, 188; mentioned, 82, 102, 119, 190, 214
Akron, Ohio, 226
Albany, New York, 146
Allds, Jotham P., 125
Altona, Germany, 221
American Architect and Building News: criticizes dumb-bell tenement, 32
American Association of Immunologists, 86
American City Planning Institute, 128
American Federation of Labor, 237
American Institute of Architects, 121
American Public Health Association, 17, 86
Andrews, Constant A., 119
Architectural League, 121
Aronovici, Carol, 81, 179
Ascension Church, 47
Association for Improving the Condition of the Poor: established, 4; views on poverty and housing, 5-6; model tenement work, 8-9, 28-29; criticizes saloon, 70; and indoor baths, 91; sponsors better housing conference, 101; Department of Dwellings formed, 119n; mentioned, 22, 35, 38, 39, 174, 207, 232, 242, 246
Association of American Pathologists and Bacteriologists, 86
Astor family, 38
Astor, John Jacob, Jr., 12
Astor, William B., 12

Astral Apartments, 36, 100
Atterbury, Grosvenor, 226, 227
Auerbach, Joseph S., 101

Babcock, Samuel D., 101
Bacon, Albion Fellows, 81, 145, 148
Baltimore, Maryland, 141, 143
Baltimore Charity Organization Society, 198
Baron de Hirsch Fund, 91
Bassett, Edward M., 240, 242
Baths, Public, 91
Belgium, 178
Bell, A. N.: criticizes dumb-bell tenement, 32
Belmont, August, 12
Beloit, Wisconsin, 227
Berkeley, California, 146
Biggs, Herman N., 86, 87
Billerica (Massachusetts) Garden Suburb, 176
Birmingham, England, 224
Boston, Massachusetts, 140, 141, 143, 175, 237
Boston Co-operative Building Company, 34, 175
Boston Workingmen's Building Association, 34, 175
Bournville, England, 224, 225, 227, 228, 237
Bowditch, H. P., 34
Brace, Charles Loring: and tenement reform in 1879, 30; mentioned, 45, 70
Breckinridge, Sophonisba, 186
Brewster, Mary, 189
Bronx, New York, 264, 266
Brooklyn, New York, 264, 266
Brown, James M., 12
Buffalo, New York, 141
Buffalo Charity Organization Society: Committee on Sanitary Conditions, 141; mentioned, 126, 143

275

Bureau of Municipal Research: investigation of Tenement House Department, 161, 163
Burnham, Daniel H., 217, 219
Butler, Edmond J.: as Tenement House Commissioner, 158-64, 168

Cadbury, George, 224
Calder, William M., 173
California: housing code, 145
Carlyle, Thomas, 127
Casework, *See* Social Work
Chandler, Charles F., 30
Chapin, Charles V., 88
Chapin, Robert C., 197
Charities and the Commons, 199
Charity Organization Society of New York: and preventive social work, 194; Department for the Improvement of Social Conditions, 128, 173; Tenement House Committee, formed, 119; significance, 119-20; recommendations to building code commission, 120, 121; opposes building code, 121; contributes to national housing movement, 140; favors of Lawson bill, 173; favors garden village, 228-29; mentioned, 36, 118, 143, 152, 153, 157, 164, 166, 169, 171-73, 199, 232.
Chester, Pennsylvania, 226
Chicago, Illinois, 141, 143
Chicago World's Fair, 217-18, 223
Children of the Poor, 65
Children's Aid Society, 30, 35, 70
Cholera: 11; and New York Metropolitan Board of Health, 23
Church Temperance Society, 95
Cincinnati, Ohio, 141, 176
Cincinnati Associated Charities, 143
Citizens' Association of New York: organized, 12; mentioned by George T. Strong, 23. *See also* Council of Hygiene
Citizens' Union, 121, 158
City: contributes to decline of countryside, 51
City and Suburban Homes Company: founded, 101; capitalization, 103; accommodations, 108, 109; rent collection and management, 108, 109, 110; Homewood project, 110-11, 227; mentioned, 102, 112, 176, 232, 249. *See also* Gould E. R. L.

City Beautiful: 219; inadequacies of, 220, 221, 229
City Club, 121, 157, 171
City Homes Association of Chicago, 141
City Inspector: opposes petition of Council of Hygiene, 13; mentioned, 4, 14, 15, 16, 23
City Planning: and housing, 215, 250, 251; origins, 217-19; shift to utilitarianism, 220
Cleveland, Ohio, 142, 143, 146
Clinton Hall, 192
Coit, Stanton, 187
College Settlements Association, 211
Collins, Ellen: friendly rent collecting, 106. *See also* Hill, Octavia; Octavia Hill method
Colorado Fuel and Iron Company, 227
Columbus, Ohio, 142, 146
Committee of Fifteen, 138
Committee of Fifty for the Investigation of the Liquor Problem, 77
Committee of Nine: prepares tenement bill, 30; mentioned, 32, 36
Committee on Congestion of Population in New York: formed, 231; organizes exhibit, 232, land and tax reforms, 234-37; and establishment of National Conference on City Planning, 234. *See also* Marsh, Benjamin C.
Committee on Improved Housing. *See* Improved Housing Council
Congestion. *See* Committee on Congestion of Population in New York; New York State Tenement House Committee of 1894
Congregationalist Board of Commissioners for Foreign Missions, 232
Connecticut: housing code, 145
Conservation, 215
Cooper, Peter, 12, 30
Co-Partnership Tenants' Council, 224
Co-Partnership Tenants, Ltd., 224
Council of Hygiene: efforts to reform health administration, 13; investigation of New York's sanitary condition, 17-20; significance, 20-22; mentioned, 27, 174, 242, 246
Coxey's Industrial Army, 50
Crain, T. C. F.: as Tenement House Commissioner, 156, 157, 158

Cravath, Paul D., 172
Crimmins, John D., 101
Croker, Richard, 122
Cross Acts, 93
Cutting Buildings, 100
Cutting, R. Fulton, 101
Cutting, W. Bayard, 101

Dahlgren, John V., 119
Daniel, Annie S.: on tenement home
  work, 210
DeForest, Robert W.: opposes Veiller as Tenement Commissioner,
  153; becomes Tenement Commissioner, 154; civic and philanthropic
  affairs, 154-55; chooses Veiller as
  Deputy Tenement Commissioner,
  155; advises Marsh, 231; mentioned,
  81, 118, 119, 124, 125, 144, 153, 166,
  169
Denver, Colorado, 142
Detroit, Michigan, 142
Devine, Edward T.: and preventive
  social work, 203; on character of
  poor, 203; reform objectives, 204-
  05; need for social planning, 215;
  mentioned, 119, 186, 187, 194, 200,
  214
Dinwiddie, Emily W.: hired as supervisor of Trinity tenements, 107;
  mentioned, 81, 114
Disease. See Public Health
Dix, John A., 170
Donneley, John, 13, 14
Duluth, Minnesota, 146, 227
Dumb-bell tenement: origins of, 29-
  31; description of, 31-32; mentioned
  93, 247

Ealing Tenants, Ltd., 224
East Side Recreation Society, 191
East Side Relief Work Committee,
  127
Eclipse Park, Wisconsin, 227
Edson, Cyrus, 89
Educational Alliance of New York,
  77
Elsing, W. T.: commends tenement
  house exhibition, 124
Engineering technology: progress of,
  factor in sanitary control, 14-15
England, 178, 221
Erie Canal, 2
Ethical Culture Society, 33, 119

Fairbanks Morse Company, 227
Fifth Avenue Commission, 239. See
  also McAneny, George; Zoning
Fifth Avenue merchants: boycott of
  garment manufacturers, 238
First Garden City, Ltd., 222. See also
  Garden City
Fish, Hamilton, 12
Flagg, Ernest, 119
Folks, Homer, 186
Ford, George B., 240, 242
Ford, James, 81, 160
Forest Hills Gardens, 227
Fort Greene Houses, 254
Foster, Roger, 89
Frankel, Lee K., 195
Frankfurt-am-Main, 221
Friendly Aid House, 192
Froebel, Friedrich, 78

Gambling, 137, 138
Gangs, 19
Garden City: described, 221-22;
  sources of appeal, 222-23; endorsed
  by housing reformers, 228, men-
  tioned, 229, 243, 244, 250, 251. See
  also Bournville; Garden Suburb;
  Garden Village; Port Sunlight
Garden City Association, 222
Garden Suburb, 223, 224, 228
Garden Village: viewed as solution
  of housing problem, 225, 227, 228.
  See also Bournville; Port Sunlight
Garment industry, 238
Gary, Indiana, 226, 227
Gaynor, William J., 232
Geary, Blanche, 107, 110
George, Henry, 240
Germany, 178, 221, 250
Gilder, Richard W.: on civic respon-
  sibility, 90; mentioned, 64, 82, 94,
  99, 101, 102, 104, 119, 127, 151. See
  also New York State Tenement
  House Committee of 1894
Gold, Michael: quoted, 61, 62, 69, 70
Goldmark, Josephine, 186, 214
Goldmark, Pauline, 186
Goodyear, Caroline, 195
Goodyear Tire and Rubber Com-
  pany, 226
Gotham Court, 20
Gould, E. R. L.: early career and
  housing research, 102; philosophy
  of housing reform, 102-03; on

housing finance, 104; favors municipal lodging houses, 105; preference for detached house, 110; recommends improved transit, 111; mentioned, 81, 107, 108, 109, 110 113, 119. *See also* City and Suburban Homes Company
Graham, Robert, 95
Grand Rapids, Michigan, 146
Greene, New York State Senator: opposes Tenement Law of 1901, 136
Greenwich House, 190, 192. *See also* Simkhovitch, Mary K.
Griscom, John, 15

Hall, John, 30
Hamburg, Germany, 221
Hamilton, Alice, 186
Hamilton, William G., 91
Harper's Weekly: and cholera scare, 23
Harris, Elisha: contributions to public health, 15, 16, 17. *See also* Council of Hygiene
Hartford, Connecticut, 141
Hartford Charity Organization Society, 143
Hatfield, R. G., 29
Hays, Samuel P., 215
Hell's Kitchen, 17
Henry Street Settlement: activities, 189-90. *See also* Wald, Lillian D.
Hill, Octavia: originates friendly rent collecting, 105. *See also* Octavia Hill method
Hoe, Robert, 29
Holls, Frederick W., 119
Home Buildings. *See* White, Alfred T.
Home economics: commended by Riis, 75
Homes Commission of Washington, D.C., 176
Homestead Strike, 50
Homewood. *See* City and Suburban Homes Company
Housing associations, 144
Housing Betterment, 144
Housing codes: opposition to, 147; mentioned, 142, 146
Housing of the Working Classes Acts, 93
Housing Reform, 145

Housing reform: objectives of, 15, 82, 174-75; environmental philosophy of, 66; relation to social work, 185-87; relation to planning, 228, 251; and social control, 252, 254-55; and Negro, 253; and problem of design, 253
Howard, Ebenezer, 221, 222, 223. *See also* Garden City
Howe, Frederic C., 236
How the Other Half Lives: contents, 57; mentioned, 49, 50, 58, 65, 248
Hughes, Charles Evans, 102, 232
Hull House, 186

Ihlder, John, 81, 145
Immigrant: Irish and German, 2, 7, 19; criticized, 46, 51, 52, 54, 55; adaptation of, 47, 98; restriction of, 53; shift in sources of, 53, 54; Italian, 54, 96; in Manhattan, 1900, 260-64
Improved Dwellings Association: formed, 30; mentioned, 36, 101
Improved Dwellings Company. *See* White, Alfred T.
Improved Housing Association of New Haven, 176
Improved Housing Council: sponsors competition, 101
Improved Industrial Dwellings Company, 35
Indiana: housing code, 145
Industrial Village. *See* Garden Village
International Tuberculosis Congress, 128
Iowa: housing code, 146

Jacobi, Mary P., 206
James, D. Willis, 36
Jersey City, New Jersey, 143

Kansas City, Missouri, 142, 143
"Katie Moeschen" case, 167
Kelley, Florence, 186, 193, 207, 214, 231
Kentucky: housing code, 145
Kindergarten, 74, 75
Kingsley House, 143
Kistler, Pennsylvania, 226
Kneeland, George J., 186
Kober, George M., 176
Koch, Robert, 84
Kohn, Robert D., 179

Laboring Classes Lodging Houses Act, 93

Land reform, 234, 235, 236. *See also* Committee on Congestion of Population in New York; Marsh, Benjamin C.

Langbourn Estate, 35

Lansing, Michigan, 146

Lawrence, James, 13

Lawson bill: introduced, 172

Letchworth, 222, 237. *See also* Garden City

Lever, William, 224. *See also* Port Sunlight

Liverpool, England, 224

Living standards, 187, 194-98

Living Wage, A, 195

Lockwood-Ellenbogen bill: defeated, 171

Lodger, 95-97, 197-98

Long Island, 227

Los Angeles, California, 143, 237

Louisville, Kentucky, 142

Low, Seth, 102, 153, 184

Lowell, Josephine Shaw: visits model tenement, 36; organizes Consumers' League, 206; mentioned, 154, 193, 194

McAneny, George: background, 238-39; introduces zoning measure, 239

McClellan, George B., 156, 157, 158, 240

McManus, Michael, 13

Mafia, 54

Magnusson, Leifur, 227

Making of an American, The, 62

Manhattan: Fourth Ward, description, 19-20; distribution of population and tenements in, Appendices 257-66

Manning, Warren H., 226

Marcus Hook, Pennsylvania, 226

Marquette, Bleecker, 81

Marsh, Benjamin C.: meets de Forest, 231; early career, 231-32; organizes congestion exhibit, 232; land and tax reforms proposed by, 234-36; mentioned, 241, 250. *See also* Committee on Congestion of Population in New York

Marshall, Edward, 89, 97, 127

Massachusetts Bureau of Statistics of Labor, 140

Mazet Committee, 69

Medical science: progress of, factor in sanitary control, 14-15

Mercantile Inspection Law, 208

Meyer, Henry C.: founds *Plumber and Sanitary Engineer,* 29; justifies prize tenement competition, 32

Michigan: housing code, 146

Mills, D. O., 101

Milwaukee, Wisconsin, 142, 145

Minimum wage, 208-09

Minneapolis, Minnesota, 142

Minneapolis Civic and Commerce Association, 149

Minnesota: housing code, 146

Minnesota Steel Company, 227

Mitchell, John Purroy, 171, 173

Model Housing Law, 145, 146, 148

Model tenement: proposed by *AICP,* 8-9; advantages of, 34; not a charity, 104; mentioned, 33, 34, 100, 101, 102, 175, 176, 246. *See also* Astral Apartments; Boston Co-operative Building Company; Boston Workingmen's Building Association; City and Suburban Homes Company; Improved Dwellings Association; Improved Housing Council; Langbourn Estate; Philadelphia Model Housing Company; Sanitary Housing Company of Washington, D. C.; Sanitary Improvement Company of Washington, D. C.; Schmidlapp, Jacob G.; Tenement House Building Company; White, Alfred T.

Model Tenement House Law, 145

Mohr, C. A., 133

Morgan Park, Minnesota, 226

Morris, Moreau, 91

Moses, Solomon, 89

Mount Union Refractories Company, 226

Mulberry Street Bend, 79n, 171

Mumford, Lewis: quoted, 218

Murphy, Charles F., 157

Murphy, John J.: as Tenement House Commissioner, 158, 162, 164-66, 169

Murray, T. F., 92

Museum of Natural History, 128, 232

Nashville, Tennessee, 142
Nathan, Maud, 207, 208
National Child Labor Committee, 214
National Civil Service Reform
League, 239
National Conference on City
Planning, 128, 234
National Consumers' League, 185, 193,
207, 211, 231, 232
National Housing Association: organ-
ized, 144; mentioned, 118, 146, 148
234
Neighborhood ethic. See Settlement
Neighborhood Guild. See University
Settlement
Nesbitt, Florence, 196
New Haven, Connecticut, 176
New Jersey: housing code, 145
Newman, Bernard J., 81
New Orleans, Louisiana, 142, 143
New York: home life destroyed by
tenement, 44-45
New York Child Labor Committee,
209
New York City Advisory Commis-
sion on the Height, Size and Arrangement of Buildings: appointed,
239; studies zoning precedents, 241;
recommendations, 241.
New York City Board of Health:
establishes diagnostic laboratory, 85;
measures against tuberculosis, 86;
educational work, 87-88; condemns
rear tenements, 93-94; child welfare services, 190; supervises food
supply, 212-13. See also New York
Metropolitan Board of Health
New York City Building Code Commission, 117, 119, 120; presents revised code, 121
New York City Building Department,
125, 127, 151, 152
New York City Commission on
Building Districts and Restrictions:
appointed, 241; cites support for
zoning law, 243
New York City Commission on Congestion of Population: appointed,
232; recommendations, 233
New York City Committee on the
City Plan, 241
New York City Committee on the
Height, Size and Arrangement of
Buildings, 239

New York City Consumers' League:
organized, 206; objectives, 206-07;
agitates for improved working conditions, 208-09; seeks restrictions on
tenement home work, 209-12; campaigns for pure food, 212-13
New York City Tenement House Department: organized, 155-56; employees, 159, 160; inspection of
tenements, 160-61; administrative
confusion, 161; delays in enforcing
law, 162-64; achievements, 165-66;
authority threatened, 169-70; existence threatened, 170-71; mentioned,
118, 181, 232. See also Butler, Edmond J.; Murphy, John J.
New York City Zoning Law of 1916:
237, 242, 243; inadequacies, 244-45
New York Civil Service Reform
Commission, 239
New York College Settlement, 95, 96,
191, 192, 193
New York Federation of Women's
Clubs, 213
New York Herald, 85
New York Metropolitan Board of
Health: established, 23; composi-
tion, 25; mentioned, 16, 135
New York Sanitary Reform Society,
30
New York School of Social Work,
155
New York State Assembly Commit-
tee of 1856-57, 2, 10, 11
New York State Board of Charities,
17
New York State Charities Aid
Association, 36, 155
New York State Court of Appeals,
169
New York State Senate Committee of
1859, 15, 16
New York State Tenement House
Commission of 1884, 33, 119
New York State Tenement House
Commission of 1900: appointed,
126, 126n; objectives and investiga-
tions, 132-34; achievements, 134-35;
combats gambling and prostitution,
137-39; mentioned, 83, 118, 140, 143,
153. See also Veiller, Lawrence
New York State Tenement House
Committee of 1894: origins, 88-89;
scope of investigation, 89; special

interests, 90; recommendations, 90, 91; studies bathing and toilet facilities, 91, 92; examines congestion, 94, 95; park bill, 99, 100; approves model tenements, 100; urges improved transit, 111; accomplishments, 114; criticizes Trinity tenements, 114, 115; mentioned, 84, 98, 113, 117, 127, 249. See also Gilder, Richard W.

New York State Tenement House Law of 1867: provisions, 26-27; mentioned, 30, 31, 135

New York State Tenement House Law of 1879: 30; provisions, 32-33

New York State Tenement House Law of 1901: provisions, 134-35; opposition to, 135, 136, 167, 168, 169; enforcement of, 159-66; upheld by Supreme Court, 167; threatened by state court decision, 169, 170; efforts of Brooklyn builders to revise, 171-73; mentioned, 158, 169, 183, 237. See also New York State Tenement House Commission of 1900

New York Tax Reform Association, 240

New York Times: criticizes dumbbell tenement, 32; criticizes tenements, 47; remarks on immigrant, 54, 55; condemns rear tenement, 94; examines tenement ownership, 113; mentioned, 13, 121, 254

New York Tribune: Fresh Air Fund, 78; mentioned, 57

Nolen, John, 220, 226, 227

Norton Grinding Company, 226

Octavia Hill Association of Philadelphia, 106-07, 141

Octavia Hill method, 105-08, 175, 247. See also Collins, Ellen

Odell, Benjamin, J., Jr., 135

Olmsted, Frederick Law, 217

Outdoor Recreation League, 191

Paine, Robert Treat, 34

Pasteur, Louis, 84

Patten, Simon, 232

Paulding, James, 191

Pennsylvania: housing code, 142, 145

Pennsylvania Society for the Prevention of Cruelty to Children, 232

People's University Extension Society, 77

Perrot, Emile, 226, 227

Phelps-Stokes, I. N., 119, 122

Philadelphia, Pennsylvania, 141

Philadelphia Housing Authority, 255

Philadelphia Housing Commission, 107

Philadelphia Model Housing Company, 107

Philadelphia Society for Organizing Charity, 198

Pittsburgh, Pennsylvania, 141, 142, 143, 237

Plumber and Sanitary Engineer: prize tenement competition, 29; mentioned, 30, 32, 33, 101

Polish Peasant in Europe and America, The. See Thomas, William I. and Florian Znaniecki

Portland, Maine, 143

Portland, Oregon, 146

Port Sunlight, 224, 225, 227, 228, 237

Post, George B., 89, 119

Poverty: middle class attitudes toward, 5; views of AICP on, 6; regarded as abnormal condition, 186-87

Pratt Institute, 36. See also Astral Apartments

Press, The, 89

Primary group, 72, 73, 76

Proctor and Gamble, 228

Proctor, William C., 228

Prostitution, 69, 70, 138-39, 208-09

Providence, Rhode Island, 142

Pryor, John, 134

Public Health: changes in, 83; and bacteriology, 84, 86, 87; diagnostic laboratory and contagion, 85-86

Puerto Rican, 253

Pulling, Ezra R., 19, 20

Pullman, George M., 50

Pullman, Illinois, 225, 226

Pullman strike, 50

Purdy, Lawson, 240, 242, 244, 250

Queens, New York, 264, 266

Raines-Law Hotels, 138

Rainsford, W. S.: praises Riis, 49; mentioned, 102

Ravage, M. C., 96, 99

Restrictive legislation: in early twentieth century, 182-83

Reynolds, James B., 82

Ribe, Denmark, 55, 56

Richmond, Mary E.: early career, 198-99; defends volunteer, 199-200; defines casework, 200-02; mentioned, 185, 186, 214
Richmond, New York, 228, 264, 266
Riis, Jacob A.: sources of popularity, 55; early life, 55, 56; emigrates to America, 56, 57; becomes police reporter, 57; hardships as immigrant, 57, 58; contempt for tramp, 58; takes advantage of opportunities, 59; love of nature, 60; attitude toward immigrant, 61, 62; idealism, 62, 63; personality, 63-64; literary style, 65, 66; compared to settlement worker, 67; condemns tenement evils, 67-71; hopes for tenement child, 71; seeks restoration of primary group, 72; public school reforms, 73-75; advocates parks and playgrounds, 75-80; favors dispersion of population, 111; compared to Veiller, 137, 249; criticizes enforcement of tenement laws, 151; and neighborhood reconstruction, 174, 250-51; and neighborhood ethic, 188; philosophy of reform, 248-49; mentioned, 49, 81, 100, 102, 104, 107, 124, 129, 130, 148, 171, 181, 190, 220, 246, 247
Riordan, Edward J., 69, 70
Riverside Buildings. See White, Alfred T.
Robinson, Charles M.: espouses City Beautiful, 219
Rochester, New York, 142
Roosevelt, Theodore: admired by Riis, 64, 65; attends tenement exhibition, 124; influenced by Riis, 124; supports tenement reform, 125
Roosevelt, Theodore, Sr.; visits model tenement, 35
Ruskin, John, 105, 127
Russell Sage Foundation, 144, 155, 199, 227
Ryan, John A.: formulates standard of living, 195, 196

St. Louis, Missouri, 143
St. Paul, Minnesota, 142, 146
St. Vincent de Paul Society, 158
Salem, Massachusetts, 146
Salisbury, Harrison E., 254
San Francisco, California, 142, 143

Sanitarian, 32
Sanitary Housing Company of Washington, D.C., 176
Sanitary Improvement Company of Washington, D.C., 176
Sayles, Mary B., 143
Schackleton, Frederick J., 69
Schenectady, New York, 146
Schmidlapp, Jacob G., 176
Schuchman, John P., 89
Schuyler, Louisa Lee: visits model tenement, 35-36
Seattle, Washington, 237
Seligman, Isaac N., 101
Settlement: espouses neighborhood ethic, 67, 188; range of activities, 188-93; mentioned, 250
Shaftesbury, Lord, 93
Sherman, Mary, 212
Simkhovitch, Mary K., 187, 188, 190, 192, 193, 196, 231
Slums: condemned by AICP, 6; description of, 18-20; outside of New York, 140-42
Smith, Alfred E., 146
Smith, Charles S., 101
Smith, John Cotton, 47
Smith, Steven: contributions to public health, 16-17; directs Council of Hygiene investigation, 17; seeks reformed health administration, 22-23; and tenement reform in 1879, 30; mentioned, 246
Social control, 250
Social engineer, 186, 203, 214, 215
Social planning, 215
Social reform: and Progressives, 185-87; 213-15
Social Reform Club, 121
Social Settlement. See Settlement
Social work: 187; casework element, 194, 200-202; and standard of living, 194; professional, 200
Staten Island. See Richmond, New York
Steffens, Lincoln: praises Riis, 49
Sternberg, George M., 176
Stover, Charles, 191
Strong, George Templeton: discusses cholera, 11, 23
Strong, William L., 127
Sweatshop. See Tenement home work
Syracuse, New York, 142, 146
Syracuse Associated Charities, 143

Tammany: delays action on tenement commission, 125; mentioned, 65, 98, 156

Tax reform, 234-37. *See also* Committee on Congestion of Population in New York

Tenement: origins, 2, 245; railroad type, 3; as speculative venture, 38-39, 112, 113; percentage of population in, 43; fosters alcoholism and "rot," 45; fires in, 92, 165, 166; overcrowding in, 94, 95, 97; prostitution in, 138, 139. *See also* Dumb-bell tenement; Appendices I-VI

Tenement home work, 97-98; 209-12

Tenement House Building Company, 36, 100, 101

Tenement House Exhibition of 1900. *See* Veiller, Lawrence

Tenement lodger. *See* Lodger

Terhune, Albert J., 12, 13

Thomas, William I. and Florian Znaniecki: on effects of material environment, 47-48; immigrant child described, 71-72; on immigrant acculturation, 99; quoted, 137

Toledo, Ohio, 142

Tolman, William H., 91, 101

Tomorrow. See Garden City; Howard, Ebenezer

Torrens Acts, 93

Tower Buildings. *See* White, Alfred T.

Tracy, Roger, 100

Trinity Church, 38, 107, 114

Troy, New York, 146

Tuberculosis, 133-34, 190

Turner, Frederick Jackson, 50

Tweed regime, 14

United Charities Building, 207

United Hebrew Charities, 89, 195

United Real Estate Owners' Association, 167

United States Sanitary Commission, 16

United States Steel Corporation, 226

University Settlement, 187, 191, 192

Utica, New York, 146

Vanderbilt, Cornelius, 101

Van Kleeck, Mary: 186; investigates tenement home work, 211

Van Wyck, Robert A., 122, 125

Veblen, Thorstein, 40

Veiller, Lawrence: describes relation between public health and housing, 83; transforms housing movement, 117, 118; proposes tenement house committee, 118, 119; as professional reformer, 120, 186; criticizes building code commission, 121; prepares tenement exhibition, 122; works for tenement commission, 125, 126; early career, 127; appearance and personality, 127-28; range of interests, 128-29; reform philosophy, 129-32; and Tenement Law of 1901, 135, 136, 142; compared to Riis, 137, 249-50; works for national housing reform, 140, 142-46; commended by contemporaries, 148; contributions, 148, 175, 183, 249; on enforcement of tenement laws, 151, 152; proposes tenement department, 153; rejected as head of Tenement Department, 153-54; distrusted by realtors, 154; compared to de Forest, 155; organizes Tenement Department, 155-56; becomes secretary of City Club, 157; criticizes administration of Tenement Department, 157-58; defends tenement legislation, 166, 169-73; relation to building interests, 168; educational efforts, 168-69; resigns from COS Tenement Committee, 173; attitude toward model tenement, 175, 176, 177; conservative outlook, 177-78; criticized by contemporaries, 179, 182; justifies opposition to government aid for housing, 180; advocates municipal slum clearance, 181-82; commends garden city, 228; mentioned, 81, 184, 211, 231, 232, 234, 243, 240, 244, 246

Vocational training, 75

Wagner, Robert F., Sr., 170

Wald, Lillian D.: establishes Nurses' (Henry Street) Settlement, 189; mentioned, 67, 139, 192, 193, 207, 231

Walker, Francis H., 50

Ware, James E., 30

Washington, D.C., 141, 176

Washington, William D'H., 89

Waterlow, Sydney: model tenements in London, 35
Weinstein, Gregory, 60
Welfare Council of New York, 155
Whitaker, Charles H., 179
White, Alfred T.: background, 34; his tenements praised, 35-36; prepares plans for model tenement, 35; Home and Tower Buildings completed, 35-36; explains objectives, 36-37; Riverside Buildings described, 37-38; mentioned, 28, 30, 39, 82, 100, 101, 104, 107, 172, 247
White, Gaylord S., 231
Whitman, Charles S., 173
Whitney, Edgar A., 69
Whitten, Robert H., 242
Whittier House, 143
Williams, C. H., 176
Williams, Elizabeth S., 191
Wilson, Charles G.: criticizes Trinity tenements, 114
Wingate, Charles F.: selected as editor of *Plumber and Sanitary Engineer*, 29; criticizes moral influence of tenement, 43, 44

Wisconsin: housing code, 145
Women's Trade Union League, 193
Wood, Edith Elmer, 146, 166, 179, 181, 183
Woodbridge, Alice, 205, 206
Woolfolk, Adah S., 95, 96
Worcester, Massachusetts, 226
Working Women's Society, 205, 206
Workmen's Home, 6, 9, 246

Yonkers, New York, 143, 146
Young, George W., 101

Zinsser, Hans, 190
Zoning: standard law prepared by Veiller, 128; origins, 229; restrictions imposed by, 229-30; and congestion, 230; sources of support, 243-44; limitations of, 244-45; mentioned, 221, 250, 251. *See also* McAneny George; New York City Advisory Commission on the Height, Size and Arrangement of Buildings; New York City Commission on Building Districts and Restrictions